COGNITIVE APPROACHES TO CULTURE

Frederick Luis Aldama, Patrick Colm Hogan,
Lalita Pandit Hogan, and Sue J. Kim, Series Editors

# NECESSARY NONSENSE

## AESTHETICS,
## HISTORY,
## NEUROLOGY,
## PSYCHOLOGY

### Irving Massey

THE OHIO STATE UNIVERSITY PRESS

COLUMBUS

Library of Congress Cataloging-in-Publication Data is available online at https://catalog.
    loc.gov.

Cover design by Lisa Force
Text design by Juliet Williams
Type set in Adobe Minion Pro

eISBN 978-0-8142-7652-5
eISBN 978-0-8142-7651-8

# CONTENTS

# ACKNOWLEDGMENTS

Let me begin by thanking those of the generation preceding mine who have emerged, unexpectedly and unbidden, to help me in my latest years: my niece, Ellen Massey of Toronto; many of my former students, among them Rick Abrams, who helps keep me up to date on scholarship, the poet Peter Grieco (quoted in this work), Ellie Valentine (who hosts me anywhere in the world), Patrick Hogan (who saw to it that this book got published), and Joan Hyde, who appears miraculously at my elbow whenever I need her; Marie-Claude and Marco Barber of Geneva, whom I first met on a rat-infested boat on the Rio Negro in Brazil; Robin and Rachel Allinson, publishers of Noumena Press; my friend and voluntary secretary Sophia Canavos; Christa Whitney, representative extraordinary of the Yiddish book center in Amherst, Massachusetts; and Sara Eddleman, who created time in her overcrowded professional and domestic schedule to copyedit a book for an old friend. Lockwood Library, in the University at Buffalo, has been my silent collaborator through the decades; recently, Laura Taddeo has been particularly helpful to me there. Wolfson College, of the University of Cambridge, with its incomparable personnel, from the kitchen and housekeeping staff and fine corps of porters to the upper administration, provided the warm, supportive, and stimulating environment that enabled me to write this book: I had special help from the Wolfson librarian, Meg Westbury, and the IT technicians, Alex Rizzo and Darryl Wilkin, showed superhuman patience in dealing with my electronic blunders. Damian

Gvirtz and his partner, Si, of London, both younger than my grandchildren, have been very kind to me. Then there is, of course, the mainstay of my life, my daughter, Rachel. Rachel has even tried to introduce a modicum of clarity into some of my foggiest sentences. Finally, I dedicate this effort to the memory of one of my teachers with a Cambridge connection, I. A. Richards.

# INTRODUCTION

## I. PURPOSE AND STRATEGY OF THE BOOK

First, I must make it clear that I do not have, as my purpose, to prove that literature, history, neuroscience, and psychology are nonsense, though I will point out significant areas of nonsense within these domains. Nor is this a book about nonsense as such. It is a book that uses nonsense as a lens, or an investigative instrument, which identifies and illuminates certain features of the several subjects that it explores, features that would otherwise not be noticed or emphasized, or that might be apprehended differently. The representative contexts in which I have demonstrated this approach have been chosen from the humanities (Chapters 2 and 4), from the psychological sciences (Chapters 5 and 6), and from the social sciences (Chapter 3). Chapter 1 is largely devoted to definitions of nonsense.

To be sure, the nature of nonsense itself is a question that I do deal with both initially (in Chapter 1) and throughout the course of the investigation, but the creation of a "final" theory of nonsense, or even of a distinctive theory of nonsense, is not my objective. For the most part, the definition and conception of nonsense in common usage, one might say, the colloquial conception of nonsense, is appropriate to my purpose; in the spirit of Ludwig Wittgenstein, I would like the term to define itself by its use. Consequently, anyone waiting for a final statement about nonsense, a crisp and novel summation of the subject, is bound to be disappointed.

Since the system of the book is primarily exploratory rather than syllogistic, the text will often seem digressive. This characteristic of the work is, largely, a by-product of its method, but it also reflects a theory of composition that I have promulgated elsewhere. I have never thought that an essential rule of rhetoric is that a book stick to its point. An undeviating attention to a topic impoverishes thought. To quote myself, in my book on German philo-Semitism, "My own occasional straying from the topic of philo-Semitism into general literary and philosophical issues reflects this belief."[1] There is undoubtedly great value in creating a structure marked by an unwavering attention to the main concern, but there is also value in a kind of writing, even of scholarly writing, that takes a chance on gobbling up things of value that cross its path. The influence of Laurence Sterne need not be entirely repudiated even where one is trying to emulate his contemporary, Kant. For this reason, I have chosen not to exclude observations and ideas that I value just because they are not directly related to my main theme, or because they stem from personal experience. Much critical writing is in any case occult autobiography, or an *apologia pro domo sua*; there is much to be gained by letting that element (or, perhaps, "elephant in the room") come out into the open.

## II. MY PAST AFFAIR WITH NONSENSE

The problem of nonsense, of that nonsense which circumscribes and defines the limits of our knowledge, is the theme which connects the chapters of this book. Nonsense has been haunting me, or, perhaps, I should say, stalking me, for far longer than I had realized. I had been trying to identify the underlying preoccupation that drove me from one to another of the various interests represented in this work when it dawned on me that they did indeed spring from a single source, but that source was not so much an idea as an obsession. Or, to put it differently, it was not so much that I had been looking for my topic, as that my topic had, under various guises, been using me as its vehicle. In fact, it was more a condition I had been in than a series of subjects I had chosen to investigate. I would go so far as to say that I have always been writing this book.

"Old Father Chaos . . . in these wild spaces reigns absolute, and upholds his realms of darkness. He presses hard upon our frontier, and one day, belike,

---

1. Massey, *Philo-Semitism*, 73.

shall by a furious inroad recover his lost right, conquer his rebel state, and reunite us to primitive discord and confusion." It was with this quotation from Shaftesbury that I opened the last chapter of my first critical book, *The Uncreating Word.*[2] Not only the quotation from Shaftesbury, but even that book's title reveals an affinity with the present enterprise. As the problem was formulated in a recent post from the "Cybernetics, Unknowability and Politics" reading group at Cambridge, "What if the unknowable was not simply a blank to be filled or a defect to be rectified, but instead an inescapable facet of everyday existence, which continually regenerates itself as we attempt to know and interact with the world?"[3] For the fact is that, after all, we are engaged in a perpetual effort to make sense out of chaos, to create a world in which we can at least pretend that we have a place. We swim in a sea of nonsense in which we are constantly trying to build islands of sense, islands that melt away beneath us. Or, to shift the metaphor slightly, we are engaged in a never-ending battle to resist the ever-encroaching tide of nonsense; even our best sentences are just sandbags in that struggle. But, obviously, it's not that we expect to win: the best we can do is co-opt the force of nonsense, find a way to make use of it, make it part of our armament, rather as in quantum tunneling, a particle is said to borrow energy from the barrier that opposes it in order to penetrate that very barrier. We use nonsense to probe the limitations of reason (see, for instance, Chapter 3). At the same time, we also welcome an end to the battle with nonsense; we find relief when we can relax, with the onset of sleep, and drift off, back into the sea of nonsense.

For this reason, Chapter 6, on the image made by chance, might be considered the central place in this book, since it is not only about our strenuous effort, but about our uncontrollable impulse to find meaning and coherence in the *disjecta membra* of our surroundings. We are constantly creating and imposing patterns in order to be able to "see" them. That is why we make a tissue of phonetic sense out of "Jabberwocky" (see below, Chapter 5 Section IV). That is why we try, with Edward Lear (also in Chapter 5 Section IV), and with Immanuel Kant (especially in Chapter 7 Sections III and IV), to peer, or to pass, out beyond the borders of "sense" in search of a higher sense.

On the other hand, precisely because we fight so hard to make sense out of everything, it becomes difficult to find any place where our thinking is not contaminated by the effort to make sense. For this reason, Chapter 5 is of special, if perhaps perverse, interest. In the verbal "intrusions" that occur when one is falling asleep (the subject of the experiment described in that

---

2. Massey, *The Uncreating Word,* 87.

3. From the Centre for Research in the Arts, Social Sciences, and Humanities [CRASSH] program, posted on October 13, 2016.

chapter), one finds a rare area, or, one might say, a privileged area, where language is still truly irresponsible. Here, our words have given up the battle, and can relax; here, our language does not succumb to the temptation of trying, against all odds, to make sense of everything. It is perhaps the one place in our normal mental processes where we can encounter true nonsense. Our "hypnagogic" language may represent some sensory retrieval, or, possibly, a sorting process. Whatever the case may be, we have, at least so far, no interpretation of these "intrusions" that would make their irregularity seem just part of another maneuver to inflict coherence on a chaotic world.

Our defenses against disorder are formidable, but hard to maintain in a universe that is itself the ultimate example of nonsense. What is the point in having this immense, or possibly infinite, pother of comets, planets, stars (with or without planets), nebulae, "jellyfish" galaxies, elliptical galaxies, galaxies with or without black holes, black holes (with or without fuzzy borders), all for the sake of this smidgen of consciousness, that is, over in a snap of the fingers, anyway? No wonder that, as William Blake said, eternity is in love with the productions of time: what else does it have to be in love with?[4] Vanishingly small though they be, the products of consciousness are the only worthwhile thing to be found in the whole of infinity and eternity. The physical universe has apparently created something (if not very much) that exceeds itself.[5] And if this is all that this boundless, eternal, infinite universe has to show for itself, it may well be ashamed of itself. (And, for all the difference that it would make, it may as well implode, in the fashion that Shaftesbury foresaw.)

Let us even allow that consciousness is more widespread than it appears to be from our limited perspective. I would like to propose the possibility that consciousness is not generated by any individual organism, but exists as a sort of virus in the universe, always ready to infect any group of molecules that achieves a certain configuration. (This is remote from the concept of "cosmic consciousness"; it is distinct from panpsychism, and has, at most, a family resemblance to the Gaia theory.) Of course, one would then still have to work out the same set of problems that beset other theories of consciousness: qualia, the variety of percepts (in the context of my theory, one would have to use a phenomenological approach), the relation of perception to concomitant events in the brain, the difference between sensory consciousness and thought (by the way, I do not subscribe to the Berkeleian adage that there is nothing in the mind that was not first in the senses), and so forth. But, even with such a

---

4. Blake, *Poetry and Designs,* 89. (No. 10 in the "Proverbs of Hell" section of "The Marriage of Heaven and Hell.")

5. Massey, "A Rationality Larger," 339–43.

generous and comprehensive theory of consciousness, it would still represent only an epiphenomenon, a ridiculously minor set of occurrences in comparison with what goes on in the universe as a whole.

In any case, now that the true nature of my topic has been revealed to me, or, to put it differently, now that I know what I am talking about, I had better explain it in more local terms. In the following chapters, I will be attempting to show how nonsense is a necessary part of our thinking. On the one hand, it is the archenemy of reason; on the other hand, reason cannot do without it; from some points of view (e.g., Deleuze, see below in Chapter 5 Section III), it is even seen as an inherent element or aspect of reason. It is, then, at the same time an opponent and a component of the apparatus that we use to contest it. An intimate part of that armament, it yet marks its limits.

Before I go on to show the ways in which nonsense functions in the five domains to which the following chapters are devoted, I will review some of the recent works that approach my topic, or, rather, related topics, from different perspectives.

## III. RECENT STUDIES RELATED TO NONSENSE

When I began to organize this book, I was concerned that some of the topics I intended to deal with might seem too outlandish, improbable, or, perhaps, even plain nonsensical, for any reader to want to engage. Who could care less about animal shapes in clouds? Who could believe that Immanuel Kant and Lewis Carroll needed to be brought into intimate contact with each other, above all in the context of nonsense? Who would want to look at a book that might have offered, as an appendix, a "Praise of Paradox"? And, finally, who would want to follow an argument that kept bordering on chaos?

I had chosen to forget an iron rule of my experience: the more personal and private the reason for one's choice of topic, the more unlikely, or even bizarre, the subject that one has fastened on, the more confident one can be that it will show up the next morning on the public notice-board. It will no doubt be hard for a reader, even for one who has had experience with this peculiar characteristic of intellectual history, to believe that I had not read some of the recently published works that have come to my attention only after having finished this work. I refer to books such as Martin Kemp's *Structural Intuitions* (2015); to Jean-Luc Marion's *Negative Certainties* (2015) (I should have known this in the original earlier); to Ben-Ami Scharfstein's *The Nonsense of Kant and Lewis Carroll: Unexpected Essays on Philosophy, Art, Life, and Death* (2015). And the latest book on chaos, Martin Meisel's *Chaos*

*Imagined: Literature, Art, Science,*[6] though somewhat more closely confined to literature and art than my own, shows parallels to mine in several respects. To begin with, of course, nonsense and chaos are related fields, though Meisel works with entirely different materials from mine (e.g., no Lewis Carroll, no Edward Lear, no neuroscience), and shows little interest in the Kantian aesthetic framework that underlies much of my work. On the other hand, he also seeks to find value in what is usually considered a negative category.

This convergence of works in the humanities concerned with the limitations and the unreliability of reason, when added to the recent collapse of the rational choice model in economics (so that only computers are now relied on to make "rational" choices), may seem to illustrate a trend. But the perception that reason is not always trustworthy is a recurrent realization. One might identify waves of preoccupation with irrationality and, more specifically, nonsense. Notoriously exemplified by Freud, this concern is brought into focus by Wittgenstein, and, at roughly the same time, into even sharper focus by Gödel, whose ideas shook the foundations of mathematics. There is another series of related studies running from Elizabeth Sewell's *The Field of Nonsense* (1952) to Susan Stewart's *Nonsense* (1978); the sequence is picked up again with Jean-Jacques Lecercle's interesting *Philosophy of Nonsense* (1994). Lecercle's book marks the beginning of what one might consider a new series, in which nonsense and its implications are viewed as part of a broader field of philosophy.

As it happens, the book which might be expected to show the widest overlap with my own, Stephen Booth's *Precious Nonsense: The Gettysburg Address, Ben Jonson's Epitaphs on his Children, and Twelfth Night* (1998),[7] is the one with which I find the least coincidence. Some of Booth's readings (e.g., of the Gettysburg Address), are interesting, but they lead to conclusions that I find deeply uncongenial. In discovering nonsense embedded in great works of literary expression, Booth seems to be confident that he has at last found "the soul of great literature" (63), as well as exactly what it is that makes a work "sublime" (60). (If so, Booth has indeed made all future aesthetics superfluous.) Nonsense is of value only because it challenges us to overcome it in favor of coherence (9) and the "organic whole" (59). (This depreciation of nonsense is enough to give it a bad name!) Too often, what Booth does is call the normal, if bold, metaphors and the normal, bold, discontinuities of a text "nonsense," and go on to draw extensive conclusions from that premise.

On the other hand, Jean-Luc Marion's *Negative Certainties* would seem to have little to do with my subject, and yet, in a subtle way, it shadows my whole

---

6. For an attempt to reconcile chaos with order, see Scott, *Chaos and Cosmos*.

7. It was brought to my attention by the Shakespeare scholar Richard Abrams.

enterprise far more closely than Booth's book does. To simplify the argument of a highly complex philosophical treatise: it asks the question, What if the only thing we can be certain of is uncertainty? and goes on from there to construct what one might call an alternative philosophy, or a shadow-system of philosophy, with uncertainty at its core. This is not the same as skepticism, of course; it also needs to be distinguished from Quentin Meillassoux's hyper-uncertainty hypothesis, which attempts to separate nature entirely from the human observer,[8] not to mention postmodern undecidability, of which we have surely had enough. In its emphasis on what is simply "given," it owes a great deal to Kierkegaard. In terms of my own pursuit, though, it shares an interest in what might be called the underside of reason; like uncertainty, nonsense is both an inherent and a subversive aspect of reason. It is no accident that, like myself, Marion had decided to offer a supplement "In Praise of Paradox," though I myself have finally decided to forego that luxury.

If that was a startling discovery, my consternation on encountering the title of Ben-Ami Scharfstein's latest book, *The Nonsense of Kant and Lewis Carroll,* can only be imagined.

I had been wondering how I could possibly justify my having created just such a concatenation in my own work, when I learned that someone else had had the same idea, and, apparently, did not consider it outlandish at all. In fact, on second thought, I found some comfort, rather than only a source of anxiety, in the fact that a well-known philosopher had ratified my choices. This realization tempered my disappointment on encountering sentences that I myself had written recently, only in different words, e.g.: "'nonsense,' the willful departure from verbal or logical conventions, has creative potential not only in literary narrative and poetry . . . but also in philosophy" (3). Or, "you can't discover new sense without . . . invoking nonsense" (4). Again, Immanuel Kant "is sometimes probably unknowable, comprising an intelligible outer Kant inhabited by a Kant-in-himself" (36). (I particularly like that one.) He "exercises the hypnotic magic of nonsensical philosophy" (36). All these lines could be paraphrases of what I had worked out painstakingly for myself. I should mention, though, that, apart from these few sentences, the body of Scharfstein's book is about topics that have nothing whatsoever to do with my own work.

The title of Martin Kemp's *Structural Intuitions: Seeing Shapes in Art and Science* was not calculated to reassure me, either, since my (long) Chapter 6 was almost entirely devoted to the image made by chance. It turns out, though, disappointingly, that this book is just about categories of forms, rather

---

8. Meillassoux, *After Finitude,* 27.

than about the psychology of forms, or about how we apprehend them. In fact, it is hard to tell what the phrase "structural intuitions" means in the first place, or whether it means anything at all. Philip Ball's *Nature's Patterns* is indeed devoted to the fact that the mind sees, invents, or "discovers" patterns everywhere. My own work, though, is concerned, not with the mere ubiquity of this process, but with its psychological and philosophical significance.

I also know of one book forthcoming that may turn out to have some bearing on my own work when it appears: Raymond Tallis has completed a study of man as the sense-making animal, entitled *Logos: The Mystery of How We Make Sense in the World*. Then, there is the volume edited by James Williams and Matthew Bevis, *Edward Lear and the Play of Poetry* (2016). Any book about Edward Lear will necessarily also be a book about nonsense, and this one is no exception. The essays in this excellent volume have much of value to say about nonsense in the context of Lear's writings, and I have had occasion to cite them, but the focus of the book is not nonsense as such. Finally, Richard Elliott's *The Sound of Nonsense* is an exhilarating, well-informed, and very well-written book. It deals primarily with sound and music in popular culture, but it has interesting things to say about Lear and Carroll, as well. It points out the pleasure we feel when music overrides sense. Its major theoretical assertion is that nonsense occurs in the moment "when sense-making is forced into code-switching." As a deliberately short book, it tends to assume, rather than probe, the connection between "sense" and music. (Elliott also, unaccountably, passes over the famous "cat" duet attributed to Rossini.) Although Elliott's interests run parallel to mine in a number of areas, there is no duplication: even when his work and mine mention the same sources, they rarely refer to the same material in those sources.

It may not be worth mentioning, but I have just learned of another book on nonsense: Raymond Moody's *Donner du sens au non-sens* (*Making Sense of Nonsense*) is of interest mainly to those who concern themselves with alternate states of consciousness, near-death experiences, and such matters. Still, the very fact that so many books with nonsense as their stated subject have appeared or will soon appear over less than two years' time is worth noticing. Not to mention that Daniel Heller-Roazen, in *No One's Ways: An Essay on Infinite Naming*, seems determined to revive the Hegelian preoccupation with negativity as such; and that his conclusion—that we sometimes say more than we know—has much to do with the conclusion of my own book.

It is perhaps necessary for me to make it clear again, then, that there is no duplication between my project and the published works in the related fields that I have mentioned above, except for, in some instances, a shared interest in the work of Edward Lear and Lewis Carroll. As far as the more philosophical studies are concerned, the material that I work with is almost entirely different, as is the methodology. There is a "family" affinity, and an awareness that a rich field of exploration is being opened up, but, apart from the sentences from Scharfstein that I have cited, there is no overlap whatsoever. But that observation should bring me to the last part of my Introduction.

## IV. THE FIVE DOMAINS

As I have been saying, this book is about the role of nonsense in the formulation of ideas, as exemplified in four general areas. I have divided these four areas into five domains. Two of my topics—metaphor and poetry (the subjects of Chapters 2 and 4)—have been grouped under the rubric of "Aesthetics" in my subtitle, simply in order to make it less cumbersome. But the book is also about the nonsense that courses through our minds at a level even below our "stream of consciousness"—as well as about the higher nonsense of metaphor and philosophy that Wittgenstein (at least, the early Wittgenstein) notoriously warned us not to indulge in. Whatever the case, it can hardly be an accident that every area I approach seems to have a node of nonsense at its core. In fact, it is enough to make one wonder whether it might not be worth one's while to probe for a creative kernel of nonsense in any field that one chose to investigate.

The easiest, and most obvious, way for me to approach the topic of nonsense would have been through literature and art. Without tracing its origins in Greece (if not earlier), one can find it as the dominant form in modern theatre, if not in literature as a whole, since Alfred Jarry in the 1890s. On the persistent appeal of Dada, see Alfred Brendel's "The Growing Charm of Dada."[9] As for art, the mere mention of surrealism says it all. However, that would have been a different book—or an entire library of books. Simpler still would have been to approach the theme through the tradition of the "wise fool," as in Shakespeare.[10] Nonsense in the arts, then, is hardly an exotic or unusual subject.

However, nonsense as a topic is also a major presence in linguistics and philosophy, and has been treated in a highly technical fashion within these disciplines: it has been dealt with by Gottlob Frege, Rudolf Carnap, Wittgenstein, and A. W. Moore, among others. It even occurs in microbiology, as

---

9. Brendel, "Growing Charm," 22–25.

10. The theme of the fool in relation to Edward Lear has been treated magisterially by James Williams in "Lear and the Fool," pp. 16–50 in Williams and Bevis's *Edward Lear and the Play of Poetry.*

"nonsense-mediated decay."[11] I will be using the term in a more commonplace manner, in the various ways in which it is generally understood, in ordinary speech. But "nonsense" in common parlance has primarily negative connotations, and the deeper, more positive associations that it carries are not at first apparent. The title *Necessary Nonsense*, then, is meant to recall this other side of nonsense.

It is probably important, though, that I sketch out in advance some of the underlying categories on which this book is framed before I launch into a summary of the work in my subject areas. There are three main general situations, a propos nonsense, with which this project is concerned: (1) one is the kind of situation in which the distinctions between sense and nonsense are challenged (Chapters 2, 4, and 7, respectively on metaphor, on inspiration, and on language as experience); (2) the second is the situation in which nonsense is perceived as transcending sense (Chapters 3 and 6, on the Baroque and on the image made by chance); and (3) the third is the situation in which nonsense appears in its pure form, irreducible to any kind of sense (Chapter 5, on hypnagogia). These are overarching categories: they have nothing to do with the specific subjects explored in the book, but they may help to clarify its underlying structure, as well as to identify its widest concerns.

To show how the idea of nonsense works its way through the book, I can begin with its role in the chapter on metaphor. How can we arrive at a metaphor without allowing it to go through a stage of nonsense? How can one thing be another, even, as often in the most powerful metaphors, another thing that seems to have been deliberately chosen to seem most unlike itself? In this case, people with damage to the right hemisphere of the brain appear to be more reasonable than supposedly sane people, since they continue to see metaphors as the nonsense that metaphors must, in rational terms, be acknowledged to be. I should perhaps also mention that, during the course of this chapter, I develop what I believe to be a new theory of metaphor.

A propos the Baroque: how could Louis XIV, the Sun King, actually be seen and thought of as Apollo? How do we cope with the nonsense of a regime, artistic as well as political, in which display and image are systematically made to exceed, frequently to a preposterous degree, reality?

In the case of John Keats, even if the conflict between poet and fanatic be resolved in the poet's favor, how could Keats, or any poet or artist, be "by mine own eyes inspired," and make himself into the source of his own *external*

---

11. Nonsense-mediated decay is a property of eukaryotic cells that suppresses errors in messenger RNA molecules, a discovery pioneered by Dr. Lynne Maquat when she was at Roswell Park Memorial Hospital, Buffalo, NY. My thanks to Dr. Joel Huberman for the reference.

inspiration? (One is reminded of Freud's "self-analysis.") How could he be at once a practicing, living poet, and routinely contemplate his activity from the vantage point (if one can call it that) of the void beyond?

A propos the (fifth) chapter on the intermediate state between waking and sleep (also familiar to Keats): where does the dissociated language of hypnagogia, subverting every principle of coherence, come from? Or is language itself permeated by some principle of nonsense? Or, again, might one venture the doubtful paradox (the "tremulous sound" of Lewis Carroll: the "Doubtful Sound" of Captain Cook), that nonsense alone lends sense to sense, as shadow helps us to know light? Not surprisingly, Friedrich Nietzsche thought so,[12] not to mention Gilles Deleuze.[13] Touching only briefly on the area of dream and dream-infused sleep, those most necessary forms of nonsense, without which we must surely die, and that occupy so much of our lives, this chapter recapitulates much of the article by myself et al. in *Frontiers in Psychology* about hypnagogic "intrusions" entitled "Intrusions of a Drowsy Mind," an article which has attracted considerable interest in psychological circles.[14] The experimental work (initiated by myself) for that publication was carried out by myself and a group of collaborators at that least nonsensical of venues, the Medical Research Council—Cognition and Brain Sciences Unit (MRC CBU) laboratories at the University of Cambridge.

As far as perception is concerned (Chapter 6, "The Image Made by Chance"): how do we incessantly lend credence to what we cannot see, trying to make sense out of visual nonsense, out of a chronically fragmented and incoherent world? As John Lennon is said to have remarked, "Reality leaves a lot to the imagination." As I have said above, we fill out the *disjecta membra* of our visual perceptions with copious supplements; are not all our perceptions, finally, to a large extent, also "images made by chance"? Or have they not, at least, had to go through a phase of "necessary nonsense" before we can even try to make something of them? And they are always threatening to fall back into that chaos, a condition to which they revert under conditions of stress or depression, when they return to the flat, meaningless state assumed by Fichte to precede our grasp of the difference between inner and outer.[15]

Cardinal Newman argues, in *A Grammar of Assent,* that there is a moment of uncertainty which precedes every decision; that we engage in a "leap of

---

12. Nietzsche, *Klassiker-Ausgabe,* vol. 3, 438.

13. Deleuze, *Logique du sens,* 87–89.

14. Noreika et al., "Intrusions." This article has recently been quoted in the *Atlantic;* the research was also mentioned online in a February 2018 article on BBC News, http://www.bbc.com/news/business-42945383.

15. Adamson, *Fichte,* 156–63.

faith" before we accede to any assertion, no matter how clearly grounded in evidence.[16] Newman, of course, had religious reasons for maintaining this position, but it is worth considering in its own right. Certainly, there are times in the history of science when the evidence for what turned out to be right was not yet adequate to prove it—and, of course, in science even the right answer is always provisional. Is there a moment of what the physicists call "superposition," during which alternatives are actually equally true (an assertion which is bound to appear nonsensical to the naïve observer), at some point during the progress of every thought?[17]

As I have been saying, nonsense does not necessarily have to have a negative connotation or express inadequacy. In conveying the ironic awareness of all that we cannot know, it transcends that very limitation, enables us to stand outside it and to appreciate its implications. What we don't know defines us. Even the attempt to capture essences in the "nonsense" of metaphor expresses the awareness of our incompleteness. In the limericks of Edward Lear, in the verses of Lewis Carroll, and—yes—even in the *Critiques* of Immanuel Kant— that ironic and tragic awareness stands nonsense on its head—or, should I say, stands it on its feet, turning it into the ultimate sense. That is an affirmation.

---

16. Newman, *Grammar of Assent*, 82–89 and passim.
17. Orr, "Being Good to Others," 27.

# CHAPTER 1

# Nonsense

## Usage and Uses

## I. SOME USES OF THE WORD "NONSENSE"

Those living with Asperger's Syndrome frequently have difficulty in distin-guishing between metaphors and nonsense (see Chapter 2 Section III.A). They are often regarded as handicapped because of this difficulty. The problem may, however, be not only psychological but also linguistic. Members of the AS community might be relieved to hear an accredited scholar in linguistics say the following: "It would be nice to have a cognitive theory of metaphor creation and decoding that could give a definitive answer to the question of whether . . . there is an identifiable borderline between metaphor and non-sense. This enigma has not yet been solved by any theory of metaphor."[1] It is enough to make one throw up one's hands and concede that "there is no real borderline between metaphor and nonsense, but only between good and bad metaphors."[2]

But this problem is only, to resort to the cliché, the tip of the iceberg. It would also "be nice to have," to begin with, at least, a generally agreed-upon definition of nonsense, if not a generally agreed-upon definition of metaphor. I had originally titled this subchapter "Metaphor and Nonsense (Linguistics

---

1. Sovran, *Relational Semantics,* 147.
2. Ibid., 148.

and Philosophy)" but that was a claim to coverage that I could not possibly have fulfilled, even if I had devoted my efforts exclusively to those domains. Entire libraries have been committed to these areas and to their interactions, since numerous major philosophers, students of linguistics, and aestheticians have been involved in the controversies devoted to these terms. Consequently, the following aspires to be little more than a very brief annotated bibliography.

For nonsense, Ludwig Wittgenstein is an obvious place to begin, precisely because he used the word in such elusive and apparently self-contradictory ways as to guarantee an eternity of dispute about what he actually meant by it. Notoriously, he ends the *Tractatus* by saying that anyone who has really understood his propositions will realize that they are nonsensical, and will discard them like a ladder that has served its purpose. In several other passages, he seems to be saying simply that statements about what cannot be fully described in language are inherently nonsensical; from this it would follow that most philosophy is nonsense; still again, he uses the word just as a delimiting factor in logic.[3] It has been further remarked that Wittgenstein's use of "nonsense" is significantly different in the *Philosophical Investigations* from the role he assigns to it in the *Tractatus*.[4] A quotation such as the following, which is based on a remark made by Wittgenstein himself (but clearly composed by someone whose native language was not English), gives one an idea of the extent to which Wittgenstein's philosophy is dependent on the concept of nonsense: "All the reflection of Wittgenstein's philosophy is a question on the possibility of crossing . . . from the hidden nonsense of the contingency of [the] language and of [the] reality to the patent nonsense of [the] philosophy."[5]

This is clearly not ground that the newly fledged philosopher can navigate with confidence. It is with the full awareness that I may be simply embarking on a *pons asinorum* that I venture any opinion about the ending of the *Tractatus*, where Wittgenstein says, in effect, what André Gide also said to his

---

3. Wittgenstein, *Tractatus Logico-Philosophicus*, 89, 4, 23, 32. Per Aage Brandt recalls to me that the Wittgensteinian concept of nonsense, according to which anything that cannot be verified is nonsense, is balanced by the "European" school, which makes a distinction between false and nonsensical propositions. Brandt associates these views convincingly with, respectively, the Spinozist and the Cartesian traditions ("A Note on the Meaning of Nonsense," personal communication, February 16, 2017). I am also grateful to Professor Brandt for referring me to an article by Hacker, "Wittgenstein, Carnap and the New American Wittgensteinians," 1–23, in this connection.

4. See, for instance, Reid, "Wittgenstein's Ladder," 150.

5. Distaso, "On *Satzklang*," 266. For the original passage in Wittgenstein on which this sentence is based, see Pitcher, "Wittgenstein, Nonsense, and Lewis Carroll," 592. In Potter and Ricketts, *Cambridge Companion to Frege*, 564, exactly the same notion seems to be attributed to Frege.

reader: "Jette mon livre"[6] ("Throw away my book"). Perhaps all that Wittgenstein meant at this point was (but I claim no originality for this view) that, in his little book, he had not been proposing a systematic philosophy, but a series of thoughts and suggestions that could be used by a reader to help him/her to find his/her own way. If this reading were correct, it would show Wittgenstein's early thought to be consistent with his later approach to language as an assortment of games.

Wittgenstein's approach, in style, vocabulary, and substance, is saturated with Frege's thinking, as he himself declared;[7] he also shared with Frege, and with other philosophers of the period, a virtual obsession with the concept of nonsense. Such a concern is hardly surprising: one has only to dabble in the subject to realize that even beginning to tug at the idea of nonsense leads to questions about the idea of sense, a doubtful link in the philosophical system, so that the entire web of philosophy threatens to come apart. This unease is apparent in a sentence such as the following: "There is some uncertainty about the question of whether the term 'sense' can be precisely defined."[8] Hardly a trivial question.

From what I understand in Potter and Ricketts,[9] for Frege, the composition of a sentence that is not nonsense excludes the collocation of two proper nouns, or of two predicates, as a grammatical unit. This seems plausible enough. On the other hand, some of the criteria by which sense is distinguished from nonsense do not seem so benign. When Carnap (very much in the spirit of Wittgenstein) argues that the criterion of sense in language is the capacity to be proven either true or false, he excludes poetry from the realm of meaning at a stroke: this is a gesture that some may find peremptory.[10] But, then, nonsense comes in a variety of forms, or flavors. For Edmund Husserl, Carnap's teacher, it divided naturally into two versions. Countersense, or "Widersinn," is produced when an adjective is used correctly (in grammatical terms) to modify a noun, but the noun is incompatible with the adjective (as in "a round square"). Nonsense proper, or "Unsinn," is created when the laws of grammar themselves are violated: in "a round or," an adjective is being used to modify a conjunction.[11]

---

6. Gide, *Les Nourritures*, 185.
7. Potter and Ricketts, 564.
8. Kjärgaard, *Metaphor and Parable*, 52.
9. Potter and Ricketts, 188.
10. Vrahimis, "Nonsense and Absurdity," 133–40.
11. Loc. cit.

A more casual, less philosophically demanding, or what one might call a behavioral, view of metaphor is to be found in the more recent work of Stephen E. Kidd, for whom nonsense is simply "language perceived as being unworthy of interpretation."[12] Of course, as in most of these cases, we can also find objections to this argument all too easily.

It will be apparent that there is no simple definition of nonsense, or even one on which one could find even moderate consensus among those who concern themselves with such matters. What does emerge from this brief glance at the topic is that it is a crucial area of intellectual investigation, well worth the attention being devoted to it. Still, one cannot help wondering whether Lewis Carroll and Edward Lear might not have taken pleasure in seeing dignified academics engage in merciless battle in the attempt to establish a single, final definition of nonsense.

Before proceeding, it may be worth our while to remind ourselves that nonsense is pervasive, and that there are many common varieties of nonsense, not all dealt with exhaustively in the formal inquiries just cited. At the risk of repetition, and at the simplest level, one might identify a half dozen (including some of the ones mentioned above). The most obvious kind is grammatical nonsense: "I will see you drank." Close behind is semantic incoherence: "A car is rolling without wheels"; a variant of semantic incoherence is mere discontinuity, or irrelevance. Another takes the form of a denial of observable events: "It never rains." Another contradicts scientific evidence, or is physically impossible: "A pig can fly." Still another makes positive statements about imaginary entities as if they were physically real: "A goblin eats an apple." These categories could be refined or subdivided (the implausible or improbable, for instance, are close neighbors of the impossible). The last two are among the most important: asserting something that is wrong, and asserting the impossible. The first of these is closely related to science, the latter to the arts and religion. (The status of philosophy itself in relation to nonsense must still be judged unclear, despite my efforts above, at least partially because even what constitutes a meaningful statement has not been decided.) To go beyond nonsense itself, and to try to define, say, absurdity, or the ridiculous, or the numerous other related terms that one could find in a thesaurus, either in themselves or in their relation to nonsense, would be an enterprise beyond the scope of this book, as well as entirely beyond my purpose.

Still, there may be some, with a passion for order, who might be eager to discriminate among the various kinds of nonsense identifiable in, for example,

---

12. Kidd, *Nonsense and Meaning,* 8.

the Lear limericks: it is obviously *impossible* to dance at the end of a bough (the old person of Slough); there is no discernible reason why the birds of the air should cause the "young lady in white" to despair (an example of *discontinuity*); the abruptious old man of Thames Ditton is guilty of (or has been subjected to) *semantic incoherence;* but such attempts to catalogue the humorist's arsenal will never tell us "what entranced all the people of Skye." (On the other hand, it might prompt someone else to compose an unkindly limerick with a rhyme like "only a fool" and "by the rule.") And I will certainly not attempt to deal with the differences between verbal and visual nonsense, which, in texts with illustrations, are often in conflict.

Obviously, I myself do not favor any one of the multiple definitions of nonsense outlined above to the exclusion of the others—and I have not even mentioned plain, heartfelt comedy, perhaps the most necessary nonsense of all. It is clear, then, that I see no need for a prescriptive definition of nonsense. I understand the desire for such a single, clear-cut definition, but, where so many major philosophers have failed, I would not expect to arrive at a final formulation of this very broad idea, nor has that ever been my purpose. As I have said before, I will instead follow Wittgenstein's own stated strategy, and allow the term to define itself, or, at least, to set its own parameters, by its use as we go along, displaying its facets in a variety of contexts.

## II. SENSE IN NONSENSE

In this book, I try to display nonsense as a participant in other areas of thought, and in other mental processes.

Whatever variety of nonsense we choose to talk about, though, it is essential to remember, once again, that nonsense can be both a positive and a negative category. On the one hand, it is the dark side of sense. To submit to it entirely is to leave us without any ground to stand on, not even the ground from which to identify and define it as "nonsense." To give up a claim to sense, by some standard, is to end up with the shapeless, pointless sort of relativism lampooned by Alan Sokal in his pseudoscientific article on the "Transformative Hermeneutics of Quantum Gravity," where categories dissolve and we can give up talking.[13] In the famous phrase often attributed to Wolfgang Pauli, this is the space in which something "is not only not right, it is *not even wrong.*"

---

13. "Transgressing the Boundaries," 217–52.

On the other hand, we cannot do without it, either. We live in a world in which every theory exists to be disproved. By some standard—and it is a standard that is not merely trivial or provocative, since every theory is bound to be proved wrong eventually—we live under a canopy of nonsense.

I have asked elsewhere whether all errors are alike. They are all alike in being errors, but that is where their likeness ends. I would argue for what I would like to call flavors of nonsense, for the individuality of nonsenses, for a realm in which every error comes trailing, if not "clouds of glory," at least the traces of its history and its genesis, its personal rags and tatters. A congenial realm of honorable nonsense.

This is not just the realm of superseded theories, in which Newtonian physics can lie down beside the theory of the ether. It is the realm of unfulfilled conjecture, where an idea does not have value only because it can be proved. (Again, that wouldn't be a permanent help either, since proof is in turn transitory, provisional.) We don't hatch an idea because we want it proved: we want it *thought about.*

Let nonsense hang, then, at least in the space between a conjecture and its provisional "proof." To take this proposition a step further, in a direction I have proposed above, I will suggest that there is a space in which nonsense is at work in the elaboration of every idea. Maybe there are even two such moments of honorable nonsense. After one has an idea, there is a brief hesitation, a second of self-doubt, before the decision to follow through is taken. Then there is a second moment: the moment in which doubt is abandoned. At that point, Cardinal Newman insisted, reason is not so much acted on as set aside.[14] We conclude on the basis of the information that we have, but we know that the information we have is necessarily incomplete, i.e., wrong. Yet we plunge in.

All of these issues have been studied intensively, if, to be sure, inconclusively, by many great logicians. Brian Josephson has pointed out the work of Imre Lakatos (Avrum Lipschitz) to me. Karl Popper had attempted to put an end to the endless arguments over the status of scientific assertions by declaring that only those that were subject to falsification qualified as scientific statements. But Lakatos insisted that "so-called 'refutations' are not the hallmark of empirical failure, as Popper has preached, since all programs grow in a permanent ocean of anomalies."[15] All scientific assertions are understood to be equally provisional. For Lakatos, a better standard of scientific value is the

---

14. Newman, passim, e.g., p. 89. It may be worth looking back at Leibniz's "degrés d'assentiment" ("degrees of assent"), from *Nouveaux essais,* vol. 4, xvi, in this context.

15. Lakatos, *Methodology of Scientific Research Programmes,* 6.

ability of a theory or "programme" to predict novel facts.[16] Objections to the falsifiability thesis have also been raised by Feyerabend and Sokal. Apparently, falsifiability is not necessarily the last word, after all: *pace* Pauli, the fact that a statement cannot be proved wrong does not necessarily deprive it of validity or value; it may be a source of great and fully verifiable ideas, crucial spin-offs from nonsense, so to speak. To demand accountability in the form of verifiability at every step in the thought process is to stifle thought in its cradle.

Perhaps some things have to be stated unscientifically (i.e., at least by Popper's definition, in a form not subject to falsification) because the means for falsification, or, rather, the possibility of falsification, remains beyond what can be conceived of at the time. At a later point in history, when more facts and techniques have become available, a falsifiable statement in the same area becomes easier to conceptualize. An example would be ancient theories of the atom, which, unfalsifiable in themselves, led to falsifiable ones.

Some parts of this debate have been formalized, or, at least, partially formalized, in the arguments over Thomas Kuhn's *Structure of Scientific Revolutions* (1962; incidentally, Kuhn's idea of paradigm shift had been anticipated by Meyer Abrams in *The Mirror and the Lamp*). What **do** we do with those dead spaces, or, perhaps, rather, hyper-alive spaces, when (say, as in the case of Renaissance astronomy) the available evidence is accounted for with a similar degree of accuracy by incompatible theories? Or when the rights and the wrongs shift back and forth, as in the recent case of Lamarck vs. Darwin (in the area of epigenetics, in particular)? Are we in the domain of double nonsense, then, until one of them turns out to be approximately right? One can easily generalize this predicament, since such an overlap, creating (my coinage) a "dead zone," or a zone of nonsense, in which rational choice alone is rendered helpless, is created by every "paradigm shift," at least in the exact sciences. And, even in the humanities, what does one do with all the stuff that is left behind when there is a change in periodization, or in opinions about what the critical causative factors in some historical change might be? For instance, do the "deciders" decide the course of history (Karl Schmitt), or do the plebs (Leo Tolstoy, for one)? A recent sample of this perennial debate: "'More than almost any other great man in history,' wrote the historian E. H. Carr, 'Stalin illustrates the thesis that circumstances make the man, not the man the circumstances.' Utterly, eternally [!] wrong. Stalin made history"[17] is the angry rejoinder. What shall we say: "What well-founded confidence?"

---

16. Ibid., 4–5.
17. Kotkin, "If Stalin had died . . . ," 35.

Where does this leave us? I have emphasized that there is, obviously and necessarily, a vast ground of uncertainty in thought; but, also, that a transitional stage in thought, a stage that might be called a reliance on a dual nonsense, is a necessary, and productive, stage, during which we have to abandon the would-be certainties of sense, and proceed in a purely exploratory spirit. We are forced into what might be called a rational irrationality. Our compass wavers, and yet we have no choice but to press on. In the end, our blind courage, though all that we have, may prove to be a better guide than we could have hoped it to be.

# CHAPTER 2

# Metaphor and Nonsense

*The following pages on metaphor represent my thoughts on that subject over a period of nearly forty years. In consequence, they exhibit overlap, repetitions, discontinuities, and even contradictions that cannot be wished away. What is perhaps worse, the extended chronology of the composition results in difficult reading: the style and even the general purpose of the writing change over time. It is not so much that the ideas alter as that the mind that thought them does. I have made an effort to diminish the impact of the most egregious changes in tone, but the fact that there are several different voices at play here cannot be concealed. The shifts in thought make for bumpy reading, and I would encourage a reader to skip the most awkward passages.*

## I. PREFACE

### A. Preliminary

As far as the content of the chapter is concerned, that does, nevertheless, admit of summary. Broadly speaking, it consists of an immersion in the phenomenology of metaphor, as I experience it (in two "flavors"), followed by a wider, theoretical discussion.

Following the Introduction (Section I.B), Section II is about what I might call ordinary metaphor, as described by I. A. Richards, Max Black, and others (voice I). Section III deals with what I would be inclined to call "ecstatic," or extraordinary, metaphor; here Andrew Marvell's "The Garden" is a relevant text (voice II). Section IV discusses the narrative element in metaphor (voice III), and the border between metaphor and nonsense, especially as understood in neuroscientific terms (voice IV). This "voice" articulates my own theory of metaphor. I hope that this sketch will facilitate access to my thoughts on metaphor, though I may not have succeeded in making them even reasonably clear. My admiration for George Berkeley and David Hume has not enabled me to achieve their perspicuity.

## B. Introduction

I have twice set my mind to understanding the ways in which metaphor is generated, and to identifying its purpose. The first time (1), I thought of metaphor as an alembic, in which the essential feature of the object could be isolated by placing the object in an environment where it could be stripped of its irrelevant associations. To achieve this result, one would first have to see the object as that which it is not, or, to be precise, as not that which it, or the manifold which it represents, is named as. The object itself would, so to speak, deliquesce, and be replaced by a more exact version of itself, leaving only its grey, fuzzy name behind.

Lionel Abel once pointed out to me that metaphor was not the only avenue for approaching essence. The phenomenological reduction was another possibility, although it has in common with metaphor the stripping away of the "*Abschattungen*," or features of the object not relevant to the pure experience.[1]

Whatever the case, the mere fact of my having begun a chapter on metaphor with a metaphor (the "alembic," above) exemplifies the seduction of this form of reasoning. Plain, expository prose just wouldn't serve. It is strange, though, to have to resort to a form of exposition which is, on the face of it, nonsensical, in order to sharpen and clarify one's meaning. Metaphor is, after all, an attempt to describe, through something else, that which one has failed adequately to describe in itself—a procedure that can only take one farther away from what one was attempting to name, capture, or describe in the first place.

But I do not wish to dwell on the ubiquity and power of the "Metaphors We Live By," attributes well known from St. Augustine, Boccaccio,[2] and, then, later, Giambattista Vico,[3] as well as William Blake,[4] onwards.

My second attempt (2) to get to the heart, or the root, of metaphor was entirely different, and much harder to describe. This time I was not concerned with what one might call the technology of metaphor, with the way in which it works itself out, but rather with its inner sources and resources. I am not even sure that the two views or perspectives can be reconciled.

My second engagement with metaphor might be better described as an encounter—an experience of almost traumatic intensity—than as an event available for analysis. I was exposed to, or, rather, confronted with, a subarctic landscape of such power that I felt myself to have become a metaphor

---

1. On the phenomenological reduction, see Husserl, *Ideas*, chapters 3–4, subsections 31, 32, 41, 44, 50.

2. For St. Augustine and Boccaccio, see Osgood, ed., *Boccaccio on Poetry*, xix and note 14.

3. Vico, *The New Science*, 36.

4. *The Marriage of Heaven and Hell*.

for my surroundings. It was an experience not identical with, but not unrelated to, Wordsworth's "visionary dreariness."[5] In my previous essay on metaphor, I had described it as the discovery of the previously hidden, unspecified essence of an object, but sheltering in another object external to itself; metaphor was something that was projected outward. (We look for something outside Achilles to represent the courage that is in him, and choose the lion to fulfill that role.) In the present situation (it was on the island of Miquelon, off Newfoundland), it was quite different: it was that I saw what was outside me through the lens of something that was already inside me. The source of metaphor was internal. As in my previous description of metaphor, one thing was also being seen through another, but in this case, the crucial thing was in me, rather than newly discovered in something outside me. In the case of the Miquelon experience, there was, so to speak, no "tenor"; the dialogue was not between tenor and vehicle, but between what one might have to call, confusingly, two tenors: the inner "voice," or, rather, object, and its external incarnation, instantiation, or projection. I was not seeing, for instance, gulls (what one might previously have called the tenor) "as" marble steps: marble steps were fulfilling themselves in the gulls settling themselves into the marl of the rocky crenellations surrounding the broad expanse of the valley.

This obscure internal element, and the (if anything) still more obscure argument in which it is embedded, are the subject of my second section on metaphor. It is presented through the medium of anecdote and description, rather than through systematic exposition; its elusive material does not lend itself to syllogistic treatment.

Before leaving my first approach to metaphor entirely, though, I must remark that the paradigm it implies has certain other implications that must be considered. First of all, metaphor is not a freezing, but a rescuing, of reality. In this sense, Keats's lament, in the "Ode on a Grecian Urn," that everything happening on that urn has become nothing more than a "fair attitude,"[6] is unjust. Not only can a successful metaphor never die; at worst, it will become a proverb, or a word. The immortalizing of essence never results in a loss; this is the understory or hidden echo that can be heard under the rather rigid surface of Ovid's *Metamorphoses*. The crawling bark that engulfs Daphne is a shelter for her essence as well as an imprisoning curse.[7] Plants, the vegetable kingdom in general, make for the ideal "vehicle," because their immobility, their quasi-lifelessness, lend themselves to complete transfiguration. As I have said elsewhere, the deictic act, the human gesture of pointing, can only be fully

---

5. Wordsworth, "The Prelude," *Selected Poems and Prefaces,* 193–366, Book 12, l. 256.
6. Keats, *Selected Poems and Letters,* 207–8, l. 41.
7. Book 1, ll. 452–568.

incarnated in a whipping reed. "And Pan did after Syrinx speed, / Not as a maid, but for a reed."[8] Plants, then, can be embodied essences. Syrinx will have more of her essential humanity in her after her transformation than before.

It may be objected that I am only seeking to revive the ancient doctrine of correspondences, whereby everything in nature expresses or exemplifies something in the mind. This is true: but what I am trying to do is show how that process actually works, as a thought is satisfied, or sanctified, in a metaphor.

I should perhaps mention that I had not fully understood the connection, or, rather, the contrast between the two versions of metaphor—what might be called the common and the extreme—when I first dealt with them. It has, consequently, been necessary for me to recapitulate my earlier thoughts in order to make my argument about the relation between the two species of metaphor.

At this point I would like to venture a detour through neighboring, if autonomous, territory. I would go so far as to say that love itself, such as Apollo's for Daphne, or Pan's for Syrinx, makes the lover too into a kind of vehicle. A plant may be chosen to incarnate, say, purity, as in the case of the lily; but the chaste lily's lover cannot avoid being caught up in the transaction. What does the lover do? The lover captures, incorporates into him/herself, and thereby rescues, the unique identity of the beloved, while the perplexed bystander is puzzled by the commotion. But the fact is, the beloved is not really conscious of his/her own identity; others are only dimly, or peripherally, aware of it; the identity of the beloved becomes a living presence, intact and secure, only in the body and mind of the lover. For this reason, I venture to call the lover a "vehicle": he/she provides shelter for the peculiar and specific personality of the beloved, as the reed has absorbed the pure, particular act of a human being's pointing.

## II. METAPHORS, COMMON AND EXTREME

### A. Metaphor: Capturing an Essence

The following section consists primarily of material from an essay of mine entitled "Two Types of Visual Metaphor." I have omitted mainly passages that concern the "second" kind of visual metaphor referred to in the title of the article; that second type of metaphor corresponds roughly to what I describe

---

8. Marvell, "The Garden," *Norton Anthology,* 1290–91, ll. 31–32.

in section (C) of this chapter ("Metaphor as Double Vision"), about my experience on the island of Miquelon (to which I have already referred). By a remarkable coincidence, I followed through, in that totally different context, and with no such intent whatsoever, on what I had tried, and failed, to do, in the previous essay.

## B. Two Types of Visual Metaphor

The insistence of Goethe, as a young man, that he wished to experience ideas or essences directly, rather than merely as abstractions, makes the subject of an amusing passage in Erich Heller's "Goethe and the Idea of Scientific Truth." Ideas, Goethe complained, should not be thought of as existing only in some metaphysical realm: "I . . . *can even see them with my eyes.*"[9]

And why shouldn't one—for what can essence be, if not embodiment in some form? I myself met Despair one evening in 2001, in the form of a tall elderly man walking down Khmelnitskovo Street (in Kiev).

With Goethe, I should like to ask once more whether we do not need to find a more regular way, or whether we do not perhaps already have a regular way, to experience essences within the phenomenal world. Jakob Böhme, too, recognized the importance of bringing together image and essence, despite their different characteristics: "Bild und Wesen welche ungleiche Dinge sind" for they "müssen dennoch beysammen seyn und einander lieben"—"after all, they must live side by side, and love one another."[10] The image is the guarantor in us of our idea of the image, and we know that it has worked by a moment of illumination, for "the Samplar of all things shineth in the mind, as the truth in the image."[11]

Jean Lefebve, in *L'image fascinante et le surréel*, suggests that certain images (perhaps potentially all phenomena) draw us toward a glimpse of what we cannot see, an object "qui ne se forme que dans le mouvement qui ne le rencontre pas" ("that takes shape only in the movement which does not encounter it"). Normally, an image refers to something "behind" itself; but

---

9. Heller, *Disinherited Mind*, 7. The present essay is an extension of theories of metaphor developed in my previous work, and some repetition of ideas as well as references that I have used earlier will be unavoidable.

10. Böhme, "Andeutung," *Mysterium Magnum*, n. pag. By my having translated "Wesen" as "essence" at this point, rather than as "being," or "reality," I was already tilting the argument in my favor.

11. Cusanus, *The Idiot*, 38. My contribution to this sentence actually foreshadows the content of Section III in this chapter.

some images—for instance, the mask, or the corpse—betray that expectation. We expect them to signal something beyond, and are caught off balance when we understand that we have always assumed there is one step more on the staircase than is actually there, that we have taken for granted the existence of something that every image points to. In that moment of betrayal, when the image refuses to fulfill its deceptive but reassuring function, we find ourselves abruptly in the presence of essence itself. "L'image, en effet . . . est notre vraie métaphysique, la seule où les mots d'éternité, d'infini et d'absolu aient un sens parce que, dans 1'image, nous les *vivons*" ("The image, in fact . . . is our true metaphysics, the only one in which the words eternity, infinity, and absolute have any meaning, for, in the image, we *live* them").[12]

Although Lefebve's formulation is an attractive one, I would say that we experience essence much more freely and frequently than he acknowledges, not only in the anxiety-provoking and particularly numinous situations that he selects for study. I would rather invoke Peirce's arguments for the widespread availability of ideal concepts in experience,[13] and perhaps even paraphrase Percy Bysshe Shelley's "Common as light is love" as "Common as love is essence."[14] (I trust that my use of the word "essence," unfashionable as the term may be, will justify itself during the course of this chapter.)

My thesis is simply this: every metaphor effects the entrapment of an essence. It does this not by some vague mystical process, but by moving the "tenor" to an environment in which we are forced to experience it stripped of its inessential attributes.[15]

I will use four examples drawn from an October walk around the lake in Delaware Park, Buffalo, New York. In the first example, I came upon a stand of reeds, each being whipped with a violent circular motion by the wind. The whipping reeds kept executing a pointing gesture, an isolated gesture, con-

---

12. Lefebve, *L'image fascinante*, 267. I am grateful to Charles Altieri for the reference to Lefebve.

13. Peirce, *Philosophy of Peirce*, 248; cf. Peirce, *Essential Writings*, 14. I have the late Lionel Abel to thank for tracing the first reference.

14. *Prometheus Unbound*, 2.5.40.

15. At this point, predictably, I began to feel some discomfort with the inadequacy of the "tenor-vehicle" distinction to account for certain aspects of metaphor, but was unable to find a satisfactory alternative. A few traces of my previous argument may be found on pp. 288 and 295 of Massey, "Two Types of Visual Metaphor." For some objections to I. A. Richards's "tenor-vehicle" distinction, see Black, *Models and Metaphors*, Chapter iii. I have chosen not to engage in the intricate investigations surrounding the fundamental issues of metaphor, ably represented by more recent scholars such as Fauconnier and Turner, not because I believe that they are unimportant, or because I think that I can casually ignore them, but, because, if I did allow myself to become involved, I would never get to the perhaps excessively simple ideas that I do wish to propose.

sisting of nothing but pointing: the essence of pointing. It was the perfect gesture, without context, which one encounters only in the natural world. The reeds expressed nothing but the perfection of the gesture that they performed. More precisely, they expressed the perfection of relationship (pointing is done *by* someone), with respect to the gesture that they performed.

In the second case, I walked under a weeping willow tree, and stopped just beyond it. Looking back, I saw among the long, yellow, drooping boughs one twig bent in a certain way that seemed to convey the very gesture or shape of an arm arched forward from the shoulder. Beyond the tree stood a bush on the right, with a few heavy, whitish leaves still attached to it. The leaves seemed to have more of leather about them than anything actually made of leather could possibly have had. Beside that bush, to the right and a little above, another one, with an army of Tartar horsemen galloping up over it, adhering to the undulations of the terrain: a wild grape vine, with its innumerable tattered, brownish, bruised leaves spreading up over the bush.

It may be only a matter of terminology, but, in all these cases, in which the idea (e.g., the imagined Tartar horsemen) suggested by the thing seen was stronger than the visible object (the grape vine), the term "tenor" begins to seem inappropriate to designate the major element in the metaphor. The situation is different from the one in which Achilles is called a lion. The essence of Achilles is courage, but the essence of a leaf is not leather. Although, technically, it is the leaf that calls to mind the leather, it is actually leatheriness that has found a means of expressing itself through the leaf. I am struck by the purple flush under certain smooth patches of bark, amid rougher brown patches, in late winter; unmistakably, it is blood that is fulfilling itself through the purple of the bark, not the bark that is expressing itself more fully through the analogy with blood. Although we usually think that the thing present is the dominant percept, the imaginary presence may overwhelm it, and deprive it of its original status as the originating force in a metaphor. What we are then left with is a vehicle without a tenor, a vehicle that has absorbed its tenor so fully that the tenor has virtually vanished (as, for instance, in Homer's "wandering similes"). At this point, one might be inclined to ask why the vehicle does not become another tenor, ready in turn to be metaphorized. The answer I would give, which I develop more fully at the end of this chapter, is that the vehicle is the beginning of a story: it is not something waiting to become part of another story.

But, to relate this observation with my previous thesis: where the idea suggested by the thing seen is not subordinate to the visible object, and the visible object is experienced as the expression of an idea more powerful than itself, metaphoric vision is the experience of an embodied essence. An actual arm in a certain position has accidental characteristics of size, shape, color, and purpose, as well as trivializing surroundings, that make it impossible for us to experience it as an essential arm with an essential bend: the twig liberates the arm from its accidents and presents its character in pure form. This is why we can experience something fully only through something else, and perhaps even why, as has so often been said, all knowledge is based on comparisons: a thing can be known in its essence only when it has been rid of its cloud of adjuncts and irrelevant particulars, and this can happen to it only when it is known through something else. Not only does the alien environment of the twig, the leaf, the reeds, the creeper, free the arm, leather, pointing, the Tartar horde, from their distracting particularizations: it isolates them by grafting them onto unfamiliar matrices, and so rids them of superfluous associations. Their essence is not merely transferred to a neutral medium, but to one that makes it impossible for any inessential connections to survive. (Leibnitz's analysis of memory, corroborated by Penfield's neurological experiments, emphasizes just how heavy an encumbrance of extraneous detail is forced upon the mind with every event, and sticks there).[16] This separation or isolation begins early in a metaphoric perception.[17]

In fact, in order for us to have noticed it in the first place, the thing we are seeing has to be doing something paradoxical, something wrong. If it is a willow twig, it is growing up in a hoop instead of hanging straight down, like the others; if it is a spray of grass, it is growing through a snow bank rather than from the earth. If it is a reed, it is gesturing, pointing at me, not doing what other reeds do. Even before the bipolarity of the experience articulates itself, before we are aware of a "tenor" calling for attention, an isolating incongruity has set in to mark the moment for metaphoric perception.

The history of paradox as an aesthetic principle, from the warnings of the Pseudo-Dionysius or of Hugh of St. Victor against "appropriate" images of the divine, such as figures of light (they favored, rather, if images should be unavoidable, vulgar and hideous embodiments of the sacred); the iconoclastic

---

16. Leibniz, *Œuvres philosophiques*, vol. 1, 22, 77–83, 124, 725; Penfield and Rasmussen, *Cerebral Cortex*, Chapter ix.

17. I am obliged to David Porush for drawing my attention to other relevant work in neuropsychology, and in particular to the late Hans-Lukas Teuber's concept of "cascade specification" (cf. "serial processing"). This was intended to provide a model for the process by which the mind narrows down the torrent of perception and allows only certain elements in the visual field to achieve prominence. (See, for instance, Michael, "Retinal Processing," 105–14, for a related approach). An analogy in the pathological realm to the metaphoric experience as I describe it in this chapter is afforded by the persistence of visual percepts in incongruous contexts, or their preempting of inappropriate areas in the perceptual field, under certain conditions of cerebral injury. See Critchley, "Types of Visual Perseveration," 267–99; Spalding and Zangwill, "Disturbance of Number-Form," 24–29, especially pp. 25–26, is marginally pertinent.

movement as such;[18] and the vogue of contradiction in critical theory; all these it should be possible, at least theoretically, to subsume under the present argument. And the more contradictory the vehicle to the tenor, the more purely we may expect to apprehend the tenor's essence.[19]

The ramifications of this theory extend for me most obviously in two directions: one, towards aleatory practices in the arts; the other, towards allegory. The given in the motion of the marionette, or in the harmonies of the Aeolian harp; the accidents of modern music, of the mobile or the computer-painting, of the novel in which one can shuffle the leaves (all apparently forms of "nonsense"), are intended to assist us in the discovery of an essence. The law behind these practices must be that all art, whether aleatory or apparently intentional, is an act of discovery, the discovery of essences. Art is the cultivation of happy accidents in which recognitions can take place. These recognitions are all recognitions of one thing through another. In this sense, all art is Rorschach—not Rorschach as self-projection, but as the capturing of one event by our having stirred up another: as if one set out early to catch dew-laden grasshoppers that turned out to fly all too well, and caught the beauty of the hillside instead. The essence can never be created: but it can always be discovered. Aleatory techniques are not a cowardly abdication of the artist's responsibility for capturing the essential image single-handed, but a recognition of the fact that it must always be something he/she finds rather than something he/she makes; so, he/she may as well set traps for it. There is a pre-existent matrix of all artistic images lying potentially, but only potentially, accessible in the things of nature (the swooping, self-enclosed gesture of the willow-tree, the pointing of the reed), at the mercy of which even the greatest artist lies; even a Turner, in his earliest, most realistic marines. Again, as Nicholas of Cusa says, the mind "is like unto one that is a sleepe, until it be stirred up by admiration, proceeding from sensible things, to be moved, then by the motion of its intellectual life, it finds described in it self that which it seeketh. But thou must understand that this description is a resplendance or shining of the Samplar of all things."[20]

Another branch of metaphor points towards the allegorical method. Let me take Philo of Alexandria as my example. What is Philo doing? Presumably, he is providing a re-reading of Genesis in terms acceptable to the Platonic Greek, or to the Hellenizing Jew. He works with two series, one the Biblical

---

18. Hugh of St. Victor, *Œuvres complètes,* 187–90. It was Hugh whose Commentary revived interest in the Pseudo-Dionysius. See also Caraher and Massey, eds., *Literature and Iconoclasm,* pamphlet.

19. See Caraher and Massey, eds., *Literature and Contradiction,* pamphlet.

20. Cusanus, op. cit., 38.

narrative, the other the philosophical discourse, and he has to read the first in terms of the second, translating as he goes. Of course, there are special problems of rhetoric, of aesthetic structure, as well as problems in presenting a thesis, that arise from this method. The armature of the presentation is a sacred text rather than a syllogism, yet the work must yield the same results as a syllogism, though ultimately to a different purpose. There is a kind of counterpoint between the two processes in the operation, interspersed with the cadenzas of unexpected association. The true beauty of the method arises from its "nonsensical" randomness: very much like rhyme, or like the arbitrary aspects of serial composition, it half forces and half permits the allegorist to fall into unforeseen insights at certain intersections of the planned with the unpredictable (for instance, the remarkable thought, with respect to Genesis 48:15–16, that God gives us the good directly and without language, whereas He can deal with our ills only by mediation, or through the Word).[21] As a complex fabric in which a blending of the intellectual and the poetic processes can be achieved, allegory has no substitute.

Yet I see a still deeper function in allegory and one which in a sense violates its own apparent aims. Allegoresis is a sustained metaphoric vision, seeing one thing as another over the long haul. Why, really? Because metaphor, a fulfilled comparison, becomes an antidote to the endless process of neutral comparison. In a searching study of Philo's allegorical method, Irmgard Christiansen argues that the allegorical interpretation of Scripture, for Philo, enables one to pass beyond the limitations of Platonic thought, which are established by two rules: (1) one can never be sure that things have their true names (cf. the *Cratylus*), and (2) as we know them, things are always contaminated by their opposites (cf. the *Gorgias*).[22] "An irrational impulse," Philo concludes, "issues forth and goes its rounds, both from our reasonings and from Mind that corrupts the truth."[23] But allegory, based on the sacred text, rescues us from the skeptical inferences that follow all too easily from the Platonic method. By making Scripture the central pillar of his allegorical work, Philo transforms comparison, often the handmaid of skepticism, into the touchstone of essence, an instrument in the repeated discovery and fulfillment of divinity through metaphor. Metaphor, then, becomes the conquest of comparison, and one can ask, Comparison, where is thy sting?

---

21. Philo, with an English translation by Colson and Whitaker, vol. 1, 421: "The good things, the food, He himself bestows with His own hand, but by the agency of Angels and Words such as involve riddance of ills."

22. Christiansen, *Die Technik*, 170.

23. Philo, op. cit., vol. 1, 457.

That every assertion is contaminated by its opposite, or eventually topples into self-negation, is perhaps the very condition of thought with which the Hegelian system was an attempt to cope.[24] That language itself is based on a process of comparison which leads us to no definable end, is a painful thought with which one can suffer for a long time.

But that metaphor may offer us a kind of double-barreled solution to these conditions is harder to see: that allegory, of all things, might be an antidote to the curse of interpretation. Yet what allegory or, more precisely, allegore-sis—reasoning through an extended metaphorical process—can achieve leads to stasis and to a sense of fulfillment rather than towards more querulous searching. There is a feeling of completion, of stopping still, in each successful metaphor, like the note of the bullfrog. Metaphoric vision, which isolates the essence in a substance other than the accidental embodiment of that essence, gives that thing rest. It craved to have its essence known: now it is known. The uneasiness of comparison is stilled. It may be said that Philo tried to pacify, on the very largest scale, much of the anxiety of thought.

To return to my previous topic, how metaphors are formed: the first thing we do when we encounter a powerful new experience is "redefine," or change, its map, break up the visual field (and I am talking largely about visual experiences, those that we tend to call "beautiful") like the fabric of a camouflaged jungle uniform. This patchwork revision of the new event is more manageable than the experience in its totality. In practice, we then tend to fasten on the salient patch and let that represent the whole. In the case of a scene that has had a strong effect, the metaphor evoked is almost necessarily a synecdoche.

When we see (rather than think) something fresh, we never see it as "itself," for to see it as such would mean merely to see it again, that is, to see it in accordance with some previous thought that we have had of it. To see something new, or as new, is *not* to recognize: it is to see unfamiliarly, to see what is not yet there. Metaphoric experience is a guarantee that we are seeing something, not as we "know" it, but as we see it. That is why it seems to us that we break it up; but there is no "it," and metaphoric vision alone enables us to recognize that there isn't one.[25]

---

24. Hegel, *Phenomenology of Mind*, "Introduction."

25. Cf. the interpretation of Hesse, "Explanatory Function," 249–59, in Ricoeur, *La Méta-phore vive*, 305–6; also Sparshott, "The Limits of Metaphor," 74–94, especially pp. 78–79. In a passage of the *Notebooks*, Coleridge seems to be groping for an explanation of the effect produced by irregular surfaces in landscape: "The looking down a dell filled up with wood rising up from unequal ground, and forming such a sweet play of Surfaces. What is the source of this peculiar pleasure?—A surface that is yet not a surface? or rather a substratum counterfeited by the deep Drapery of the true Substratum?" *Notebooks*, vol. 3, entry 3990.

The effect of this kind of vision, which overwhelms what we know with what we see, breaking it up into parts none of which corresponds with what we "think" we are seeing (as a row of cars in a snowy parking lot is seen from an airplane, the light catching each one in a blaze that produces shapes incongruous with the structural elements of a car, anything but whole cars), is to leaven the scene, to rid it of its heaviness, of its "itness." Each of the parts then becomes lighter, and can be lifted off, as if with an airship: the object's self, its torpid weight, is conquered. The parking lot becomes an airfield. It is no longer an empty space with cars in it, it is a dazzling patched surface of far-flung rows, coruscating objects in procession, each part glitter, part color, part shadow, anything but car. Beauty creates a self-evacuating space into which essences can, and must flood.

Where there is a surplus of the present experience, the metaphoric rendering of it can never be adequate. Still, we are refreshed, and our unendurable burden, "the heavy and the weary weight / Of all this unintelligible world, / Is lightened,"[26] by contact with essence through metaphoric perception. Even in our confrontations with overpowering beauty, we have some appropriate response, so that the whole scene can be lightened, relieved of its reality, lifted off from its squat, pinned-down condition, and, like a dirigible, felt to tug powerfully at its moorings.

## C. Metaphor as Double Vision

In the first part of this chapter, "Capturing an Essence," I described what I might call the common experience of metaphor, in which the essence of one thing is expressed through another. This is an event that can occur anywhere, and at any time: it does not require an extraordinary situation to give rise to it. I see a late autumn wasp crawling and stumbling on a ledge at my elbow, and I imagine a baby "floundering" on my windowsill. It is, for some reason, a poor metaphor, but that doesn't matter: the point is that it is easily generated, and, what is more important, the process, or what one might even venture to call the mechanism, by which it is produced is easy to understand: a feature of one thing is made more noticeable by being attributed to something else of which it is a more salient feature. As Carl L. Hausman puts it (though he is in error about the original meaning in the transfer being "marginal"), "Metaphors play

---

26. Wordsworth, "Tintern Abbey," 108–11, ll. 39–41.

on the transfer of some marginal meanings of one term to the central meaning of the other term."[27]

In the following section of this chapter, something quite different is described. I found myself immersed in a scene in which there was no question of looking beyond what I was seeing, for a better equivalent of what lay before me. The metaphors, if one can call them that, imposed themselves, instead of being invoked. In the earlier case, the object would solicit an image to represent it; in the present case, the image arose from within to embrace the object. This image came up from some inner reservoir and emerged to engage my perceptions.

I will try to gloss a few lines from Andrew Marvell's "The Garden" to clarify my meaning. Marvell writes:

> The mind, that ocean where each kind
> Does straight its own resemblance find;
> Yet it creates, transcending these,
> Far other worlds, and other seas;
> Annihilating all that's made
> To a green thought in a green shade.[28]

The mind contains the equivalent of everything outside itself, but it transforms some of these mere things into a reservoir of perfected, transcendent images. Or one might say that it contains a minor reservoir (a reservoir of mere practical equivalents), and a major reservoir (or, to borrow from Marvell's poem, a garden) in which the images are matured into their perfected selves. From this second reservoir or garden, it can draw materials to enhance and magnify the physical world. To pluck a sentence from William Empson's *Some Versions of Pastoral,* "A hint of the supreme condition is thus found in the actual one." Through this process, "all that's made" is rescued rather than "annihilated."[29] In terms of the experience on Miquelon which I describe below, a companion image in that reservoir was waiting to rise and greet each gull as it settled into the ground, and transform it into a step on the way to heaven.

The problem with conveying such an experience is not exactly that it is site-specific; it does require, though, a situation in which one is entirely subor-

---

27. Hausman, *Metaphor and Art,* 26.

28. Marvell, "The Garden," ll. 43–48. A different approach to "The Garden," an approach for which the entire issue of metaphor is largely irrelevant, can be found in Ryan Netzley's "Sameness and the Poetics of Nonrelation." Here, the emphasis is on a "subtractive poetics," which recalls Elizabeth Bishop's "One Art," or Robert Louis Stevenson's "The only art is to omit."

29. Empson, *Some Versions of Pastoral,* 130.

dinate, in which one is not doing something, or initiating a reasoning process. But, as is the case with all other quasi-mystical moments, in order to be communicated to any significant degree, they should really be happening while one is telling about them. The following passages on Miquelon are an attempt to convey the raw reality of the experience, "wie es eigentlich war" ("as it really was"). It is expressed in the incoherent language that came to me at the time; perhaps that language, hard as it is to accept, can recreate something of what it actually felt like to be there. The principal idea in this section is that metaphor is an imperfect image seen through a perfect one.

The original notes are in bold type: commentary and interpolations are in standard type. It will be seen immediately that the passages involving French are even less coherent than the others, grammatically as well as conceptually. As it happens, I do know French, but I have let these passages stand as they were originally written, whatever may have prompted them to come out in that way. Only "nonsense" could convey fully what I meant: there was no other way. Those who may not wish to struggle with this unedited "tangled bank" of notes and commentary should skip to the next section.

<hr />

**Life is just a source of the images with which we construct the images of the perfection that is in us.**

**Metaphor gives one a bit of that perfection—it is an experience of life seen through an image of perfection—that is, seen through one of those images of perfection that well up in us, made up of the imperfect images in life: it is an experience of life brought into association with a vision, therefore made like** (i.e., made similar to) **the perfect image. It is an imperfect image seen through a perfect one.**

(What I seem to have had in mind was a pattern with three components: first, an unformed potential for perfection in us; second, experiences of real life borrowed to give a face, so to speak, or some specifiable form, to that perfection; third, another stage, at which the experiences of life would be seen through the lens of that perfect image. The real experience then is sanctified by its association with the perfect experience. If Achilles is like a lion, it is because that lion is no ordinary lion, but the imaginary lion, the vision of a lion, that we carry in us. A metaphor is a real experience brought under the aegis of an imaginary experience, of a perfect vision that has employed the materials of life to give form to a "moment" of perfection. And we carry within us a lode of visions that can be exploited by life to realize its own perfection.

It is the disintegration of these inner visions in the aftermath of a death that Max Wickert seems to be describing in "Ave atque Vale":

> The solitude where I am not alone
> Commences now. All images I made
> Melt to the memories I made them from.[30])

**Life and all its visions and its pleasures is just a detraction from vision. That's why watched sex is better than lived sex—simply because the imaginary can be perfect and an experience is only an experience.** (Although the assertion now seems merely ludicrous, I think I know what I meant at the time.) **What is needed is to shut one's eyes.**

(Here the point seems to be that one does not have to bring the inner visions to light by drawing them up through the temptation, so to speak, of an experience in real life that yearns to be justified by a metaphor; one can go back directly into, and dwell in, that world of visions, an autonomous world which can only be diminished by being forced into a transaction with the real world. It might be straining a point to invoke Marvell's "Garden" again at this point, but there is a moment in that poem which matches up precisely with what I was trying to say here:

> And so the mind, from pleasure less,
> Withdraws into its happiness. . . .[31])

**Une falaise, des cailloux dans l'eau.** ("A cliff, pebbles in the water." Apparently, a vision I was having while falling asleep. Not merely a memory image of the shore as seen during the day, but one of those visions cobbled from the elements of reality of which I have been speaking: brief as it is, a perfect image, a central example of the kind of experience that I have been attempting to describe. It will be apparent that, at some times during this event, I dwelt on the importance of external stimuli for evoking the inner vision; at other times, I rejected the external and dwelt entirely on the inner dimension of the experience.)

**En parler ? Surtout ne pas la chasser. Il n'y a que la vision elle-même. Il n'y a pas de moyen entre elle et la vie. Laisse-la arriver. Ce qui est dedans.** ("Speak of it? Above all do not drive it away. There is nothing but the vision itself. There is no middle ground between it and life. Let it come. That which is within.")

---

30. Wickert, "Ave atque Vale," 42, ll. 1–3.
31. Marvell, "The Garden," ll. 41–42.

(The following passage derives from a familiar domestic situation: I complain of being disturbed just as I am about to fall asleep. The grammar of the French begins to deteriorate further around this point.)

**Elle l'a chassée, elle l'a gâtée, en ne restant pas dans mes bras et me *laissant* m'assoupir dans l'autre monde, le monde en moi; je me sens comme une vessie distendue de beauté, pression pénible; la beauté doit couler de moi, trouver des issues.** ("She has driven it away, she has spoiled it, by not staying in my arms and letting me drift off to sleep in the other world, the world within myself; I feel like a bladder distended with beauty, painful pressure: beauty needs to run out from me, find openings.")

(Beyond this point, the notes become a mixture of "Joual"—my native Montreal dialect of French—and English. I was probably dipping into French simply because I was in French-speaking territory at the time.)

**Au moment de *relaxer*, de m'endormir, pour que les visions sortent, viennent, et maintenant elles restent en moi, incomplètes, car il faut qu'elles viennent, afin d'être *fulfilled*; à moins qu'elles ne soient articulées dans des visions spécifiques la beauté reste douleur—belle, mais pourtant douleur, incomplète, et toujours [*running the risk* d'être]** (transcript uncertain here) ***overwhelmed* par la vie, par la vie extérieure, toujours en danger de se *collapse* sans avoir été formée en formes saisissables donc parfaites et, donc, éternelles.** ("At the moment of letting go [me laisser aller], of falling asleep, so that the visions can emerge, can come out, and now they remain in me, incomplete, for they have to come out in order to be fulfilled [comblées], unless they are articulated in particular visions beauty remains pain—beautiful, but pain nevertheless, incomplete, nevertheless, and always running the risk [courant le risque] of being submerged by life, by outward life, always in danger of collapsing [s'effondrer] without having achieved forms that can be seized in their perfection, and that thereby can become eternal.")

(There appear to be two "moments" of beauty, then: one in which it is turned inward, self-contained, complete in itself, not even aware of any outside world: and another in which it cries out for articulation.)

(The following embarrassing interjection reflects the yearning and disappointment experienced when the presence of the perfect forms is felt, but they remain just beyond reach:)

**Groan, groan, groan—that's what I want to do—groan.**

**I feel as if I were a visitor from another world forced to participate in this one, where everything is "non" (in French)** (i.e., where everything conspires to negate this state of being).

(The next paragraph refers to a scene that is described in greater detail later on.)

A metaphor is an exterior image (the gulls) seen through the lens of an interior image (the steps being laid).

Maybe the stained glass of St. Julian has to do with the seeing of the experiential through the internal—or of using the experiential to help see the internal.

It's perhaps a way of combining the quality of the two images in the idea of "seeing through," yet in the same dimension, or at the same level, therefore it's seeing *not* through. (One doesn't see *through* stained glass: one sees the glass; but it's still glass, translucent though not transparent).

(In Flaubert's story, "The Legend of St. Julian the Hospitaller," we are told at the end that what Flaubert has written is approximately what can be seen in the stained glass window at a church near where he lives.[32] I was suggesting that it could be understood in terms of the idea I have proposed. The actual event is experienced through the inner event; there is an act of fusion, and a glow radiates from their reaction. This is the most parsimonious possible conclusion. The inner consumes the outer as Christ consumes Julian at the end. At that point, there is no longer any need for an inner and an outer, much less for a "tenor" and a "vehicle"; they illuminate each other mutually, and completely. The space between them vanishes, and what we are left with is the stained glass.)

The gulls climbing the hill—placing steps in the face of the hill so that one could éventuellement (possibly, potentially) climb—the scene is itself a metaphor (allegory) for the experiential's placing steps for, or serving as steps for, the inner vision.

(A scene in which gulls flew one by one up the face of a distant hill and settled one above another was the occasion for this entire rhapsody. It presented an image of steps, and gave a visual embodiment to the very principle that it was later used to illustrate—the ascent of *the image of an ascent* to its embodiment in the real world. In terms of my model, what happens is simply this: the gulls settling into place in an ascending sequence are seen through the inner image of a marble staircase.)

(To repeat: I was on the island of Miquelon, on the cape of the Eagle's Nest, a high, steep-sided peninsula with a broad depression or valley near its tip, ringed by crenellations that wall off the sea beyond. In this shallow valley, well over a mile wide, there lie three small lakes surrounded by grey-green tundra, with the peculiar flat profile of arctic lakes. Coming across the valley from the right was an irregular line of gulls, widely spaced, pure white in the

---

32. Flaubert, "Saint-Julien L'Hospitalier," 623–48.

sunlight, and so far away that they seemed to be barely moving, flying with excruciating slowness.

As they passed over the lakes and reached the opposite wall of the valley they settled, one by one, on the distant slope across from me. They were not directly above one another, but they seemed to be setting, in sequence, the pure white steps of an irregular marble staircase into the hillside.

This scene is the main thing that I have been trying to write about).

**The reason for the poignancy of metaphor is precisely that it includes the experiential—the mortal, and imperfect, what goes towards death—in association with the perfect.**

At one point, I had intended to take up the relation of paradox to metaphor, and to thought as such, in an Appendix, but abandoned that effort as excessively ambitious. For the present, I merely want to acknowledge the obvious fact that my theory of the imagination has affinities with several previous theories, although it was not conceived in terms of any of those theories, and can, I believe, be distinguished from all of them. The basic vocabulary can be found, among many other places, in Kant, who speaks of the "Chiffreschrift . . . wodurch die Natur in ihren schönen Formen figürlich zu uns spricht" ("coded writing . . . by which nature speaks to us symbolically through its beautiful forms"), complete with seven colors corresponding to seven virtues.[33] Or, in the Bernard translation: "The imagination . . . is very powerful in creating another nature, as it were, out of the material that actual nature gives it. . . . Thus we feel our freedom from the law of association (which attaches to the empirical employment of imagination), so that the material supplied to us by nature in accordance with this law can be worked up into something which surpasses nature"[34] ("was die Natur uebertrifft").[35]

To see how these issues are addressed from different points of view, one might look at passages from later authors. Here is a familiar fragment from Coleridge: "In looking at objects of Nature while I am thinking, as at yonder moon dim-glimmering thro' the dewy window-pane, I seem rather to be seek-

---

33. Kant, *Kritik der Urteilskraft*, 226–28. To anticipate my argument in Chapter 6: it is only if we are prepared to recognize nature's language as universally intelligible that nature can speak to us. Nature speaks to us, through what we call beauty, on condition that we recognize that what it is saying to us it is saying to everyone, and we will want to spread the "good word." See also the quotation from Coleridge, n. 36, below.

34. Kant, *Critique of Judgment*, 157.

35. Kant, *Kritik der Urteilskraft*, 246.

ing, as it were *asking,* a symbolical language for something within me that already and forever exists, than observing anything new."[36]

I myself suggest, rather, that novelty or discovery, not the mere confirmation of a prior relationship, is the essence of the encounter between the inner and the outer images.

In *The Linguistic Moment,* Hillis Miller says, "According to this personifying symbology, things of the outer world are properly symbols of qualities in man's subjective world. This correspondence is validated by the resonance of both with the supernatural center that is their source. Williams rejects this personification as firmly as he rejects metaphor."[37]

Miller's phrasing is close to my own, but the idea is not the same. In this case, the outer is, again, an exemplification of some principle that is within one; for me (and I speak of the Miquelon kind of "image," if one can call it that), the subjective quality is radically different from the outer "thing": the outer is not just an instance of the inner. The inner image has its own identity (although it may be attired in clothing, so to speak, borrowed from the outer world), and has been created independently. There is no prior collusion between the two.

In *Ursprung des deutschen Trauerspiels,* Walter Benjamin says, "Jedes Gefühl ist gebunden an einen apriorischen Gegenstand, und dessen Darstellung ist seine Phänomenologie" ("Every feeling is bound to an *a priori* object, and the presentation of the object provides the phenomenology (physical instantiation) of the feeling").[38] In this formulation of the problem, it is the object rather than the inner feeling that is given *a priori,* but the allegorical structure is the same. The study of the object displays for us the features of the feeling to which it is bound; the object becomes the lens through which one views the inner thing. This is my principle reversed.

## D. Two Views of Metaphor: Conflict or Reconciliation?

The question is, then, Is a reconciliation of the above two versions of metaphor, as represented in Sections II.B and II.C of this chapter, possible, or even desirable? They arise under very different circumstances or conditions. As I have said, one requires no highly specialized environment, affecting the whole person: it can happen, or be generated, anywhere, and at any time. An encounter with something that "begs" to be metaphorized is all that is neces-

---

36. Coleridge, *Notebooks,* vol. 2, entry no. 2546.
37. Miller, *Linguistic Moment,* 369.
38. Benjamin, *Ursprung,* 150.

sary, and one is available to perform that function for it—to "service" it, so to speak. The other is a much more passive experience, in which the whole organism or being is submerged in an overpowering environment.

Are the materials that come into play in the metaphorizing situation the same in both cases? The process, at least, is certainly different: in the first case, the image is *summoned* to fit the occasion by the person who produces the metaphor, and there are, at least in principle, other appropriate metaphors that might have been proposed; in the second, it imposes itself, and there is no alternative. The gulls couldn't have been anything but marble steps. The rules have been set for us. We can't play with them.

In the second case, it isn't that we are trying to do justice to the object, or helping it to fulfill itself. It is already fulfilled, before we get to it.

Can we say that the images in the first situation come from a shallower stratum than in the second? That they are, or what results from them is, "mere" metaphor? ("Prends l'éloquence et tords-lui son cou!"[39]) That the two things are so radically different that they inhabit different categories of experience, and might even have to have different names? That, in fact, they have nothing in common?

One (A) is a figure of speech, or a rhetorical device, no matter how beautiful or impressive; perhaps we have to let it go at that, and acknowledge that it is, finally, just a figure of speech. The other (B) is a change of state, of the whole person: what was inside instantiates itself in what is outside.

It is almost a matter of sequence. In A, the object appears first; then there is a groping, a searching, in the effort to provide it with its most suitable or evocative "other." In B, it is the inner image that has lodged itself in the outer object, before one has even thought of a "metaphorizing" process, or tried to bring them together.

Simply to talk about "images," as though one were talking about the same thing in both cases, is misleading. Images are involved in both, both result in things that look like images, but the word is appropriate only in the first case. The second process results in stones; slabs of stone; impenetrable, solid surfaces for which there are no alternatives. They are lode*stones* for the image, bypassing the observer. They go directly to/come directly from the reservoir; the transaction is between them and it. You are not called upon to participate; you are only the shutter, or the gate.

What is the source of the images in the first process? It can't be what I have called Marvell's *major* reservoir, full of the perfected, seasoned and idealized materials of life, that are just waiting for a lodging in an object in the outside

---

39. Verlaine, "Art poétique," 126–27, l. 21.

world, an excuse to materialize. Perhaps the furnishings of "ordinary" metaphors come from some sort of halfway house, a place where there is a work in progress going on, a purgatory, or holding area, before they can sink into perfection, and, having vanished from conscious sight, gain currency—and, with luck, eventual agency, as summoned visions—in the unconscious. In any case, they haven't ripened; but they will do for the nonce.

So it's not that one kind, (B), is better than the other, (A); they are different from the beginning, behave differently, and serve different purposes. It is not so much that one kind of image comes from here and the other from there. It is that both the word "image" and the outcome mean different things. Having any part of the vocabulary in common just creates confusion. I am inclined to call the first one metaphor and the second simply "vision."

(Just a coincidence with Raymond Roussel's "La Vue.")

Nevertheless, that distinction, important though it be, is not uniformly crucial to my argument in the remainder of this chapter, and I will refer to it only as needed.

## III. METAPHOR AND NONSENSE

### A. Metaphor and Nonsense

It is natural to think of nonsense as a defensive strategy when deployed rhetorically. In such a role, it would seem inappropriate to identify it with metaphor, which is constructive: metaphor tries to make things better, to improve or even to leap beyond them. At its most exalted, one might associate nonsense, at best, with the *via negativa* in theology, but it is usually connected with satire, though it acquires a stronger moral meaning with the Greek Cynics' repudiation of "normal" social behavior (Diogenes in his bathtub), or with Ezekiel's disgusting practices as reported by Blake in "The Marriage of Heaven and Hell": "I then asked Ezekiel, why he eat dung, & lay so long on his right and left side? He answer'd, 'The desire of raising other men into a perception of the infinite.'"[40]

Nonsense, then, may have as powerful a moral and metaphysical purpose as any other form of expression. In fact, in its typical role as the subverter of logic, sabotaging the claims of rationalism, it is inherently transcendent in its

---

40. Blake, "The Marriage of Heaven and Hell," [Plate 13] in *Poetry and Designs*, 93. We can add to the pedigree of nonsense the fact that Franz Schubert belonged to a "nonsense society" ("Unsinngesellschaft") in Vienna in 1817–1818, a prototype for many such associations in later centuries. See Bostridge, *Schubert's Winter Journey*, 226.

orientation. When Lautréamont introduces us to "the chance meeting on a dissecting-table of a sewing-machine and an umbrella,"[41] he is not only undoing the pretensions of metaphor to provide us with a better imaginary world; he is demanding that we grapple in earnest with the limitations of our mind. "L'autonomie! Ou bien qu'on me change en hippopotame."[42] The foundations of reason are not laid by ourselves; "Maldoror" is maddened by the insecurity that this realization provokes.

As the other side of sense, then, nonsense is inescapably wedded to the transcendental. One can talk about it in practical terms, try to hedge it in or define it, but, in its use, it is connected to such language only by a negative valence. It may come off a different launching pad from metaphor, but it is aimed in the same direction. In its very creation, it provides an escape from the rationalism that dogs it, and at which it thumbs its nose.

While retaining clearly in mind the fact that metaphor and nonsense have similar goals, one may still consider some of the differences in the ways in which they pursue them. Or, to put it differently, what exactly distinguishes a metaphor from a nonsensical expression? (See below, Section III.B.)

This is a seasoned problem, and its indurated surface does not provide much of a purchase for the naïve reader, or even for the would-be philosopher. At first glance, there does not seem to be much reason why we would experience a metaphor as anything but nonsense. Achilles is clearly not a lion. The problem is somewhat mitigated by our replacing the word "metaphor" with the word "simile," but this is just an evasion. All the attributes and characteristics of the lion that are different from those of Achilles spring to mind as soon as we compare them; these secondary characteristics are too striking to ignore. To say that the lion is the incarnation of courage doesn't help; it still has a tail.

What is still harder to explain is that the secondary characteristics of the "vehicle," precisely those attributes that the tenor and the vehicle do *not* share, often play an essential part in the effect of the comparison. In fact, these unrelated attributes, rather than the obvious link between the two items, may make the metaphor (or simile) either powerful or feeble. What is more, these apparently irrelevant elements in the pairing (like the supposedly inert stretches of DNA, or the "insulation," the glial cells or white matter, of the brain) can come alive, exerting an attraction so seductive that the original reason for the comparison may be entirely forgotten, while the author (and, hence, the reader) goes off in pursuit of these random attributes. As Kant puts it, at such

---

41. For the French, see Ducasse, *Œuvres complètes*, 322.
42. Ibid., 279–80.

moments the central image "eine Menge von Empfindungen und Nebenvor-stellungen rege macht, für die sich kein Ausdruck findet" ("arouses a swarm of sensations and associations for which no expression can be found").[43]

The naked, cold Ulysses has sought shelter under some bushes; "as a man hides a brand beneath the dark embers in an outlying farm, a man who has no neighbors, and so saves a seed of fire, that he may not have to kindle it from some other source, so Odysseus covered himself with leaves."[44] By the time we have reached "that he may not have to kindle it from some other source," we are far from the beach and the dead leaves, even far from Odysseus and his plight, deeply concerned instead about the lonely farmer on his distant homestead.

One may have to tug at the thread of relevance until it nearly comes undone, to threaten the reader with a real non sequitur, with genuine non-sense, in order for a metaphor to achieve its greatest intensity. This principle accords with the general opinion, voiced repeatedly from Coleridge through Paul Reverdy on to André Breton, that the more dissimilar the vehicle from the tenor, that is, the greater the incongruity, the greater the effect.[45] Clearly, we want to be teased with nonsense.

As we have seen, though, a single view of metaphor omits aspects that come back to complicate the issue; the same is true, in even greater measure, when we try to define the relationship between metaphor and nonsense. But, to add another level of complexity to what may already seem to be an impos-sibly layered problem, I would like to look into the matter from another per-spective: what contribution could neuroscience possibly make to the study of this very specific issue, the relation of metaphor to nonsense?

Actually, it might in fact contribute to the simplification of the question, though, as will eventually become apparent, in a disconcerting way.

## B. Metaphor, Nonsense, and Neuroscience

One might assume that metaphor would not lend itself easily to neuroscien-tific study. This may be true, but, if so, it has not deterred the neuroscientists: there is, in fact, a vast body of highly technical literature on the subject. One might say that it has become a specialty, even a subdiscipline, in its own right.

---

43. Kant, *Kritik der Urteilskraft,* 249.

44. Homer, *Complete Works,* 85.

45. Breton, *Manifeste du surréalisme,* 34. Breton quotes Reverdy: "Plus les rapports des deux réalités rapprochées seront lointains et justes, plus l'image sera forte" ("The more remote and well-defined the relation of the two realities, the more powerful the image will be").

There is an enormous amount of disagreement about the localization of metaphoric functions (including, for instance, proverbs, irony, satire, humor in general, and some other forms of ambiguity) in the brain. The popular assumption is, of course, that the right hemisphere is superior in holistic and "creative" tasks, and, in spite of continuing uncertainty and inconsistency in experimental results, many (but by no means all) neuroscientists do agree that the right hemisphere is more regularly involved in the processing of metaphoric and quasi-metaphoric language than the left. In fact, even when the results of a study are inconclusive, or do not obviously support such a conclusion, the scientists involved sometimes appear to accept it as a general principle that just does not happen to be proved by their particular experiment.[46] If the right hemisphere is especially important in the comprehension of metaphors, what, then, happens when, perhaps as a result of insufficient connectivity, it is found to be compromised? It is apparent that, in some cases, particularly in those exhibiting Asperger's syndrome, the ability to react, or respond, appropriately to metaphoric language is, in fact, reduced.[47]

When studying subjects diagnosed with Asperger's Syndrome, "electro-physiological research found no differences in the ERP's for processing novel metaphors compared to processing unrelated word pairs, in contrast to neurotypical controls. Thus, when persons with AS processed novel metaphoric and unrelated two word expressions, their N400 amplitudes did not differ, suggesting that they process novel, potentially meaningful semantic relations as if they are meaningless. In addition, when persons with AS processed novel conventional and novel metaphors their N400 amplitudes were significantly more negative compared to neurotypical controls. . . . These findings suggest that for persons with AS, integration of novel metaphoric meaning is as difficult as the integration of unrelated, nonsensical meanings."[48] To someone with AS, the phrase "silent tears," or, to take a more obvious example, "green

---

46. For a typically ambiguous report, see, for instance, Mihov et al., "Hemispheric Specialization," 442–48.

47. A review of the relevant literature by Faust and Kenett, "Rigidity, Chaos and Integration," 1–10, provides pertinent information, not only at the behavioral but also at the neurophysiological level. The same issue is reviewed in the context of punning, by Jacobson, in "Your Pun-Divided Attention," 17: "Brain injuries to the right hemisphere can be associated with humor deficits in some people."

48. Faust and Kenett, 5. Even Ludwig Wittgenstein, for all the wry humor that he sometimes evinced, may not have been immune to such confusion, if Fania Pascal is to be credited. When she was ill, she responded to Wittgenstein's inquiry about her health by exclaiming "I feel just like a dog that has been run over." Instead of saying something like "Don't be foolish," or "You're exaggerating," Wittgenstein "was disgusted. 'You don't know what a dog that has been run over feels like.'" See Frankfurt, *On Bullshit*, 24.

thumb," may make no more sense than the phrase "violin tiger."[49] Stephen E. Kidd suggests that all of us, not only those suffering from a cognitive deficiency, find ourselves in this predicament when confronted with comedy: we are not really sure that we know the grounds for differentiating between metaphor (as joke) and nonsense, or "crazy talk," and need to be constantly reassured that someone else does know.[50]

But, the point is, nonsensical meanings, whether they be judged as nonsense for logical or for physiological reasons, are not *meant* to be integrated. If, for the subjects with AS, the metaphors were simply nonsense, not as a matter of subjective choice or judgment, but at the physiological level: if their brains tell them that metaphors are nonsense, why should they be made to think that there is something wrong if they see nothing meaningful in these expressions? Why expect them to "connect remote associations into a new and appropriate linguistic product"[51] when they do not of their own accord find the new "product" appropriate? (For an analogy from another domain: how could one convince a person who lacks libido that he/she should regard someone else as a sexual object?) And it is apparently not only those who have a particular mental profile who may find metaphors implausible. The professor of literature cited by Ion of Chios finds Socrates's quotation, "The light of love shines on purpled cheeks," ridiculous (Socrates had made a handsome waiter blush; a propos Wittgenstein, see footnote 48, above).[52]

Obviously, one could explain, laboriously, to someone with AS that it is appropriate to say that Achilles is a lion because a lion is "synonymous" with courage, so it is not ridiculous to call Achilles a lion. But a metaphor is not just an exchange of neutral information. It cannot just be understood: it has to be experienced. The problem is that an explained metaphor is not a metaphor at all. It is the act of mind that, in a flash, identifies what is happening in the exchange of identities, that creates the metaphor. The removal of this little piece of understanding, an apparently trivial injury, strikes at the very heart of the aesthetic state; or, to venture another metaphor, it opens up a gulf into which the whole aesthetic enterprise could vanish. I quote myself on this issue, though in an entirely different context: "If we wanted to restore the metaphor-generating function to a brain from which it had been excised, what, exactly, would we be trying to put back? Could we put the potable tear

---

49. Gold et al., "Semantic Integration," 132.

50. Kidd, 186. On the disquieting element in comedy see also Abel, *Important Nonsense*, 51–65.

51. Faust and Kenett, 5.

52. In Davidson, "Laugh as Long as you Can," 33–35.

back in the hand of Elizabeth Bishop's 'Man-Moth'[53]? Could we help him find his way back through the subway? If one were trying to replace someone's lost capacity to name carpentry tools, or even the lost capacity to use function words, one would know exactly what to look for; but what would a capsule of imagination look like? What would be the thing that we were reinstating?"[54] What instructions could we give the patch of tissue that we would be using to replace the missing part?

The difficulty of deciding between the literal and the genuinely metaphoric remains, or, perhaps, grows even more acute if we shift the ground to the consideration of catachresis. The leg of a chair is not really the "leg" of a chair to us. We no longer think of it as a metaphor, if it could be said ever to have been one. The metaphor has been entirely absorbed into its practical function; it certainly no longer has any "shock" value (if it ever did have any), yet it would not occur to us to search for another, or a better, alternative. A live catachresis, though, can still present us with the same kind of problem as, for instance, the "silent tears," or any other of the metaphoric phrases used in the experiment mentioned above: in exactly what way do they "mean"? I can think of no way to convey the sound of the comet 67P trundling through space other than what the announcer on the radio said of it: it was the sound of marbles being poured into a biscuit tin.[55] No other possibility comes to mind. It seems at once metaphor and literal statement, tightly superimposed, or united. But, to the AS subject, presumably, there would be no resonance: only the literal meaning would come through. We, on the other hand, are left with the surplus. It is that surplus, that margin of something that either means or doesn't mean, but that is indisputably there, that we have to deal with.

Proof of what we usually call sanity, then, lies in our ability to experience nonsense as sense.

## C. Metaphor and Nonsense, Again (Linguistics and Philosophy)

One can hardly do better, in initiating any discussion (and, by implication, defense) of metaphor, than to cite the sentence from Nietzsche that E. F. Kittay uses to end her book on this subject: "The drive towards the formation of metaphors is the fundamental human drive."[56] On the other hand, as far as

53. Bishop, *Complete Poems*, 15–16.
54. Massey, *Neural Imagination*, 94.
55. Announcer for the BBC (November 16, 2014).
56. Kittay, *Metaphor*, 327.

definition is concerned, metaphor is not much better off than nonsense, since "a precise criterion cannot be formulated as to whether an arbitrary isolated expression is or is not a metaphor."[57] However, what metaphor may lack in the way of a definition, it more than makes up for by the multiplicity of the theories that surround it. There is some limited agreement among the spokespersons for these theories that the history of ideas about metaphor can be divided roughly into periods, which are associated with individuals, such as I. A. Richards in the 1930s (who coined the terms "tenor" and "vehicle"[58]), with Max Black[59] in the 1950s, who may have weakened the foundations of the "comparison" notion of metaphor, and moved towards an "interactive" theory, and particularly with George Lakoff, who is considered responsible for the so-called "contemporary" theory of metaphor (no longer very contemporary, since it dates from the 1970s), which holds metaphor to be primarily a conceptual rather than a verbal phenomenon: it is "a cross-domain mapping in the conceptual system."[60] As Kittay puts it, metaphor is a transfer of meaning, not between terms, but between semantic fields.[61] In Tamar Sovran's version, it entails withdrawing to a level of abstraction that enables us to see the coherence among the disparate elements of the metaphor.[62]

Predictably, there are also aestheticians who hold "post-contemporary" views: the Metaphor Analysis Project at the Open University, under "Theories of Metaphor in Discourse," offers four: "Conceptual Metaphor Theory" (which is still largely Lakoffian), "Context-Limited Simulation Theory," "Lexical Concepts and Cognitive Models Theory," and "The Discourse Dynamics Framework." No fewer than seven semantic theories are listed by Eva Feder Kittay in her article in *Encyclopedia of Philosophy Supplement*[63] and, in her book she cites six concepts of metaphor from Scheffler (1979).[64] There are now computational or computer-based approaches to metaphor[65] which churn out not merely metaphors, but narratives, as well. Along the way, Paul Ricoeur wrote extensively on metaphor;[66] Mark Turner and Gilles Fauconnier offered

---

57. Kjärgaard, 23.
58. Richards, *Philosophy of Rhetoric*, 96.
59. E.g., *Models and Metaphors*.
60. Lakoff, "Contemporary Theory of Metaphor," 1.
61. Kittay, "Metaphor," *Encyclopedia of Philosophy*.
62. Sovran, 124–26.
63. Kittay, "Metaphor," *Encyclopedia of Philosophy*.
64. Kittay, *Metaphor: Its Cognitive Force and Linguistic Structure*, 178.
65. Ibid., 9.
66. Ricoeur, *Rule of Metaphor*.

a "blended space" approach to metaphor;[67] and Sam Glucksberg and Boaz Keysar proposed a "class-inclusion" model.[68] Not only the theories, but the technical vocabulary, as well as the frank neologisms that the theories engender, gradually become unmanageable.

It is hardly surprising, though, that metaphor should require such an army of interpreters, since its varieties and functions are multifarious, going far beyond the literary. Metaphor "is present in political, economic, scientific, artistic and other discourses";[69] George Lakoff would have added the field of mathematics.[70] At least since Vico (a crucial precursor whom Lakoff has a surprising tendency to ignore), it has been argued that it is in fact the primary constituent of language, or, at the very least, of the substantive (nominal) element of language. Of course, it has also been objected, especially by Benjamin Lee Whorf,[71] that metaphor does not play as pervasive a role in all languages as it does in the Indo-European group. It is possible that the famous telegram sent by A. R. Luria after his trip to Uzbekistan, proclaiming that "The Uzbeks have no illusions," implied that they have no metaphors either.[72] In any case, at least in the instances with which we tend to be familiar, it still inhabits language in the form of innumerable "dead metaphors" and simple expressions that we don't think of as metaphoric (Lakoff makes much of these: "path" or "road" can serve as an example). It wins and loses political advertising campaigns. What is more, it works in the sciences in the form of the "model" or "paradigm" (a term familiar from the social sciences, whether in Meyer Abrams, Thomas Kuhn, or Michel Foucault); the "model" is in turn not far from the concept of "theory" itself: in these ways, it can be seen to pervade thinking, language, and method from top to bottom.[73] It is a far cry from the view of metaphor as a decorative device in literature to a view of metaphor as the very engine of thought (*pace* Jacques Derrida[74]).

---

67. Turner and Fauconnier, "Conceptual Integration," 183–204.

68. Glucksberg and Keysar, "How Metaphors Work," 401–24. For a good review of the literature, at least up to 1986, see Kjärgaard.

69. Tretjakova, "Contemporary Theory of Metaphor."

70. Lakoff and Nuñez, *Where Mathematics Comes From.*

71. Whorf, *Language, Thought and Reality.*

72. Allik, "Do Primitive People Have Illusions?" 40.

73. For a brief summary of modeling theory, see, for instance, Windt and Noreika, "Integrate Dreaming," 1096–98.

74. Derrida, "La mythologie blanche," 1–52.

# IV. A NEW THEORY OF METAPHOR

## A. A New Theory of Metaphor: Metaphor and Reference

The title that I have given to this section of my chapter on metaphor may well sound grandiloquent; I hope to justify it, but I would not be surprised if I were to discover that my idea is not as original as I am assuming it to be. On the other hand, if there is some plausibility to it, and if it has not previously been offered as a central thesis, then it may be understood as cutting through vast thickets of sophisticated but painfully inconclusive argument. It would be a fine example of the parable about Columbus and the egg.

It will be seen that my own interest in metaphor, as displayed in the earlier portions of this chapter, is decidedly old-fashioned. I am not concerned with the (abovementioned) pervasive role of quasi-metaphors in general discourse, with the social role of metaphors, with the proportion of verbs to function words in metaphors, with the status of metaphors in logic (a subject explored rigorously by Kjärgaard and exhaustively by Kittay), or with many of such other interesting and legitimate approaches to the subject which avoid the literary realm. My center of interest remains metaphor in literature, and, particularly, in poetry. This is not only because of my natural preference for the aesthetic domain; it is also because I think that the two central problems of metaphor are still to be found, and must be confronted, in that sphere.[75]

These two problems are (1) What, if any, is the "referent" of a metaphor, or, to use an alternative formulation of the same question, What is its cognitive content? and (2) What are we to do with the "superfluous" elements in metaphors—the elements that do not overlap between tenor and vehicle? I will try to deal with these problems together.

It might be possible to declare at least the first issue, which also entails determining the "cognitive content" of metaphor, moot, but only if one followed the strategy of Mogens Kjärgaard in declaring the metaphor to be a "speech act" or a "performative" act that does not require a referent;[76] but few have had recourse to this device, and even Kjärgaard himself may be caught looking for the metaphor's "content" here and there in his work. Setting this

---

75. As an aside, I have mentioned above that, for the purposes of the latter part of this essay, I would not, for the most part, be distinguishing between the two types of metaphor that I have identified. It is not clear to me that "extreme" metaphors participate in a narrative in the same way as "common" metaphors do, though I have not yet been able to capture the difference. (See also below, Chapter 2 Section IV.B.)

76. Kjärgaard, 19.

approach aside, we can hardly deny the presence of cognitive content in numerous metaphors, and, indeed, in whole classes of metaphor. Whatever their previous history, the innumerable metaphors incorporated into ordinary language as "dead" metaphors carry exactly the same amount and quality of information as any other ordinary terms. Using the vocabulary of the field, Eva Kittay speaks of the class of "constitutive" metaphors which organize scientific thought:[77] surely no one would deny that, for all its obvious shortcomings, the assertion that "the brain is a computer" also carries information. Catachresis, often employed when nothing else will do to convey information, can hardly be said to be empty utterances: I have cited above the example of the comet's sound being like that produced by marbles being poured into a biscuit tin. Proverbs, too, obviously carry information, although they are not always consistent! The framing, and the intensification, created by metaphors, both give us a kind of meaning: as has often been said, they draw attention to, and increase one's awareness of, things that might have passed unnoticed: the increase of understanding that they produce is like that provided by washing a window.

What, then (once more), is the problem? If metaphors are so obviously instruments of knowledge, why do they have such a dodgy reputation among philosophers and speculative linguists? Why are innumerable books and papers written in the attempt to define their contribution to cognition?

I would be inclined to say that, whatever other characteristics it may have, the central seed or crucial component of metaphor is not referential: its reference value, if any, is an accidental byproduct, or unintended consequence, of its nature. It does not refer to something outside itself that anyone can point to. Paradoxically, it even draws one away from the very thing the perception of which it is meant to intensify. One might say that metaphor is a predatory form of narrative that makes off at the first opportunity with the essential characteristic of its tenor. To put it simply, a metaphor is the beginning of a story.

What I have been calling the wandering simile, also known as the epic simile, or the Homeric simile, is the critical example. The proof of the fact that no "live" metaphor (i.e., no metaphor that has not become indistinguishable from ordinary language) is paraphrasable is that the epic simile, which is a simile that has been "given its head," so to speak, is not paraphrasable. The reason why it is not open to paraphrase is that it contains elements that have nothing to do with the tenor, and all efforts at paraphrase necessarily focus on the attributes of the tenor.

---

77. Kittay, 325.

It is not fully clear to me why metaphor seeks to draw one away from the tenor, or why we should wish to be drawn away from the tenor. Perhaps, in accordance with my own argument, it is because we crave essence, and are always in pursuit of essence. On the one hand, the metaphor gives us the essence of the tenor, but, on the other hand, it abstracts us from the tenor. After what might be called an initial honeymoon, or, to borrow a phrase from Saul Kripke, an initial baptism, in which tenor and vehicle illuminate each other brilliantly, the vehicle begins to detach itself, and go its own way. Perhaps it is only if a metaphor or catachresis becomes a cliché, or a proverbial expression, that it can retain something of its referential force ("it knocked the wind out of my sails"). The Homeric metaphor, in particular, drifts imperceptibly across the dividing line from referentiality, hypnotizing one, or anesthetizing one against excessive awareness, so that one will not notice the discontinuity. We may sometimes even choose to forget the tenor entirely: we do not always remember that Keats was talking about the blind Homer when we repeat,

Aye on the shores of darkness there is light.

The following opinion may have been articulated elsewhere, but, if so, I have just not run across it: as I have said above, I think that every metaphor is the beginning of a story. We are drawn in; we want to know what comes next. Homer is simply honoring that impulse when, at the end of Book 5 of the *Odyssey,* he stops to draw our attention to the pebbles that cling to the tentacles of the octopus when it is torn away from the rocks, as the skin is being ripped from the hands of Odysseus when he tries to cling to the rocks on the coast of Phaeacia, in order not to be dragged out to sea and drowned. Why, at this point, of all places, pause to mention the pebbles? The same happens when Homer describes the red-hot stake being driven into the eye of Polyphemus, as if a blacksmith were tempering iron, "and the metal screeches steam and its temper hardens."[78] What has the hardening of the iron to do with that extreme and immediate event? What did the upland farmer's need to go to a neighbor to get a coal to restart his fire have to do with Odysseus sheltering under a bush?

It is certainly true that the deliberate inclusion of apparently irrelevant details makes the comparison seem more natural, less forced, almost inevitable: it makes the metaphor seem less of a device. But that is not the main point. The parts of the vehicle that do not overlap with the attributes of the tenor are simply parts of the new story. There is nothing "extraneous" there.

What is the "reference" of a story? What is it "about"? What is the "reference" of a metaphor? It is the same question, and equally inappropriate.

---

78. Homer, *The Odyssey,* 223.

## B. Metaphor and Essence (Again)

The feeling of hubris, of having "had the last word," inevitably ends, where metaphor is concerned, with embarrassment, if not humiliation. How could one imagine having brought the millennia of conversation about metaphor to an end?

I was sitting on the screened-in back porch of my son's house in Port Hood, Nova Scotia, when I realized, yet again, that I had not grasped the nature of metaphor fully. Like the speaker in the Kipling poem, I was "looking downward, to the sea," over the great field sloping to the channel that separates Cape Breton from Port Hood Island. There were two files of Queen Anne's Lace, one to the left, the other more or less central, meandering down through the field. At the distance from which I was seeing them, and with my poor vision, they looked, not like the commonplace flowers with ragged tops (belying their lovely name) that I "knew" them to be, but almost like globular, dazzling white mushrooms in the sunlight, proceeding in clear if not strictly orderly fashion towards the channel beneath.

These mushrooms were far more beautiful than their "parent" flowers, and were disposed in a far more purposeful manner. (Were they on their way to a funeral?) In any case, I was experiencing a metaphoric vision, in which one thing had been transformed into another before my eyes.

At this point, it became apparent to me that my model of metaphor, or of metaphoric structure, was still inadequate. In that model, the essence of the "tenor" is captured by a "vehicle" that displays the essential feature of the tenor in heightened form. But, on studying the scene before me, I realized that what I was seeing was not the essence of the flower, but the essence of the (imagined) mushrooms. The flowers were only a trampoline that enabled the mushrooms to leap into existence. In my trying to seize the essence of the tenor, the tenor had slipped out of my grasp, and I had, in fact, seized the essence of the vehicle. And there was now nowhere left to go, and no need to go any further.

This is a process that seems illogical, even counterintuitive; it is, nevertheless, unmistakable. There is a danger, then, for the tenor, in entering upon the metaphoric transaction. On the one hand, it must reach towards the vehicle for its fulfillment, for its moment of transfiguration: for the only means by which it can be fully itself. On the other hand, it may then turn out to have been cannibalized, as its "alter ego" makes off with its most valuable possession. Like a virus, the vehicle borrows the vital element of the tenor to enrich itself, to make its own essence prevail. Apparently, in the service of the metaphor, it ends up turning the tables on its master.

It can then go its own way. The mushrooms gather and join each other in a procession that grows denser as it approaches its terminus, as it moves down towards the focus of the funeral, that invisible gathering point just above the sea.

I believe that the above arguments, in outline, are broadly applicable in the field of metaphor. On the other hand, I must also acknowledge what is probably obvious to most readers: in the attempt to reach a general understanding of the metaphoric event, even with this supplement about mushrooms and flowers, I have still avoided the uncomfortable, complicating fact that not all metaphoric events are the same, so that some of my examples, intended to be paradigmatic, may not illuminate all other cases. For instance, in the flower/mushroom example that I have just cited, although there was no "extreme," overwhelming scenario (as in the Miquelon events cited previously), there was also an immediate, unconscious transfer from flower to mushroom, with no moment of choice in-between. (On the other hand, the example lends strong support to the claim that metaphor is narrative). Again, although I have been emphasizing the separability of vehicle from tenor, or the independence of the vehicle, there are some situations in which the vehicle cannot be separated from the tenor at all, and therefore cannot be very well thought of as asserting its own essence, or of starting its own narrative. I have already hinted that "extreme" metaphors may not lend themselves to narrative extension; for instance, what is the "narrative" in what I have called simply "vision," or in the "pebbles in the water" (see above, Chapter 2 Section II.C)? Again, I think of the iridescent cloud, or blur, of the tiny white-breasted swallows that swung in and out of position, in their comings and goings, on the naked twigs of a bush reaching out over a lagoon in the Peruvian jungle, and I can think of no story that would start with that cloud, or that would want to be separated from its precious tiny particles.

Not the whole story, then.

## C. A Transition (With Apologies for a Change of Tone)

Before proceeding, I find it necessary to consider a problem, or question, that lies just beyond the horizon of this entire enterprise, but casts a shadow back over it. As I approach my topics, one by one, I will find myself with some unresolved question that lingers after each area of investigation has been explored. Let me call it a margin of "nonsense": some space in which the rule of verifiability or of disproof (it's either true or false, right or wrong) cannot be made to apply. I will not, at least at this point, offer a list of examples.

The question is, Do all of these unresolved questions, uncertainties, things which words haven't been able to settle, end up in the same place? Is there a Hell, or a Paradise, of the unresolvables, where they all vanish into a stew of indifferent nonsense, indistinguishable from one another? In that dark night of Wittgenstein's exclusion zone, in which what cannot be proved is not worthy of mention, are all cats gray? Is every unsettled question identical with every other? Or do they all carry some unmistakable mark of their origin with them into their positivist doom? (See above, Chapter 1 Section II.) Is nonsense completely democratic, that is, is all nonsense equal, or the same? I am not enough of a logician to know whether Leibniz's law, the "Identity of Indiscernibles," applies in this situation. In any case, I will leave this question for reconsideration.

# CHAPTER 3

# The Baroque

## Nonsense in Prospect and Retrospect

> Marduk amuck and the manlike buttercup
> blurt ungrammatical drivel scot-free.
> —Peter J. Grieco, *At the Musarium* [21801–21900]

## I. NONSENSE, BETWEEN WORDS AND IMAGES

The baroque, as a style, is associated less frequently with literature than with the visual arts. But, in either domain, the Baroque is almost too easy a target for the discovery of abundant nonsense. Inherent in its very definition (or in any of its definitions) is the idea of an excess of display over substance, or even of an attempt to evade the responsibilities of meaning. Its espousing of the grandiose, the excessive, the unnecessarily intricate, make it the natural abode of nonsense. If put in terms of tenor and vehicle, the vehicle has repudiated the tenor; in terms of percept and perceiver, the perceiver has vanquished the percept. In terms of form and content, content comes in a poor second.

Not far behind this sufficiently disconcerting complex of issues lies another, ancillary source of perplexity for anyone seeking order and coherence in thought: the relation of image to word. This is an issue that one does not need to worry about as long as verbal language is clearly dominant; a visual illustration is understood to be subordinate to its text, and does not have to correspond to it in all its particulars. When the symbol outweighs the thought, though, it forces us into an act of interpretation for which we are poorly prepared. The masturbating "Blessed Ludovica Albertoni" by Bernini is a good example.[1] What are we expected to say about her? In a paradoxical sense, con-

---

1. The sexual implications of beatific ecstasy were understood long before our time. On Bernini's St. Theresa see, for instance, Forsyth, *Remarks on Antiquities,* 105.

ceptual art may have put us in the same dilemma: although it may seem to be only an illustration of a verbal theory about art, it is intended to shock us into an act of interpretation, for, lacking an art object, there is no help for us but to get to work interpreting. This is the up-to-date way to "épater le bourgeois."

The relation between images and words formed the staple of aesthetic discourse for much of the 1980s and 1990s, culminating in the work of Jean-François Lyotard.[2] This is not the place to revive those debates in all their subtlety; for present purposes a few obvious points will suffice. Seeing is believing, and a picture is worth a thousand words. But what, exactly, does the picture *mean*? (We are reminded of our long-suffering "metaphor," about which the selfsame question keeps cropping up: what does it *mean*?) As long as an answer that satisfies us in verbal terms remains unavailable, we are unsatisfied.

There are many ways to try to bridge the gap between seeing and speaking, but they can only be partially successful. As there is no way to make a Mercator projection correspond point for point with a globular map of the world, so there is a space between these two forms of representation that refuses to be collapsed, or even to diminish. To try to translate a picture into words produces a distortion that is a form of what I would call "necessary nonsense," that province of thought in which an unavoidable clash of categories takes place. It is not for nothing that we think of Lear and Carroll in terms of their illustrations: nonsense resides in the space between words and images, or, rather, is created by our attempt to reduce it. Just putting them side by side reminds us of the point. Nor are we unduly surprised when the two occasionally slip entirely out of alignment (as so often happens with, for instance, Blake's illustrations). But I will not dwell further on this problem.

Obviously, the Baroque is far too large a topic for cursory treatment, particularly as I have chosen to pursue the subject into recent times. I have therefore confined myself to one major theme: symbolic form. I have subdivided that theme in the following fashion: the Baroque and symbolic form; pure vs. symbolic form; theory of forms in Germany, practice of form in France; Freud and symbolic form; pure vs. symbolic form; and the ensuing confrontation with nonsense in the twentieth to the twenty-first centuries.

At the time when I was first working on this chapter, there was a major Baroque exhibition on at the Victoria and Albert Museum in London; I decided to indulge myself and began my paper with a Baroque fantasy, a prologue/cadenza, or what some might call a display of Baroque historiography, in both senses of the term.

---

2. Lyotard, *Discours, figure,* 105.

## II. THE BAROQUE AND SYMBOLIC FORM

It has become fashionable to speak of the Baroque as not only a local phenomenon coinciding roughly with the Counter-Reformation, but as a movement extending from the seventeenth into the twenty-first century, and having to do with the uneasy relation between object and perceiver and, possibly, with the relation between symbol and referent more broadly. These two relations cannot well be separated, since, especially in the arts, symbols inevitably intervene in the relation between the perceiver and the object of perception. I myself am inclined to think of the Baroque as characterized by an excess of symbol over referent, and also, as has often been said, by a preponderance of the visual medium; it is something that we usually think of as inclined to the spectacular or even as marked by a degree of bombast. In William Egginton's more searching exploration of the issue, the Baroque is understood as an expression of doubt in the integrity of the referent, in the reality of any subject of representation.[3]

The relation between the symbol and the thing symbolized, though, has changed gradually during the course of the past four hundred years, and one may even be able to identify some phases in that change. When Louis XIV had himself dressed up as Apollo and went on stage, the scene was not entirely ludicrous; it was understood that some characteristics of Apollo actually attached to the king. At that time, it could also make sense to refer to the king as "The Crown," because something of the king, likewise, attached itself to the crown. The synecdoche was not just a figure of speech. We find it difficult to understand why the "emblem" was such a popular form of graphic art at this time, but, if we posit a real symbiosis of symbol and referent, of the picture and its interpretation, the currency of the genre begins to make sense. By the time of Blake, though, the unity of the genre had been compromised, and Blake's contemporaries were unable to read his illustrated poems in the same spirit as that in which the readers of the Abbé de Chesneau had presumably received a page of the "Most Adorable Sacrament of the Eucharist," showing how the efficacy of pigeon's blood in curing eye disease illustrated the efficacy of Christ's blood in curing our spiritual blindness—much as Blake would have liked them to do so.[4]

As the relationship of symbol and referent became more tenuous, the bond between the two eventually loosened to the point of rupture, though a real severance of the connection is obviously impossible. What did happen,

---

3. William Egginton, "Baroque as a Problem of Thought," 143–49.
4. Chesneau, *Emblèmes sacrez*, 80–81.

though, in practical terms, is that pageantry, at least, finally became meaning-less; objects could no longer be invested with the honorific significance previously transferred to them by their human or institutional referents. The love affair between symbol and referent was coming to an end.

The extended transition during which secular categories gradually replaced the sacred has been studied intensively by Hans Blumenberg, among others. Tellingly, Blumenberg remarks: "Probably nothing in the terminology of aesthetics is as instructive in regard to the problematic of secularization as is the concept of a 'symbol.'"[5] This is true not only of symbolic objects, but of entire human functions or activities. Among the fraught examples that come to mind is Bernini's use of female sexuality as a symbol for divine ecstasy (see, for instance, the abovementioned "Blessed Ludovica Albertoni," in the Victoria and Albert Museum's own "Baroque" exhibition; it is interesting to observe that, in Western cultures, female sexuality can be associated with the sacred, whereas male sexuality is always regarded as profane). Another is Bach's resorting to the terminology of commercial accounting ("Kapital und Interessen," "Es ist bezahlt, du bist quittiert!") ("capital and interest" and "It's paid up, we're even!") in Cantata 168, to symbolize the budgeting of moral values.

Along with the decline of the Baroque order, in which the excess of external show can already be seen as a symptom of the loss of confidence in the symbol-referent relation, a new aesthetic theme begins to emerge. During the eighteenth century, the sublime gradually becomes a major category in the history of the arts. The sublime is what happens when the Baroque effort to make the symbol adequate to the referent has been abandoned, and the symbol loses its prestige.[6] (Some might argue, though, that the "overreaching" characteristic of the Baroque is precisely what led to the sublime.) What occurs next, with Kant, is an attempt to establish an iconoclastic regime, in which the whole symbolic realm is subject to degradation. For Kant, at least, there is no way to incarnate a thought. What survives this assault is the so-called Romantic symbol, more personal, subjective, and perhaps less secure than the symbols of the "*ancien régime,*" which were usually selected from an approved repertoire of Classical or religious sources. In fact, the whole category of the "aesthetic" seems to emerge during the eighteenth century as way of providing a home for, and dealing with, the newly unanchored and (*pace* Coleridge) attenuated

---

5. Blumenberg, *Legitimacy of the Modern Age,* 111.

6. For a different reading of these complex developments in intellectual history, one which emphasizes the possibilities of aligning the sublime closely with the Baroque rather than pitting them against each other, see Battistini, "The Telescope in the Baroque Imagination," 3–38 (especially 24), and Cascardi, "Genealogy of the Sublime," 221–42, both found in *Reason and its Others.*

symbolic order.[7] In the nineteenth century, the Baroque reappears, though not in fully sacralized form, in Victorian visual extravaganzas.[8] In terms of this imagined trajectory, the struggle to rescue symbolic form—that is, a form that has an intimate relation to its referent—is a rearguard action, in which, as we shall see below, physiological and psychological thinking eventually replaces religion as the glue or matrix holding symbol and reality, and perhaps even percept and perceiver, together. From the fluid and ambiguous relations surrounding the Romantic symbol, a psychological residue settles, as a result of which the subjective element comes to occupy the entire field. The movement may be said to be from the sacred to the subjectively sacred to the completely subjective. In the perceiver-object relationship, the response of the perceiver is now not only dominant: it becomes, in a sense, all that we can know. Even when confronted with an abstract shape that has no meaning in itself, we immediately bind to it by the categories of our own needs. Meaning is not inherent in the natural world, nor is it something that is supplied by God. We see parallel lines, and we think and feel stress, stretching, order, and so forth; we see converging lines, and we experience convergence. None of this is in the lines themselves. (Vico is not far behind here: man makes himself the measure of all things). Extrapolated to our general encounter with the world, this view reduces the object of perception to a mere colorless stimulus. The sacred in the object, or even the only subjectively sacred, is no longer available, and the density of perception is gone. The numinous has to be transferred to abstraction: hence, perhaps, the phenomenon of Cubism.

This schematic overview of symbolic form and its history since the seventeenth century is, obviously, oversimplified, and open to objection at any point. The area in which the remainder of this chapter proceeds is more limited, and the arguments are perhaps less speculative. I will have to leave the question of where exactly the symbolic form issue in late nineteenth-century aesthetics fits into the history of the Baroque and its battle against the abstract sublime for later; there is more than enough to do to trace the history of symbolic form in the very local arena in which I wish to pursue it. Some might wish simply to transfer the issue, at least in the realm of art, to the twentieth-century conflict between abstraction, as a possible representative of the sublime, on the one hand, and the latter-day Baroque extravagances of Expressionism and postmodernism, on the other.

---

7. Cf. Blumenberg, 112.

8. See, for instance, the program at CRASSH in Cambridge, UK on May 7, 2015, entitled "Exhibiting Belief: Materiality and Religious Display in the Nineteenth Century."

## III. PURE VS. SYMBOLIC FORM

Intellectual history, with its innumerable interlaced or overlapping strands, seems more like a scribble or a tangled web than a rhizome, or even a net. One does not know how to begin to organize it, and any order imposed on it appears arbitrary. One way to look for order is by a process of exclusion: by extracting from the mass of data, and then grouping, certain phenomena that can plausibly be contrasted with another group of phenomena. The discovery, or creation, of symmetry (of what, in Luhmann's terms, might be called a "system") makes simplification easier.[9]

One way to produce such simplification, or grouping, in the nineteenth-century aesthetics of form, is to distinguish between those approaches (later associated with Cubism) which emphasize the basic geometrical forms in their pure abstraction, and those which stress the anthropological aspect of form. The latter is sometimes known as symbolic form; it is that aspect of form which reflects or expresses human needs or interests. Of course, in practice these two approaches sometimes overlap. Johann Friedrich Herbart and the theorists of the "Golden Section" (still a live concept in architecture) are sometimes taken to represent the first, or abstracting, tendency. Robert Vischer, whose name is associated with the concept of empathy, is connected with the second, which tends towards the psychological.[10]

In this chapter I will deal mainly with the latter group of ideas, and will try to disentangle the strands of a web that connects late nineteenth-century speculation in the psychology of aesthetics to Freudian thought. Inevitably, the abovementioned topic of empathy, an idea that points far beyond Freud to the now famous (or perhaps infamous) mirror neurons, will have to be taken into account.[11] These neurons, as is now well known, lie in or near areas in our brains that would normally be aroused in us by emotions that we see in others' faces; they are perhaps what enable us to recognize other people's expressions.

The great theorist of empathy, Theodor Lipps, may be said to provide a bridge between the abstracting and the psychologizing approach to forms. Lipps has a strong interest in the elementary forms, but, at the same time, he attributes a psychological function to these basic forms; in accordance with his understanding of empathy, we are thought to invest them with vitality, and to experience shapes and lines as stresses. The interaction of these stresses produces what we experience as optical illusions. These illusions or distortions of reality are a symptom of the clash between form and expression, that

9. Scheibmayr, *Niklas Luhmanns Systemtheorie*.
10. See Mallgrave and Ikonomou, *Empathy, Form, and Space*.
11. See below, footnote 32.

is, of the shapes that are there and the impulses with which we endow them. Lipps devoted a work entitled "Aesthetische Faktoren der Raumanschauung" (1891) to this subject.[12]

In exploring these themes in the intellectual history of the late nineteenth century, I went through the first thirty volumes of the *Revue philosophique de la France et de l'étranger*, edited by the famous psychologist Théodule-Armand Ribot from 1876 on. The first and most striking impression that one has is that the subjects of research which attracted attention in the international community of psychologists at the time are among those that are still being actively investigated now: not merely cerebral localization, lateralization, and the nature of memory, but the aphasias, preverbal thought, inner language, subvocalization, the amusias, lucid dreaming, differences between color and luminance, synaesthesia, the brain's revision of "raw" perception, and the nature of attention, as well as the dreams of animals and the psychology of lesser organisms. The second impression that one has is that there is an overwhelming preoccupation with the nature of space. The Kantian assertion that space is an a priori form in perception gradually loses support. There is a ferment, an upheaval in the understanding of space during the nineteenth century under the onslaught of the new geometries of Carl Friedrich Gauss, Bernhard Riemann, and Nikolai Lobachevsky, and hardly an issue of the *Revue philosophique* lacks an article on geometry, on space-time, or on the idea of dimensionality. It is easy to see how the counterintuitive features of the new geometries and the accompanying movement in physics could have created the disorientation that was fertile soil for the "nonsense" movement, particularly in English and Russian literature, of the later nineteenth and early twentieth century. It is also easy to see how the urge to push beyond three dimensions would have fed into Cubism, with its "nonsensical" treatment of space, and how the dissatisfaction with the older notions of space and time created a breeding ground for the physics of Poincaré and Einstein. Incidentally, many German psychologists and physiologists appear as both authors and subjects of commentary in numerous issues of this journal, although it was edited in France.

Henri Bergson's 1888 *Essai sur les données immédiates de la conscience* is also interesting in the context of Cubism.[13] Bergson seems to have realized

---

12. Lipps, "Aesthetische Faktoren der Raumanschauung," 217–307. Many of the following remarks appeared, after parts of this chapter were delivered as a lecture, in my book *The Neural Imagination* (2009). I have retained them as material to my description of the Baroque, and to maintain the continuity of my theme. I am reprinting this material with the kind permission of the University of Texas Press.

13. Bergson, *Données immédiates de la conscience*.

that German "psychophysics," especially as exemplified in the work of Gustav Fechner, supports the view of reality that, as we understand it, subtends Cubism: namely, that the mind does not operate as a continuous flow, but employs fixed, separable quanta of experience (59, 63); that time itself can be understood in terms of spaces (65–66); and that, therefore, at least by implication, discontinuities need not be shunned (22). In a way, then, Bergson's virtual diatribe against Fechner can be read as an attack on Cubism, and the "nonsensical" view of reality that it represented, *avant la lettre*. Bergson's well-known attachment to the idea of continuity and uninterrupted flow, and his association of grace itself with process (22–23), represents the opposite of the German method, which culminated not only in Cubism but in quantum physics, as well, which even Einstein found nonsensical. (Nevertheless, a phase of what might be called French Cubism, even more *avant la lettre,* can already be found among the neoclassical artists of the eighteenth century such as Claude Nicolas Ledoux and Étienne-Louis Boullée, though it does not appear to have overflowed into the nineteenth century. The sixteenth-century Mannerist Luca Cambiaso is also sometimes considered a precursor of Cubism.[14]) It is apparent, by the way, given the fact that quite a few of the German artists and theorists were themselves physicians or psychologists, that the aesthetic and the psychological streams of thought were closely allied in Germany.

## IV. THEORY OF FORMS IN GERMANY, PRACTICE OF FORM IN FRANCE

It is a curious fact of intellectual history that, although the foundations of Cubism in art were clearly laid in France, by Paul Cézanne, and although there was such a strong tendency towards abstraction in French painting at the time that even Vincent van Gogh, struggling to defend a "naïve" reality from its inroads, at one point succumbed to its pressure,[15] the theoretical foundation for the movement was provided by German psychologists. Yet, I have not been able to find any evidence that Cézanne was familiar with the Germans' work, and I do not think that Bergson's antipathy to the German school was unique among thinkers on such subjects in France. What adds to the complication of this interaction, or, rather, lack of interaction, is the apparent failure of the Germans to respond to Cézanne in his time. They were in the best position to recognize the revolutionary implications of Cézanne's proto-Cubism, but they

14. For Cambiaso, see Melikian, "Exhibition." For a 1624 abstract etching by Giovanni Battista Bracelli, see Halpern, "Robots and Algorithms are Taking Over," 26.

15. Van Gogh, *Painted with Words*, 339–40.

showed no early inclination to accept his work. When Paul Cassirer brought twelve works by Cézanne to Germany for a one-man show in 1890, not one of the paintings was sold.[16] Apparently, they did not make enough sense.

As I have said above, in the development of perspectives on the plastic arts during the nineteenth century, it is possible to distinguish two views: (1) the belief that basic geometric forms as such are the essential constituents of the visual arts; and (2) the more psychologically oriented opinion, which insists that we respond to visual forms because we experience them as symbolic of our own bodily attitudes and needs. The theoretical underpinnings of the first opinion may be traced all the way from Plato's interest in the five possible geometric solids and Plotinus's musings on symmetry and unity, through to, in the nineteenth century, other German aestheticians, such as the previously mentioned Herbart and Fechner (physician and physicist),[17] Robert Zimmermann, Adolf Goeller, and Cornelius Gurlitt. (Fechner's work on the aesthetic hierarchy among geometrical forms had been anticipated by the eighteenth-century English aesthetician Francis Hutcheson). The second strand (deriving from sources as ancient as Vitruvius's *Architecture,* as well as from the anthropomorphism prevalent in Renaissance architecture) is closer to our immediate purposes; it is associated with the attempt (especially prominent in the work of Wilhelm Wundt) to find a specific physiological basis for both behavior and subjective experience.

A quotation from Arthur Schopenhauer might serve to introduce this subject: "What is imagination? A very complicated physiological occurrence in an animal's brain, whose result is a consciousness of a picture or image at that very spot."[18] But, if it is just a "physiological occurrence," how can we attribute any meaning to it? As for symbolic form (for which Heinrich Wölfflin was later to propose a neurological correlate), Johann Gottfried Herder had already argued, in 1800, that forms are inherently anthropomorphic, that is, that they have expressive bodily values.[19] Robert Vischer (1873) emphasizes the sympathy (i.e., identification) or discord of the body and its systems, especially the visual system, with what it perceives.[20] We have the "wonderful ability to project and incorporate our own physical form into an objective

---

16. Turner, ed., *Dictionary of Art,* vol. 6.

17. See Phillips et al., "Fechner's Aesthetics Revisited," 263–71. Most of the references for this following section of my paper are taken from Mallgrave and Ikonomou. A more comprehensive review of the same material was published in the following year by Braungart, *Leibhafter Sinn.*

18. Mallgrave and Ikonomou, 10.

19. Ibid., 18.

20. Ibid., 22–23.

form."[21] For Hermann Lotze (also a physician) in 1868, even two straight lines necessarily convey a symbolic meaning; again, we resort to a kind of nonsense in order to lend meaning to our surroundings.[22] Vischer again: we have "an unconscious need for a surrogate for our body-ego," on the basis of simple nerve sensations, where "every phenomenon provokes a related idea of the self in sensory or motor form." The phenomenon "becomes an analogy for my own structure." One moves with a landscape, "guided by kinesthetic imagina-tion . . . mediated by the reflex stimuli of sensitized nerves."[23] This seems to be an automatic process: there is no "sense" involved here, either.

It will be noticed that all of the above quotations are from German sources. I have not been able to discover much work on either the psychology or aes-thetics of empathy among the French contributors to the *Revue philosophique* during the years relevant to this discussion, with the exception of a debate in the February, March, and June issues of 1890 between Georges Sorel and Charles Henry over the merit of the latter's concept of *dynamogénie,* which seems to follow the familiar pattern of explaining our positive or negative responses to shapes as a function of muscular stresses.

For Theodor Vischer (the father of Robert Vischer, mentioned above), architecture was an orchestration of forces and forms symbolic of emotions and meanings.[24] But, at least for Heinrich Wölfflin, all this talk of self-pro-jection into abstract forms, or animation of abstract forms, lacked precision, and he preferred a more objective description of the process. "Instead of an inexplicable 'self-projection,' we might perhaps imagine that the optic nerve impulse directly stimulates the motor nerves, which cause specific muscles to contract."[25] (Again, as in the case of the quotation from Schopenhauer above, meaning is entirely lacking from the equation here.) Wölfflin seeks support for his opinion in what he refers to as the "recently championed theory that the comprehension of human expression is mediated by a sympathetic response."

Here we find ourselves, of course, in the thick of the concept that domi-nates this field, but over which I have not lingered: the rich and complex con-cept of empathy (*Einfühlung*), a term usually thought to have been coined by Robert Vischer (1873), but actually present or implied throughout the centu-ry.[26] There is an automatic transfer of feeling from object to subject—we feel what we see. To put it in Berkeleian terms, a thing is that which provokes a

---

21. Ibid., 154.
22. Ibid., 20.
23. Ibid., 101.
24. Ibid., 19.
25. Ibid., 155.
26. Ibid., 71, n. 57.

sensation in us. In a sense, we are never even entirely ourselves—we are our percepts.[27] The psychologist whose writings are most often associated with the theory of empathy is, as I have mentioned above, Theodor Lipps.

For nineteenth-century psychologists, empathy was not a feeling confined to relations with other humans, but involved our response to our surroundings in general. Lipps explored both possibilities in two magisterial essays: "Aesthetische Faktoren der Raumanschauung" ("Aesthetic Factors in our Perception of Space," 1891),[28] and "Das Wissen von fremden Ichen" ("The Knowledge of Other Selves," 1907).[29] The first is an incredibly detailed (eighty-nine pages, in large format) study of basic shapes, lines, and stresses, with numerous stark, unadorned drawings to drive home Lipps's points. It is very hard to imagine that such thinking would not have contributed to the development of Cubism and other forms of abstract art, and, indeed, one can see a direct line extending from German nineteenth-century psychology to the simplified forms of the "Blauer Reiter" school and the Bauhaus movement in Germany. The influence of German psychologists, for instance, Wundt, Hermann von Helmholtz, and Adolf von Hildebrand, in the development of Russian movements in art, such as Kazimir Malevich's "Cubo-Futurism," is even more striking.[30]

Lipps's second essay is an equally extended consideration of the puzzling fact that we seem to understand the expression on other people's faces quite automatically. As far as I can understand this difficult text, I gather that Lipps's essay has a negative outcome. After going through all the plausible explanations that he can think of, and finding all of them unsatisfactory, Lipps seems to resign himself to the conclusion that empathy with others is an irreducible fact of psychology: simply a given.[31] It was not until the 1990s that major progress could be made in this area, with the discovery of the now-familiar mirror neurons. It must be acknowledged, though, that not all psychologists believe that the mirror neuron theory accounts for the phenomenon of empathy.[32] It is a provisional explanation, at best; like most scientific explanations, accepted until a better one can be found.

---

27. Vischer seems to have been aware of this perplexing difficulty. See ibid., 25.

28. Lipps, "Aesthetische Faktoren der Raumanschauung," 217–307.

29. Lipps, "Das Wissen von fremden Ichen," 694–722.

30. See Zhadova, *Malevich*, 45–46, 323–25. Dr. Antje von Graevenitz also tells me that Marina Abramovic did a performance piece based on Theodor Lipps's work in the 1970s, but Dr. von Graevenitz may have been confusing Theodor Lipps with Thomas Lips.

31. For an exhaustive study of simulation theory, an outgrowth of empathy theory, see Goldman, *Simulating Minds*.

32. See Saxe, "Against Simulation," 174–79; Gopnik, "Cells that Read Minds?"; and Shetty, "Mirror Neurons Not All They Are Cracked up to Be," 9. The controversy goes on.

It would be a pity to leave the theme of the scientific influences on artistic movements around 1900 without mention of yet another German physician, biologist, psychologist, or whatever exactly Ernst Haeckel was. In his gargantuan work, *Kunstformen der Natur (Aesthetic Forms in Nature)*, of which I have seen only the second volume, he offers, on his very first page (p. 1), the familiar argument that all human art forms are anticipated, but in a superior degree, by nature (see below, Chapter 6 Section I.B.1).[33] In the actual (fifty) plates of overcrowded illustrations, close to folio size, Haeckel presents us with a multitude of organisms, from the vanishingly small to the fully vertebrate, with their innumerable fantastic curvilinear shapes, as material for art. At first glance, it may seem only visual nonsense, with diatoms juxtaposed with antelopes, but one soon realizes that this is really Art Nouveau, **more** than *in nuce*, in full bloom, in all its abundant splendor. Haeckel is perfectly explicit: modern artists, and the new, powerfully developed applied arts industry ("Kunstgewerbe") will find a wealth of material and of inspiration in his pictures ("Vorwort" ["Preface"], p. 2. The hint of reproducibility, of the industrial production of art, in "Kunstgewerbe," is also worth noticing).

## V. FREUD AND SYMBOLIC FORM

There remains one other historical connection to be worked out: the sources of Freudian thinking, again in the brew of mid-nineteenth-century German aesthetics. Once one accepts the idea that every form embodies some human desire or impulse, that we are constantly anthropomorphizing our surroundings, it is only a short step to the sort of somatic symbolism that Sigmund Freud practiced. Actually, the chronology of this development is not entirely straightforward. The notion of symbolic form was everywhere at the time. It appears in one version in Charles Baudelaire's "Correspondances"; it may even be lurking behind the Duchess's remark, to Alice (in Wonderland), "Everything's got a moral, if only you can find it." The link between the thing and our interpretation of it is pretty arbitrary. Out of this atmosphere (or, perhaps, fog) a remarkable work was precipitated: Karl Albert Scherner, in *Das Leben des Traums (The Life of Dreams)* of 1861, has by far the strongest claim to being Freud's major forerunner.[34] Scherner took what had been primarily an aesthetic theory and made it the basis of his dream psychology. For Scherner, most of the images in dreams are to be understood as symbols of parts of the

33. Haeckle, *Kunstformen der Natur.*
34. Scherner, *Das Leben des Traums.*

body, of bodily states, or of bodily desires: the role of sexual impulses and of the sexual apparatus is worked out in particularly explicit detail. Scherner's contribution was picked up by Vischer in 1873 and used to reinforce Vischer's own aesthetics.[35] Two years later, in 1875, another of what one might call the "projectionist" aestheticians, Johannes Volkelt, wrote at length about Scherner in his book *Die Traum-Phantasie* (*Dream Fantasy*), attempting to draw attention to what he considered Scherner's crucial contribution to psychology.[36] (It was Volkelt's theory of symbolic projection [1876] for which Wölfflin tried to find a neurological grounding in his 1886 "Prolegomena to a Psychology of Architecture.") At some point after that date, but necessarily before 1899, the year of the *Traumdeutung* (*The Interpretation of Dreams*), Freud found his way to Scherner's work, apparently via Volkelt, whom Freud cites extensively. Freud ended up owning two copies of Scherner's *The Life of Dreams,* both of which he underlined heavily.

I first drew attention to Freud's debt to Scherner in "Freud before Freud: K. A. Scherner (1825–1899)," in 1990. Scherner is an interesting but mysterious figure, heavily buried under the sands of intellectual history.[37] He never wrote the promised second volume of his work on dreams; in fact, the only other book of interest that he produced was a guide to the Tatra Mountains. His health, both mental and physical, appears to have been precarious. Many other factors have contributed to his obscurity: among them, I am told by members of his university (formerly Breslau, now Wrocław), were his poverty, his choice of neighborhood in which to live, and his membership in the dissident group of the "old believers," who were presumably contemned by Scherner's peers, especially at a university under ecclesiastical control. That university has apparently made no attempt to commemorate his presence there, though his biography would be well worth a full-length study. He was also eclipsed by more famous philosophers, such as Wilhelm Dilthey, and Lipps himself, who followed him at Breslau. Not least among those who were responsible for the failure of his reputation, however, was Freud. Freud refers to Scherner frequently, and offers him the highest praise; at the same time, he is extremely careful to avoid citing precisely those passages in Scherner that clearly anticipate his own ideas. In any case, it is interesting to see how Freud, who began, of course, as a neurologist, allowed himself to be seduced by the psychologized remnant of an aesthetic theory in Scherner, to change course in midcareer, and to notice that some of his major ideas are derived from that theory. It is also interesting to realize that the *Traumdeutung,* a work that

---

35. Mallgrave and Ikonomou, 100.
36. Johannes Volkelt, *Die Traum-Phantasie.*
37. Massey, "Freud before Freud," 567–76.

came to be regarded as the founding text of a revolution in psychology, actually represented a retrograde movement, the revival of what was, by 1899, a fading paradigm in aesthetics. Incidentally, the unconscious also appeared, at the same time, to be a fading concept in psychology, before Freud revived it.

Without confronting the familiar questions concerning the general validity of the Freudian system, it may be worth recalling that it cannot avoid involvement in the issue that I mentioned in the introduction to this chapter: the difficulty of translating images into words. A visual image has an irreducible ambiguity about it, and attempts to eliminate that ambiguity may lead to nonsensical results. I am reminded of an argument between two psychoanalytic interpreters of Goethe, one of whom argued that the great mountain in the "Harzreise im Winter" was symbolic of the breast, the other, of the penis. If any assertion that is not subject to disproof must be judged to be nonsense, then we have a pretty likely candidate right here. There are ways around "naïve" Freudianism, but the problem persists. Too deep an investigation into the relationship between symbol and word leads to the precipice of nonsense.

## VI. THE BREAKDOWN OF FORMS: NONSENSE TO THE RESCUE, IN THE TWENTIETH AND TWENTY-FIRST CENTURIES

Of course, phrases such as "symbolic form" (though, for the most part, in a much more general sense than the one in which I have been using it), now associated primarily with the name of Ernst Cassirer, have also had a strong career in the twentieth century.[38] Aestheticians such as Rudolph Arnheim may be considered disciples of Lipps; Susanne Langer is another well-known theorist of symbolic form, as is the lesser-known Matila Ghyka; and as late as 2004, we still find advocates of the significance to be found in elementary forms (and, indeed, proponents of a universal grammar of forms), such as Peter D. Stebbing.[39] It is interesting to note that Stebbing, in his "A Universal Grammar for Visual Composition?" (2004), still finds it necessary to invoke the authority of Alexander von Humboldt.[40] And a famous experiment conducted at Smith College in 1944, using simply triangles, a square, and a circle, showed that, when these were set in motion, most viewers, instead of dismissing them as visual nonsense, promptly endowed them with human character-

---

38. For a somewhat dismissive article on Cassirer and symbolic form, see Simpson, "A Positive Future," 14–17. A group of scholars based at the University of Glasgow published three volumes of papers on Cassirer between 2003 and 2008.

39. See Zaidel, *Neuropsychology of Art*.

40. Stebbing, "A Universal Grammar," 63–70.

istics and an accompanying narrative.[41] Nevertheless, the large and focused school of thought that concentrated its attention on the concepts with which these authors have worked was a product of the nineteenth century.

The dialectic, or dialogue, between artists and authors who espoused pure form, on the one hand, and expressive form, on the other, also continued, of course, beyond that time, though any designation of the outstanding partisans on either side is bound to be somewhat arbitrary. Piet Mondrian, not only in eschewing subjectivism but also in adhering strictly to the straight line (he found even curved lines objectionable) might be considered a prominent spokesperson for absolute form without "meaning," though Malevich or any number of others could just as well be nominated. In literature, someone like Raymond Roussel, who built entire novels on arbitrary structures of puns, or Alain Robbe-Grillet, in rejecting the psychological "meaningfulness" of natural forms (whatever autobiographical references his impenetrable surfaces may have concealed), might fall into this same camp. On the other hand, Pablo Picasso after Cubism, and perhaps James Joyce before *Finnegan's Wake,* using formal devices mainly to further deeply subjective ends, might be classified with the interpretive school, those who did not value form for form's sake, but for its human meaning. Of course, the fact that one is left with a plethora of artists and writers who are not readily identifiable with one group or the other makes apparent the fact that applying principles of symmetry and simplification in historiography creates as many problems as it solves—if not producing what can be dismissed as mere nonsense—and can be said to be, at best, a necessary evil. Yet the thought that a different selection of examples, or a different frame of reference, might bring one to different conclusions, is not exactly calculated to reassure one, either. Perhaps, as I have suggested more than once before, we have to develop a category of respectable nonsense, or, better, a hierarchy of nonsenses, that maintain their identity to a greater or lesser degree in the great universe of ideas. Or, perhaps again, we need to be more charitable to ourselves, and value whatever knowledge or information each attempt at thought leaves us with, rather than require a strict accounting at every step (see above, Chapter 1 Section II).

But to return briefly to one of the questions with which I began: is there, after all, some way in which we can relate the recent state of the arts to the continuing history of the Baroque in its interaction with the abstract or sublime? The effort may not be beyond reason, especially since the affinities between the Baroque and certain features of the modern/postmodern con-

---

41. Heider and Simmel, "An Experimental Study of Apparent Behavior," 243–59. The narrative imperative is everywhere. Meaning itself seems to arise when facts are set in motion by narrative.

dition have not gone unobserved, and some of the connections have already been outlined. When Walter Benjamin wrote his thesis on the German drama of the Baroque (*Ursprung des deutschen Trauerspiels*), with its emphasis on fragmentation, disorder, and the predominance of surface over depth, he was obviously describing his own time at least as accurately as the culture of the seventeenth century. One need hardly mention the Theatre of the Absurd, or Daniil Kharms's still earlier, pioneering writings. After Guy Debord's founding work, *La Société du spectacle,* the Baroque arises again as a major issue in the work of Gilles Deleuze, particularly in *Le Pli*; the dismantling of orderly structures made Deleuze, even more than Derrida, the high priest of postmodernism.[42] The strong connections of Deleuze and Félix Guattari to the ideas of the Baroque has been emphasized once again in the work of Gen Doy.[43]

The title of Christine Buci-Glucksmann's book on the Baroque aesthetic, *La Folie du voir* (*The Madness of Seeing*), could as well be applied to our own age.[44] As Per Aage Brandt puts it, "We . . . pull picture-blankets over our eyes."[45] Certainly, it may be fairly said that visual representation has run wild, and we no longer even bother to ask whether there is anything more "real" behind it.[46] Besides, if the Baroque involves a surplus of form over content, and if we consider the increasing proliferation of forms, so that no work seems valuable unless it actually inaugurates a form, the Baroque would seem to have reached its apogee. (The way forms have proliferated has a certain homology with the way in which, in the economic sphere, the privatizing process has replaced the disintegrating body of governmental responsibility). As for the form-content issue in the arts, the very notion of "content" has come to appear obsolete: it implies a division that is no longer even recognized.

At a certain point, discussions of the form-content dilemma begin to blur the boundary between philosophy and fudge: nevertheless, they cannot be entirely avoided. Why is "content" under such overwhelming assault? In addition to the "serious" reasons that I offer, it may be simply because that universal scapegoat, the force that is in the process of expelling print, has driven the heart out of content as well. For postliterate societies, words are an accompaniment of video and of popular music; their fixed presence on a page, asserting something that is meant to be pondered, arouses only bewilderment. Maybe "content" has also become identified with the dangers of positivist poli-

---

42. Debord, *La Société du spectacle*; Deleuze, *Le Pli*.

43. For instance, Doy, *Picturing the Self.* I am grateful to Professor Ann Colley for this reference.

44. Buci-Glucksmann, *La Folie du voir.* See also Jay, "Scopic Regimes of Modernity," 19.

45. Brandt, *These Hands,* 157.

46. For an example of a violent reaction against the tyranny of the visual, see Mars-Jones, "Sight, Sound and Sex," 43–45.

tics, with attempts to reshape the world in conformity with credos which lead to very concrete and disastrous consequences (the "grand narrative" illusions).

For James Porter, though, the precarious state of content has even deeper causes.[47] On the one hand, form is always an arrangement of *something* (75); or (quoting George Santayana), "Form cannot be the form of nothing" (72). But, when we come down to it, matter (i.e., content) is, at best, "dirt's noble relation" (25). In fact, to speak bluntly, "Matter is the dirtiness of form" (124). Hence the efforts in Georg Wilhelm Friedrich Hegel (73), or in Friedrich Nietzsche (80), the effort to make form its own content. Yet, without content, we move toward the ascendancy of nonsense.

Henri Michaux, for instance, speaks of his attempt to sabotage meaning, "content," or referentiality, by using words "without etymological memories" ("sans souvenirs étymologiques"), words that, "referring us to so many 'high-speed forgettings,' lose their signifying function. They become disconnected from their referential value, which depends on the memory of language" ("renvoyant à autant 'd'oublis à grande vitesse' et perdent ainsi leur fonction de signifiant. Leur valeur référentielle, mémoire de la langue, est désamorcée").[48]

It is interesting to see a poet such as Peter Grieco looking for a place where meaning ("content") need not be ashamed of itself. Grieco writes poems in which he confines himself to the vocabulary available in certain word-count frequencies, including proper nouns; the commonest would be in the range 1–100. In the place of a title for each poem, the word range is given. From the range 1001–1100 (with some adjustments) we get:

> . . . Wonderful start. Drink? He's
> proved his courage provided a sufficient
> passion, though the board questions this.
> Military access. Ears! Attack! Worse loss.
> A mighty movement mentioned. The crowd
> had spoken, but, at a glance, the higher fee
> in dollars couldn't doctor a safer path.
> This is serious. A father's built for
> sorry, for grace, pride, for his dog, Jack.
> All repeated forms of the same vain dream.
> The class smiled. Heads shook. Any questions?[49]

---

47. Porter, *Origins of Aesthetic Thought*.

48. Quoted in Gillain, "'Participer au monde par des lignes' (Henri Michaux) ou comment taire le bruit des mots : petit éloge du silence," in *Représenter à l'époque contemporaine*, 324.

49. Grieco, from "Portraits: for Phil" (manuscript), ll. 5–15. Quoted by permission of the author.

Adding some words from the range between 21801 and 21900 (i.e., still moderately common words), produces:

> Marduk amuck and the manlike buttercup
> Blurt ungrammatical drivel scot-free.[50]

The slightly more esoteric series 31601–31900 yields the wonderfully comic:

> Not to extrude on your farsightedness
> But is that tofu in your backpack?[51]

It is hard to tell whether meaning ("content") is struggling to conceal itself or to break free in such passages, meticulously constructed to aggravate the dilemma. In either case, the joke is on us. And so, the Baroque effort to minimize the authority of content over form is given its belated victory—but in the court of nonsense.

The epistemological aspect of the problems emphasized by the Baroque shows a similar evolution. The destabilization of the object-perceiver relation continues apace, as we become more and more aware of the endogenous nature of our experience. The philosopher Johann Gottlieb Fichte had already made this aspect of our condition abundantly clear, but we now have the scientific means to connect the minutest quiver of our minds to an inner, neurological source. Who can say, under these conditions, what a "percept" means?

To look further: what the arts will look/sound/feel/read like when we have become the prostheses or functional appendages of our self-installed technological apparatus or "chips," I cannot tell. I will not go so far as to say that it will not matter.

———◇———

In considering the Baroque, then, one not only has to deal with the manifestations of nonsense which one encounters within it: one begins to see the value in these very prodigies of nonsense (e.g., Louis XIV as Apollo, once again) as a means of probing a fundamental issue, the relationship between form and content.

---

50. Grieco, "[21801–21900]," ll. 1–2, *At the Musarium*, n.pag.
51. Ibid., "[31601–31900]," ll. 1–2.

# Salutary Nonsense

## Keats, Kant, and Madame de Staël; or Inspiration vs. Fanaticism

## I. A SOURCE FOR POETRY

It might seem not merely insensitive but downright offensive to associate the name of John Keats, even in the remotest sense, with the idea of nonsense, especially after our having encountered some of its extreme manifestations in the previous chapter. In fact, for that reason, I had at one point considered omitting the present section entirely. On reconsideration, though, I realized that it was not only *not* an insult to the memory of Keats to write about him in this context, but that the issue that Keats himself raises insistently—Is what I am writing really inspired, or is it just nonsense?—lies at the very heart of this entire inquiry. At the root of Keats's uncertainty lies the age-old anxiety about poetry: how can you tell the poet from the madman? Or, to put it in terms of my previous confrontation with this challenge: who is right about metaphor, the person whom we identify as exhibiting the characteristics of Asperger's syndrome, and who sees nothing but nonsense in a metaphor, or the person who enjoys, or may even revel in, the metaphoric experience? In that case, though, it is the "madman" who insists on strict standards of rationality, and the "normal" person who luxuriates in what is, at least on the face of it, nonsense (see Chapter 2 Section III.B).

Traditionally, of course, poetry was also associated with religion, or could even be said to have been inseparable from it. "Inspiration" was the breath of

God. It would hardly be suitable for me to try to deal with the subject of religion in general at this point, but, given Keats's preoccupation with the problem of inspiration, it does not seem inappropriate to consider that topic in the context of religion, even though Keats does not seem to have given much evidence of religious conviction as such.

The first two questions that confront one, if one does decide to take up the relation of poetry to religion, are (1) does poetry come from some divine source? and (2) if so, how can one tell whether any particular poem derives from that source?

As far as the first question is concerned, it is usually answered in the affirmative, even by avowed atheists, since everyone uses the word "inspiration," or some equivalent, even if that equivalent be only a certain "je ne sais quoi." In this respect, though, Keats was, or, rather, deliberately placed himself, in an unusually difficult position, since, in his "Ode to Psyche," he explicitly denied the existence of any extrapersonal source for his art, declaring himself to be "By mine own eyes inspired."[1] This assertion immediately put Keats in a quandary with respect to the second question, that is, whether his own work was in fact "inspired." If his poetry came from himself alone, where could its seal of approval, or stamp of authenticity, come from? He was caught in a tautology: if Psyche, whom he himself, he tells us, had elevated to the status of a major divinity, is his Muse, is she also the guarantor of his creativity? It is hardly surprising that Keats (as he tells us, particularly in "The Fall of Hyperion: A Dream") was troubled by the question of whether his writings were genuine poetry or just private complaining. Having rejected the traditional sources of poetic utterance, he found himself under the increasing necessity of finding some alternative authority. But he never did find it. At the end of "Ode to Autumn," he still stands alone; he appeals to nothing, and to no one, for support: like the swallows, he will have to make do for himself. Even the strange person of "Moneta," under whose shadow he belatedly tries to find shelter, offers him not reassurance, but once more only a warning of his inadequacy as a freestanding being: "I sure should see / Other men here, but I am here alone."[2] Moneta's response: "What benefit canst thou do, or all thy tribe / To the great world? Thou art a dreaming thing, a fever of thyself."[3] Who would need his maunderings?

Not that Keats was the only poet who worried that his thoughts might not have universal resonance, might just be narcissistic babbling, not much more than nonsense. Even William Wordsworth, usually a determined wordsmith,

---

1. Keats, "Ode to Psyche," *Selected Poems and Letters,* 203–5, l. 43.
2. Ibid., "Fall of Hyperion," 235–46, ll. 159–60.
3. Ibid., ll. 167–68.

was concerned that his "associations must have sometimes been particular rather than general," and that "my language may frequently have suffered from those arbitrary connections of feelings and ideas with particular words and phrases, from which no man can altogether protect himself."[4]

Such doubts, of course, have ancient roots. Plato, as is well known, was of two minds about the trustworthiness of poetry, though he did finally acknowledge that some poetry, and some poetic performance, was divinely inspired, but he seemed unsure just what to do, at least in the context of statecraft, with this grudgingly acknowledged conclusion. The debates over the centuries about inspiration sometimes have overarching theological and political implications, whether in the horrifying realism of Euripides's *Bacchae,* in which Pentheus's failure of "inspiration" results in his being literally torn to pieces, or in the recurring iconoclastic wars, in which disputes over the literal presence or absence of the divine in icons—were they real, or were they visual nonsense?—had deadly consequences. The Protestant Reformation made it more difficult to delegate the responsibility for the confirmation of the divine presence, whether in objects, persons, or utterances, to a higher authority, throwing the burden of rescuing the immediacy of God, so to speak, on individuals. But, perhaps with the memory of the terrible Anabaptist revolt fresh in mind, in chapter 32 of *Leviathan,* Thomas Hobbes demolished, with devastating clarity, and a century before David Hume, all modern claims to sense in inspiration, all spokesmanship for the divine.[5] And so, whether in political movements such as Anabaptism, in the dissenting sects during the seventeenth century, or, later, in philosophical systems such as Friedrich Schelling's, divinity gradually becomes something dependent on human actions to be sustained or to be bodied forth, rather than something given. With the diminution of confidence in the prior existence of a vivifying principle, there is either an attempt to coerce inspiration, or, at least, to create a vacuum in oneself where God, or a god, may (one hopes) rush in and do the rest. Getting the guardians of consciousness to drop their vigilance, whether by chemical means, by excessive exertion, by extreme relaxation, or by whatever will stupefy the mind and allow access to a higher principle, is the next step, or forlorn hope.[6]

Even in the case of George Herbert, a convincingly religious poet if there ever was one, there is an underlying paradox. Herbert does not content him-

---

4. Wordsworth, "Preface to the Second Edition of *Lyrical Ballads* (1800)," *Selected Poems and Prefaces,* 161.

5. Hobbes, *Leviathan.*

6. On the surrealists' attempt to achieve such a condition, see Caillois, *Cases d'un échiquier,* 192–216.

self with creating the conditions for God to gain access to his spirit: he draws God towards him; he enjoins God to inhabit him. By making demands of his Muse (God himself), Herbert violates the very principle of inspiration, which presupposes self-effacement, while appearing to honor it: in this sense, prayer flies in the face of poetry. An appeal on behalf of the self is inconsistent with the subordination of the self, usually associated with every kind of aesthetic event. Of course, Herbert manages to have it both ways through what might be called his "modest hubris": "I aspire / To a full consent,"[7] he says, "not my groveling wit, / But thy silk twist let down from heav'n to me, / Did both conduct and teach me, how by it / To climb to thee."[8]

There is a surprisingly substantial bridge which can be discovered between George Herbert and Immanuel Kant, one that not many may have noticed. If one sets the passage from "Discipline" cited above beside one in which Kant produces a different personification, one finds a strikingly similar thought. I quote the Herbert passage more extensively. Herbert:

> Throw away thy rod
> Throw away thy wrath;
> O my God,
> Take the gentle path.
>
> For my heart's desire
> Unto thine is bent:
> I aspire
> To a full consent.
>
> Not a word or look
> I affect to own
> But by book,
> And thy book alone.[9]

Here is the passage from Kant: "You[r] sublime great name . . . requires submission, and yet seeks not to move the will by threatening aught that would arouse natural aversion or terror, but only holds forth a law which of itself finds entrance into the mind and yet gains reverence against my will (though not always obedience) before whom all inclinations are silenced."[10]

---

7. Herbert, "Discipline," *Poems of George Herbert*, 169, ll. 6–7.

8. Herbert, "The Pearl," 80.

9. Ibid., "Discipline," 169.

10. Fenves, "The Scale of Enthusiasm," 131; Kant, *Gesammelte Scriften*, vol. 5, 86, 118, hereinafter referred to as AK.

Of course, Kant had strongly iconoclastic leanings; he was uncomfortable with the physical imaginary in any form, and found superior power in abstract entities, which he did not hesitate to create (and then apostrophize) as need arose. This tendency to personify and glorify abstractions is particularly striking in *Critique of Judgment* #29, where Kant not only inveighs against images, but attributes an overwhelming power to the disembodied idea of the ethical. But in this case,[11] one would assume that the "great name" whom Kant addresses in the above passage, from AK vol. 5, 86, in terms remarkably similar to those employed by Herbert in "Discipline," could be no one other than God. In fact, the addressee is, like Morality in *Critique of Judgment* #29, just another of Kant's personifications, but this time, it is Duty ("Pflicht")! (Cf. Wordsworth's address to the "Stern Daughter of the Voice of God!"[12]) So similar are the terms in which Herbert and Kant apostrophize their respective deities (for it is hard to ascribe to Duty, in this context, any status lower than that of the divine), that Peter Fenves's commentary on Kant is equally applicable to Herbert: "Duty makes possible the apostrophe to duty, hence to *itself,* by silencing all other voices, including Kant's. . . . Inasmuch as it [duty] is 'someone' singled out in the address, it comes forth, or withdraws, as a You through which the I itself is defined: a You by virtue of which the 'authentic self' is a self in the first place."[13]

Here is Herbert, in "Complaining":[14] "I am thy clay, that weeps / Thy dust that calls." Or, in "Clasping of Hands," "Lord, . . . I am thine, / If mine I am."[15]

To whom, then, is one to appeal for inspiration? To God? To the personification of an abstraction? Or is it really sufficient, as Keats seems sometimes to have believed, to rely on the Self itself? By the time of Keats, of course, such thoughts had proliferated, and, chief among these recurring doubts, for a self-authorized poet such as Keats, had to be the question: how can you tell whether you are really inspired if there is no one to inspire—to breathe into—you? When Keats points to his own hand, he can describe it as his "warm scribe,"[16] but whose "scribe" is *he*? How can one make sense of this circularity?

Keats was apparently attempting to add a category of secular or self-induced inspiration to the roster of possible sources of poetry. After all, the author need not necessarily be thought of as drawing his/her material from a divine source. Just because something (poetry) cannot be produced by delib-

---

11. Kant, *AK,* 86.
12. Wordsworth, "Ode to Duty," *Selected Poems and Prefaces,* 184–85.
13. In Fenves, 131–32; emphasis in the original.
14. Herbert, "Complaining," 134, ll. 4–5.
15. Ibid., "Clasping of Hands," 147–48, 147, ll. 1–2.
16. Keats, "The Fall of Hyperion," *Selected Poems and Letters,* 235–46, l. 18.

erate effort, it does not necessarily follow that it must be of extra-human origin. Yet even Keats, for all his insistence that he is "By mine own eyes inspired," felt the need to project a part of himself as a mythological Muse— his "Psyche true," on whose authenticity he insisted, although her psychological and even neurological attributes might be thought to compromise her status. But if Keats's Psyche could, by a sort of self-affirmation, prove that her creator, Keats, was a real poet, why would Keats later have such serious doubts about his standing before Moneta? How secure was the category of secular inspiration?

## II. IS THIS POEM REAL, OR IS IT NONSENSE?

As I have said above, if the first question in the relation of poetry to religion is, Does poetry come from some divine source? then the second follows naturally, How can you tell whether, by any criterion, a particular poem, or a poet, is inspired? Although the question may have grown more fraught after the Reformation, and still more so with the rise of physiological psychology in the late eighteenth century, it had to be there, of course, from the very beginning. Not that any practical gauge of divine intervention in the poetic process ever was, or could have been, developed: in the end, critics simply ascribe inspiration to poems that they like. Plato ridiculed poets who try to gain acceptance without the divine afflatus; he claimed that it takes a *prophetic* madness to gain access to "the chiefest blessings granted to man."[17] Yet, although genius may require madness, madness is no proof of genius, as Horace famously pointed out at the ending of the *Ars Poetica*. Still, for lack of a firmer criterion, this is the one invoked repeatedly, from Aristotle through Seneca[18] to John Dryden's assertion (soon to become a cliché) in "Absalom and Achitophel": "Great wits are sure to madness near allied; / And thin partitions do their bounds divide."[19] There are, apparently, three forms of discourse: (1) the rational speech of sane beings; (2) the irrational but valued speech spoken, or thrown off, by mad poets; and (3) the nonsense spoken by the merely mad, who, when they imagine themselves to be real poets, are sometimes called "fanatics."

During the eighteenth century, as will become apparent in the following pages, this problem reappears in the debate over enthusiasm versus fanati-

---

17. Plato, "Phaedrus," *The Dialogues of Plato*, vol. 1, 250.

18. Seneca, *Treatises*, 100.

19. Dryden, "Absalom and Achitophel," *The Restoration and Eighteenth Century*, 56–83, part 1, 61, ll. 163–64. The first scientific support for this adage appeared in the *Guardian* for June 9, 2015, p. 1, in an article entitled "Gene Study Hints at Surprising Source of Artistic Genius."

cism, representing, respectively, true and false inspiration (or, sometimes, as above, mere madness). Since this issue is raised explicitly in Keats's "The Fall of Hyperion: A Dream," it is important to be aware of the intellectual context in which that problem was formulated in the years leading up to 1819, the date of the poem, where it appears in a familiar passage:

> Fanatics have their dreams, wherein they weave
> A paradise for a sect; . . .
> . . . . . . . . . . . . . . . . . . . . . . . . . . . . . . . . . . . . . .
> Whether the dream now purpos'd to rehearse
> Be poet's or fanatic's will be known
> When this warm scribe, my hand, is in the grave.[20]

The contrast is stated in harsher terms by the judgmental figure of Moneta; far from offering the suppliant [Keats] reassurance, she declares flatly that "The poet and the dreamer are distinct, / Diverse, sheer opposite" (199–200): the dreamer presumably being classed with the fanatics.

Of himself, Keats declares, "Sure a Poet is a sage; / A humanist, physician to all men. / That I am none I feel, as vultures feel / They are no birds when eagles are abroad" (189–92). But, then, somewhat contradictorily, Keats, who had just compared himself to a "vulture," whom the imperious Moneta had accused of being nothing more than "a dreaming thing, / A fever of thyself" (168–69), suddenly assumes a judicial stance, "Judge of all present, past, and future wit,"[21] and consigns all pseudopoets to perdition. He would gladly give his life, he says, to see "all mock lyrists, large self-worshippers / And careless Hectorers in proud bad verse" (207–8) "sprawl before me into graves" (210). At least at this moment, Keats has no trouble in distinguishing true poetry from false, and, presumably, he would not think that he had the right to make this distinction if he did not believe in the authenticity of his own poetry.

## III. KANT, COLERIDGE, AND MADAME DE STAËL

But, to get down to one of the more specific points that I am trying to make in this chapter: the terms, and the tone, in which Keats raised the issue of the "fanatic" versus the true or inspired poet make it sound as if it were something familiar to him, something routine and rehearsed. Now, it is certainly

---

20. Keats, "The Fall of Hyperion," *Selected Poems and Letters,* 235–46, ll. 1–2, 16–18.
21. Pope, "The Dunciad," *Selected Poetry and Prose,* 409.

true, as I have been emphasizing, that the general topic had been a commonplace since ancient times. That it had been revived in theological terms in the controversies over religious dissent in England during the seventeenth and eighteenth centuries is also well known. William Hogarth's famous satire of Methodism in "Credulity, Superstition, and Fanaticism" bears a subscript from I John 4:1 that could almost be used as an epigraph for this chapter: "Believe not every Spirit, but try the spirits whether they are of God: because many false Prophets are gone out into the World."[22]

Still, the specific formulation of the issue, especially as a problem in aesthetics, as a contrast between an unwholesome "fanaticism," on the one hand, and a genuine poetic impulse (often, in this context, equated with "enthusiasm"), on the other, which we find in Keats's "Fall of Hyperion," was elaborated primarily in the late eighteenth century by Kant. I must make it clear, though, that no "smoking gun" has been discovered, proving that Keats had read the specific passages, inspired by Kant, in either Coleridge or in Madame de Staël, that would have led to his own formulation of the issue. What can be shown is that the subject was popularized by these two widely read authors, both under Kant's influence, in Keats's time; that Keats had read extensively in Coleridge;[23] and that Keats's phrasing bespeaks a striking familiarity with the topic, as well as with the particular terminology in which it was being discussed in the early nineteenth century.

The Kantian background of the "Schwärmerei-Enthusiasmus" antagonism, the rich soil from which Keats's casual remarks can be seen to have eventually emerged, is reviewed in the magisterial article by Peter Fenves, "The Scale of Enthusiasm." Fenves cites several key passages from Kant, e.g., on p. 123: "This ambiguous appearance of phantasy [Phantasterei] in moral sentiments that are themselves good is enthusiasm [Enthusiasmus], and nothing great in the world has been done without it. Things are altogether different with the fanatic (visionary, Schwärmer). The latter is actually a lunatic with a supposed immediate inspiration and great intimacy with the powers of heaven. Human nature knows no more dangerous delusion."[24]

The gist of Kant's pronouncement is clearly echoed in the language of Keats's "The Fall of Hyperion." The question remains, though: through what channels did Keats become so familiar with the vocabulary of Kantian reasoning that he falls into it as if it were a commonplace? (The similarity between Kant's remark, in the *Anthropology*, that, "as far as *character* is concerned, a

---

22. Hogarth, *Credulity, Superstition, and Fanaticism*, 1762, etching.
23. See Lau, *Keats's Reading of the Romantic Poets*, especially pp. 69–86, for a careful examination of the evidence.
24. Ibid., 123 [AK, vol. 2, 267].

peculiarity of the poet is that *he has no character,*"[25] and Keats's insistence that the poet "has no character . . . no Identity" may be no more than a coincidence, though.)[26] Since Keats did not have direct knowledge of German philosophy, he would have had to become acquainted with it through some intermediary or intermediaries.

One of the Continental authors who helped to introduce Kant's ideas to England was Mme. de Staël. She was tutored in German philosophy by Henry Crabb Robinson, a prominent figure in the English literary society of his time, who was thoroughly steeped in German culture. Mme. de Staël's *De L'Allemagne* appeared in England before it was published in France, where Napoleon banned it. Mme. de Staël's works were very popular in England; *Blackwood's* termed her novel *Corinne,* "perhaps the most original work, either of poetry or of prose, which has appeared in our time."[27] Coleridge and Mme. de Staël had met, on September 2, 1813.[28] *De L'Allemagne* was widely reviewed in England, by William Hazlitt among others.[29] In the chapter entitled "Of Enthusiasm," Mme. de Staël begins by warning the reader that "many people are prejudiced against Enthusiasm; they confound it with Fanaticism, which is a great mistake. Enthusiasm, I repeat, has no resemblance to fanaticism, and cannot mislead as it does."[30] Moreover, "enthusiasm alone can counterbalance the tendency to selfishness; and it is by this divine sign that we recognize the creatures of immortality."[31] We are reminded of Moneta's insistence that "none can usurp this height . . . / But those to whom the miseries of the world / Are misery, and will not let them rest" ("Fall of Hyperion," ll. 147–49).

In her final (twelfth) chapter, Mme. de Staël declares "with confidence, that of all the feelings of the human heart enthusiasm confers the greatest happiness, that indeed it alone confers real happiness, alone can enable us to bear the lot of mortality in every situation in which fortune has the power to place us." And again: "Poetry and the fine arts are the means of calling forth in man this happiness of illustrious origin."[32] Here we have the identification of poetry with enthusiasm, which de Staël had consistently contrasted with fanaticism: the homology with the contrast described by Keats becomes apparent. (It must be remarked, though, that the somewhat wooden translation fails to do justice

---

25. Scharfstein, 33.

26. Keats, *Selected Poems and Letters,* 279.

27. Anonymous, "Observations on Mme. de Staël's Posthumous Work," *Blackwood's* 4, 635.

28. Coleridge, *The Friend,* xxxi.

29. Hazlitt, "Madame de Staël's Account," 162–66. See also Hazlitt's articles of February 17, March 3, and April 8, reprinted in *Collected Works.*

30. Baroness Staël Holstein, *Germany,* 397.

31. Ibid., 389.

32. Ibid., 403, 406.

to the palpable, if perhaps effusive, fervor [or enthusiasm] of Mme. de Staël's prose.)

I have mentioned that Mme. de Staël and Coleridge met on September 2, 1813. One could not say that Coleridge himself held a consistent position on the fanaticism-enthusiasm issue, but, then, he was not alone in this vacillation. Still, in the "Statesman's Manual" (1816), he chides the seventeenth century divine Richard Baxter for confusing Fanaticism with Enthusiasm, which he here defines as an unusual vividness of ideas "or of the obscure inward feelings."[33] In a *Lay Sermon,* he emphasizes the fact that Jacob Behmen was an enthusiast in the strictest sense, as not merely distinguished, but as contradistinguished, from a fanatic."[34] In the *Lay Sermons,* also, Coleridge recalls the "ancient wisdom, that nothing great was ever achieved without enthusiasm."[35] An 1820 annotation of Coleridge's on *Pilgrim's Progress* is cited on this same page (fn. 1), to the effect that "No two qualities [are] more contrary than Genius and Fanaticism. Enthusiasm indeed . . . is almost a Synonym of Genius."[36]

In his *Biographia Literaria* (1817), Coleridge had also rung the changes on fanaticism, genius, enthusiasm, superstition, and related terms.[37] In the same context, he cites the familiar derivation of the German word for fanaticism, *Schwärmerei,* from *Schwärmen,* to swarm (like bees), a form of thinking or behavior that creates an unhealthy uneasiness. (It is interesting that the condition referred to is presumably an individual experience, yet the term implies a crowd or collective insanity—or, perhaps, merely surrendering to a fashion rather than hewing to one's own reason).

It seems uncommonly sad that the principal detail which Coleridge remembered, or invented in retrospect, from his meeting with Keats on April 11, 1819, near Highgate, was his own remark to his companion, Joseph Green, "There was Death in that hand."[38]

## IV. THE "SELF" AND THE SOURCE OF POETRY

But to set aside the historical context for Keats's anxieties about the inspiration or lack thereof behind his poetry, and to return once more to the question

---

33. Coleridge, *Lay Sermons,* in *Lectures 1818–1819,* 56.
34. Ibid., 481.
35. Ibid., 23.
36. Loc. cit.
37. Coleridge, *Biographia Literaria,* in *Selected Poetry and Prose of Coleridge,* 124.
38. See Lange, "A New Coleridge-Mills Letter," 769.

itself, which is the one with which I began this chapter: what is the source of poetic inspiration, and how could Keats's predicament as a poet who could neither quite attribute his inspiration to a suprapersonal source, nor claim it conclusively as his alone, be resolved?

What are the circumstances in which artistic creation occurs? They are enormously diverse, ranging from despair through indignation to serenity. The one thing they have in common is that none of them exhibits the executive authority of the self as a primary feature: in other words, we cannot produce a creative event by commanding it to happen. What is more commonly assumed is the contrary: that a surrender of the self is required in order for the creative process to set in. The poet, Keats tells us, must be passive: "Let us open our leaves like a flower and be passive and receptive."[39] But, as Andrew Bowie puts it: "Which bit of the self actively decides that it itself is going to be passive?"[40] The case is further complicated by the fact that Keats famously denied that he even had a self (279)—he could just as well have been a sparrow picking about the gravel (259). Indeed, we are told that what distinguished the great poet was "negative capability" (261). Yet this was the same writer who, somewhat like Oedipus, insisted that he was the source of his own creations: he is a self-made man. How can we reconcile this manifesto of autonomy in the "Ode to Psyche" with the repudiation of the active ego?

It is surely a quixotic endeavor to attempt, yet again, a definition of the self, or even to review some possible concepts of the self, in order to place Keats along that spectrum. Still, the effort, no matter how superficial the results, cannot be entirely avoided. What are some of the possible selves that Keats was vacating or denying in order to make way for poetry? It is hard to know where to start.

I will skip the well-known, if still unsettled, Hume-Reid arguments over the discontinuous self. Perhaps one could begin with those who deny the self or the reality of the self entirely. Arthur Rimbaud tells us, in a lapidary line, that the self is "another"—"Je est un autre." But what, then, is the thing that the "autre" has left behind? There are many such general statements, hardly warranting specific references. Thomas Metzinger has offered the idea of the "self-model" as a replacement for the illusory self. For Ronald Melzack, the self is just a "neural signature." For Heinz Lichtenstein, its place is taken by an "identity theme." Even in Freud, neither the "I" nor the "it" is exactly a self. Or is it that the "self" is only an artifact of the "we," a local intensification of a social process?

---

39. Keats, *Selected Poems and Letters*, 266. References in this paragraph to Keats's letters are from the aforementioned Bush edition.

40. Bowie, *Philosophical Variations*, 63.

Assuming, for the moment, the individuality of the self, we never catch ourselves in the absence of thought: perhaps the practitioners of Buddhism are capable of achieving an entirely evacuated self, but, for the most part, we are condemned to a consciousness which is inhabited by things, thoughts, or both. We are always churning out words or images, even in reverie. As Paul Valéry dared to say, "Personne ne médite" ("No one meditates").[41] We never know a pure blank or vacancy from which our thoughts emerge. Does it follow, then, that thought itself is as much of a self as we can know, rather than a that-which-thinks? Or is the "self" an entity that, as Michel Foucault would have it, emerges only from the practice of confession?[42]

A simplification (or perhaps merely an evasion) of the question would be to say (to allow myself a paradox) that, in addition to all the non-selves, there are a great many changing selves, or that the word means something different at different times. Sometimes we can think of the self as merely a matter of location; as Keats himself points out in his letter on the "vale of soul-making,"[43] psychological events have to happen somewhere. Pain (even reflected pain) has to happen somewhere, to someone, and not to someone else. Then, again, one could make a distinction between the active self ("It's mine!") and the epistemological self that is, at least partially, the passive subject of impressions.

Then there are the really difficult, obscure selves that operate below, or behind, our consciousness. Some of these we can detect, or, rather, they force themselves on our attention by interfering with what we think of as our conscious behavior (but who guides *that*?). And does the self that generates dreams (and, sometimes, preplans dreams) belong to the same category as the one who writes an essay about dreams? For me, the most deeply hidden are the selves that compose aesthetic forms without any intention on our part[44] and those, even more profoundly obscure, that work on some puzzle that has lodged in our brain and emerge with an unforeseen answer some hours, days, or years afterwards. This unconscious creative elaboration is described, among others, by Henry James; for more about James's Preface to *The American,* see Chapter 5 Section V.[45]

---

41. Valéry, *Monsieur Teste,* 27.

42. Such questions are examined in detail in Dolgopolski's *The Open Past,* see especially p. 138.

43. Keats, *Selected Poems and Letters,* 289.

44. See Massey, *Find You the Virtue,* 118–119.

45. James, *Art of the Novel,* 22–23. See Chapter 5 Section V for further discussion.

## V. TRANSIENCE AND PERMANENCE

"Here lieth one whose name was writ in water."

As I have said, perhaps too often, Keats was, by choice or by destiny, in an unusually precarious and liminal position. It was not only that, as he often claimed, he had no self, and therefore could not even evacuate his self and let inspiration occupy the vacancy. It was not only that there was no divinely authorized standard by which his poetry could be judged real or, alternately, nonsensical. It was also that he seemed to have consciously assumed a position between the permanent and the transient, taking up residence inside the deadly paradox of time. Keats chose to take hold of the proverb *ars longa, vita brevis* from the wrong end. It is not that he said "Evil, be thou my Good," but "Transience, be thou my Permanence." It is not in the spirit of more recent artists who have reveled in destroying or undoing their own work (Jean Tinguely, Christo): it is, rather, holding fast to transience rather than casting it away together with art, holding fast to it, and, "In midst of other woe / Than ours,"[46] forcing us, continuously, to face it. Art is the lasting proof that life cannot last.

That is why one should not take "Here lieth one whose name was writ in water" as merely a cry of despair. Keats was always, by choice, standing on the world's brink, looking, but finding nothing beyond it: "Till Love and Fame to nothingness do sink."[47]

"Where are the songs of spring? Aye, where are they / Think not of them."[48] The songs of spring offer the false promise of a secure future. The work of art is transience itself. For the artist, it cannot be permanent; no matter how elaborately worked out, it is always improvised, gone in a flash, "Consumed with that which it was nourished by."[49] But, in the same instant, it returns to haunt mankind with its lure and its warning. How true what Friedrich Schiller said, that it is, and can only be, elegy, satire, or utopia. It cannot occupy real time.[50] If the Grecian urn is "a friend to man" (l. 48), who needs an enemy?

But, is it also possible to have absorbed this lesson too deeply, and, for this or some other reason, to have adopted too rigidly ascetic an attitude towards art? Escorting Marshall McLuhan through the Albright-Knox Gallery in Buffalo, New York, at a time when the collection was more diverse than it is now,

---

46. Keats, "Ode on a Grecian Urn," *Selected Poems and Letters*, 207–8, ll. 47–48.
47. Keats, "When I Have Fears," 133, l. 14.
48. Keats, "To Autumn," 247–48, ll. 22–23.
49. Shakespeare, "Sonnet 73," *Love Poems and Sonnets of William Shakespeare*.
50. Schiller, "On Simple and Sentimental Poetry," *Aesthetical Essays of Friedrich Schiller*.

I was amazed by the depth of knowledge and understanding of art and its history that McLuhan displayed. At the same time, McLuhan assured me, it was not to museums that he turned when he was in search of spiritual experience.

For me, at least, McLuhan was applying too rigorous a standard. Art does, still, offer moments of perfection, no matter how transient: if one will, moments when divinity, like Percy Bysshe Shelley's "Spirit of Intellectual Beauty," drops in among us. Even in the less canonical forms of art (e.g., for one, in Gilbert and Sullivan!) one can find precious oases of blessed relief from the inadequacies of life. Perhaps simply because we lack Keats's honesty, for us ordinary mortals, the poet, even Keats himself, remains, in spite of himself, "a friend to man" (yes, even in the "Grecian Urn"!), a "physician to all men" ("Fall of Hyperion," l. 190), providing a refuge in which one can dwell briefly, if not a sirens' isle on which to hide, like the cowardly reader of Anton Chekhov's "Ward 6."[51] As a trampoline to help launch us beyond itself, and beyond ourselves, art/poetry is something for which we have no alternative.

But none of this would have been a central concern for Keats, as primarily a provider, and not just a beneficiary, of art. Rejecting the entrenchment of art as a fixed object of worship—an outcome that Plato dreaded, and that has been purged periodically in the waves of iconoclasm that have racked and are still racking history—Keats, rather like Constantine Cavafy, whom E. M. Forster describes as "Standing at a slight angle to the universe,"[52] chooses to maintain a solitary and precarious vigil at the edge of his "wide world."[53] Poised between everything and nothing, he cannot be said to be "inspired," but he cannot—if we dare to use such an expression with respect to Keats—be said to be just blowing his own horn, either. Keats's is an unsupported voice, sometimes unsure of itself, but never unsure of its intent.

Other poets, after Keats, have confronted similar uncertainties. If Keats was having such a difficult time in identifying a source of inspiration, to what, or to whom, could later authors, even more distant from religious certainties, turn as guarantor of their poems' authenticity? A century ago, Anna Akhmatova lamented, "golos Muzi yelye slishni"—"the Muse's voice is scarcely heard."[54] But now, surely all talk of inspiration is obsolete nonsense: we now

51. For Chekhov, see Massey, *Find You the Virtue,* Chapter 3: "Escape from Fiction."

52. Forster, *Pharos and Pharillon,* 91. Interestingly enough, iconoclasm, which plays such a large role in the Abrahamic religions, does not seem to have figured significantly in Chinese history.

53. Keats, "When I Have Fears," l. 13.

54. Akhmatova, "Somewhere There is a Simple Life," *The Complete Poems,* vol. 2, 410, l. 14. Elsewhere she speaks of writing poetry as merely taking dictation: "And find the lines, dictated, simply there / Lying in place upon the snow-white page." See "It Happens Thus," vol. 1, 154, ll.

know that the poet alone is responsible for her/his work. Nevertheless, when it comes to a poem such as Mark Strand's "Prediction," once more, a force beyond the poet's control is evoked, and that force is again, as it once was in Shelley's "Ode," the wind. This time, though, the wind does not sustain the poet, but obliterates the very possibility of poetry:

> . . . the wind rising
> And taking the moon and leaving the paper dark.[55]

<hr/>

The last word? Apparently not, at least in a different register, for someone like Leonard Cohen, who could just as well be channeling George Herbert. God speaks again, in a tolerant if unmistakably authoritarian voice. He will put up with Leonard, with all his faults, because, in the end, Leonard will obey him. In terms of his physical appearance, Cohen is described as dressed in a slightly pompous, conventional bourgeois fashion. He hardly seems to be someone who is poised, waiting to answer the call of duty. At best, he would make a most reluctant prophet. Nevertheless, when the time comes, God tells us, "He does say what I tell him / Even though it isn't welcome." Not that he has had any choice in the matter; we are informed that it is not in his power "to refuse."[56]

Maybe what we really need is a dose of such salutary quasi-nonsense, to wake us up and rescue us from the brink of too much "sense."

<hr/>

Keats, though, had the courage of his convictions. For all his religious velleities, he would not hand over the responsibility for his voice to anyone, or anything, else.[57] As I have said, his is an unsupported voice. But who wants to listen to a mere mortal? For all his bravery, then, Keats created a middle ground, and invented a Muse for himself in the person of Psyche, half myth, half mind. What drove Keats to this extreme measure?

<hr/>

15–16. On the silencing of the poetic voice by uncongenial circumstances, compare Alexander Blok: "All sounds have stopped. Can't you hear that there are no longer any sounds?" in Figes, *The Russian Revolution, 1891–1924*, 784–85. I am grateful to Sophia Canavos for having found this quotation.

55. Strand, "Prediction," *Darker: Poems*, 29.

56. Cohen, "Going Home," *Old Ideas*.

57. See also Ducasse (the comte de Lautréamont), the line quoted previously: "L'autonomie! Ou bien qu'on me change en hippopotame" ("Independence! Or let them change me into a hippopotamus"), 322.

We cannot do without a Muse; or without something, someone, or a Someone, in thinking about art. For anyone who even tinkers with art knows that, at the moment when we feel that we are expressing what is most intimately ours, we are, as Anna Akhmatova declares flatly, taking dictation. To put it another way: even if we reject the conventional definition of inspiration as that which breathes something into us, we know that, by any definition, inspiration is that which summons from us that which was not ours to give.

# CHAPTER 5

# Neural Nonsense

## Neuroaesthetics, Hypnagogia, and the Aesthetics of Nonsense

> Oh! W! X! Y! Z!
> It has just come into my head—
> —Edward Lear, "Mr. and Mrs. Discobbolos"

## I. NEUROAESTHETICS AND ITS DISCONTENTS

One might have hoped that the scientific study of the mind could answer questions such as those raised in the above chapter on Keats, concerning the difference between genuine poetry and random raving. Neuroaesthetics as a discipline began to enter popular awareness about a dozen years ago, with the work of Margaret Livingstone, Semir Zeki, and V. S. Ramachandran. Of course, the introduction of any new approach to the arts is likely to be accompanied by exaggerated claims (think Marxist analysis, psychoanalysis, discourse analysis, "New Criticism," structuralism, Bakhtinian "heteroglossia," Deleuzian rhizomatics, etc.), and neuroaesthetics was no exception. I attempted to outline the limits of its possible achievements in *The Neural Imagination* (2009); on close inspection, at least according to my judgment, these limits turn out to be extremely narrow. Least of all could this method be used to adjudicate in matters of taste. But neuroaesthetics isn't necessarily a bad thing. It's like a cobra—you just have to be careful which end you pick it up by. If you begin by assuming that neuroscience will eventually tell you what art is, you've had it: you have already ceded the essential ground, and you will be fighting a rearguard action from then on. If, on the other hand, you understand that neuroscience can tell you many interesting things that are tangential to art, or that go to make up art, you may safely pursue neuroaesthetics, and art itself will remain safe. John Keats, who immersed himself in studies of the brain as a medical student, was not afraid that neuroscience would undermine poetry, as we can see from his "Ode to Psyche." To be sure, Benjamin Libet could prove that our own brain "knows" what we are going to do long before we do it.[1] But presumably Keats's brain also "knew" the poem he was composing before he composed it, and Mozart's brain "knew" the music he was composing before he performed it. For that matter, my brain presumably "knows" the sentence I am writing before I write it. Does that also go to prove that I am nothing but the passive plaything of my material instantiation? Even if it is only my unconscious or preconscious that is speaking, it is still *my* unconscious. All that this approach has done is move the problem of the source of consciousness one step back, without bringing us any closer to solving it. What Keats understood, when admiring Psyche (the embodiment of thought), is that it takes a mind to marvel at a brain.

But to return to the question of neuroaesthetics. In all my explorations of the subject, I myself have found only one place, in music, where neurology may gain a purchase on art, though there are undoubtedly others, some perhaps related to dance, and some related to humor, as Tristan Bekinschtein's article on puns may begin to demonstrate.[2] I myself have wondered all my life how composers succeed in making wonderful songs out of terrible texts. As Joseph Addison puts it, "Nothing is capable of being well set to music that is not nonsense."[3] Pondering this problem, I began to wonder whether the solution might have something to do with the interaction of the hemispheres. Speaking on the related area of poetry, Iain McGilchrist (in interview) says that poetry has to steal a march, so to speak, on the dominant hemisphere:

"Our initial apprehension of the world . . . is a holistic impression from the R. H. This information is then apprehended sequentially by the L. H. . . . but in order for us to have an integrated understanding, it must return to the R. H. where it is re-presented . . . as a whole . . . we are used to seeing, seeing differently, and then seeing again."[4] Poetry piggybacks on this process: as McGilchrist puts it, poets "have to smuggle in their jewels by distracting the officers of the L. H."[5] The nonrational and musical elements of poetry survive

---

1. Libet, *Mind Time,* 45.

2. Bekinschtein et al., "Why Clowns Taste Funny," 9655–71.

3. Addison, *The Spectator,* 42.

4. "Poetry on the Brain: The Moon and Other Clichés." Interview by Ange Mlinko with Iain McGilchrist, May 16, 2012. http://poetryonthebrain.blogspot.co.uk. (This blog has since been removed.)

5. Ibid.

the journey and find shelter in the R. H. In my own wording, "In poetry, the right words give one access to the nonverbal."[6]

It seems to me possible that, in the case of sung poetry (i.e., song), a transaction between the hemispheres is also involved, but in a different way. It is understood that the right hemisphere does not deal with language as easily as the left hemisphere. When the right hemisphere finds the words for a song dumped in its lap, so to speak, not knowing quite what to do with them, it adopts them—but strictly on its own (i.e., musical) terms. It strips those lyrics of their own inherent musicality, of their musical DNA, and fills them with its own power, overwhelming the semantic content of the original text. A simple example: in a famous section near the end of the "St. John's Passion," "Ruhet wohl, ihr heilige Gebeine" ("Rest well, ye sacred bones"), the word *wohl* would normally be read with a rising inflection, whereas Bach gives it a heavy downward beat.

In other words, "Music can run away with meaning whenever it chooses to do so."[7] The result is a fusion or marriage, but a marriage in which music is dominant and dictates the terms. This amalgam, once created, appears to have its own cerebral niche, since it is possible to arrest normal speech by transcranial magnetic stimulation without interfering with the subject's ability to sing songs.[8]

Thomas Carlyle said that we are nothing but music.[9] Similarly, Adam Zeman says that "We, ourselves, are music."[10] I myself argue that music is the fourth state of consciousness, in addition to wakefulness, non-REM sleep, and REM sleep.[11] That music is rooted in the very basis of our being seems to be shown not only by music's ability to survive major brain damage, but by its ability to influence behavior or elicit a response even when there is scarcely any brain at all.

I spend my summers in Nova Scotia, and three years ago I was listening to the CBC when I heard a program about a microcephalic child in Halifax who benefited from music therapy. On further inquiry, I was able to make contact with her foster mother, Willa London; Willa kindly brought the child to see me. (Kymiah is now Kymiah London: she has been officially adopted). Kymiah

---

6. Massey, *Neural Imagination,* 75.

7. Ibid., 121. Housman apparently regarded this situation as unfortunate. "European music . . . when added to words, which express emotion with precision, becomes, strictly speaking, nonsensical." See Keegan, "Housman Country," 29.

8. See Stewart et al., "Transcranial Magnetic Stimulation," 433–35.

9. Carlyle, "On Heroes," 116–17.

10. Zeman, *Portrait of the Brain,* 200.

11. Massey, *Neural Imagination,* 122.

has a beautiful face, but, at 5 years of age, she was unable to hold her head up or make any orderly limb movements, and her fists were more or less permanently clenched. I was able to hold her; she was quite soft and limp. She did smile, though, and even laughed if joggled or had her cheeks lightly pinched. Kymiah had been not expected to live beyond her third month. Now she was involved in active programs of physical therapy, and had regular meetings with the music therapist and guitarist, Anna Plaskett.

As can be seen from the following image, Kymiah's skull was largely filled with cerebrospinal fluid. She had a brain stem, a cerebellum, and a pituitary gland that enabled her to grow. The image of her skull shows the severity of her condition if compared with that of a normal skull and even with that of what is usually considered a microcephalic child.

I have a number of other images of Kymiah's skull which apparently contain some contradictory information; in one image, there is evidently some sign of a cortex. Whatever they may show, it was evident that Kymiah was surviving with extraordinarily little brain.

Having seen and held Kymiah, I found it astonishing that she responded to music to the extent to which she did, though Björn Merker observes, in an important article, that microcephalic children respond to sound even in the absence of an auditory cortex.[12] In a video taken during one of her music therapy sessions, she is much more active and responsive than she was when I saw her; she is obviously stimulated by the music, vocalizes, and at one point almost seems to be trying to imitate the pitch of the instrument. It is clear that music has meaning for her: it is not mere nonsense.

I have said above that the interaction of music and words in song is the only area in which I have thought neuroscience might find some purchase on aesthetics. But, it will be objected, doesn't neuroscience have a great deal to tell us about acoustics in music, about color relations in painting, about, say, memory in literature? It does, indeed, but it is not able, to the best of my understanding, to discriminate between aesthetic events and ordinary perceptual or psychological experiences. It can account, as Margaret Livingstone explains, for the shimmer on the water in a Monet painting by the confusion of luminance with color intensities,[13] but it cannot tell us what sets such a picture apart from examples of visual paradox in an ophthalmology textbook, or, for that matter, from impressionist or postimpressionist techniques used in an advertising poster chosen at random. Caught in her own neuroaesthetic trap, Livingstone ends up by admitting, "I find enlarged magazine images to have

---

12. Merker, "Consciousness without a Cerebral Cortex," 63–81. It is not inconceivable that other parts of the neural apparatus take over, to some degree, the functions usually served by the auditory cortex.

13. Livingstone, *Vision and Art*, 150–53.

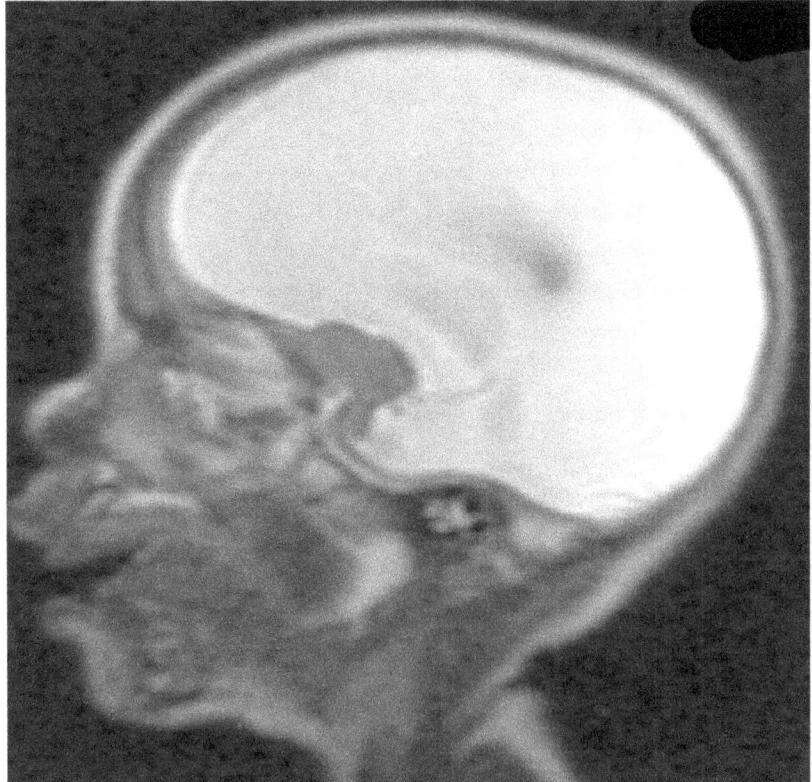

FIGURE 1. Image of Kymiah London's skull.

colors that are just as visually interesting and just as lively as Post-Impressionist paintings."[14]

This is where the confusion between perception and art leads us: vision, no matter how complex and interesting its characteristics, is not in itself aesthetic. In *The Neural Imagination,* I say that art "does not do what the brain would be doing anyway of its own accord. Art emphasizes 'inappropriately.' Art does not duplicate the natural percept: it cancels the natural percept and replaces it with another. In a melody, for instance, what it cancels is the note as it existed outside the melody; in a song, the word as it existed outside the song. Similarly, in rhyme, meter, or other poetic devices, it works at cross-purposes to the perceptual brain, continually defying our prosaic expectations and linguistic norms."[15] Art, Semir Zeki says, "liberates us from the fortuitous

14. Ibid., 48.
15. Massey, *Neural Imagination,* 43.

view,"[16] but (and again I quote myself) "only by creating a view that is systematically at variance with the one provided by ordinary perception."[17]

These are my general observations on neuroaesthetics: it gives us unlimited information about the "how" of a work of art—how it produces its effects— but very little about the "why," the meaning or the value of the work—and virtually nothing about the unique characteristics that distinguish one work from another and determine importance. For a more detailed discussion of all these matters, see my book, mentioned above, *The Neural Imagination,* or Raymond Tallis's *Aping Mankind.*[18]

## II. THE EXPERIMENT, NONSENSE, AND METAPHOR

My second topic is "the Experiment." This rather vague and mysterious title refers to a special undertaking of the Medical Research Council's Cognitive and Brain Sciences unit in Cambridge, UK. I had noticed, all my life, that, at sleep onset, I would often experience what I can only call "intrusions": words or phrases that diverged from the images and actions current in the mind at that time. They are rather like the disconcerting adjectives that Edward Lear often introduces in the last lines of his limericks: the "*incongruous* old Woman of Smyrna," the "*intrinsic* Old Man of Peru," the "*abruptious* old man of Thames Ditton." This divergence, for me, is virtually diagnostic of sleep onset; it marks a threshold of relaxation and a moment of recognition that one is entering another mental world. A friend of mine, the neurologist Daniel Glaser, formerly of the Wellcome Institute, says that he has come to regard these as precious moments, to be "revered"; Edgar Allan Poe went so far as to claim that they give one "a glimpse of the spirit's outer world."[19] In the ecstatic language characteristic of those who have first come to realize the special nature of this state, Poe goes on to speak of "a class of fancies, of exquisite delicacy, which are *not* thoughts, and to which, *as yet,* I have found it absolutely impossible to adapt language. . . . They arise in the soul . . . at those mere points of time where the confines of the waking world blend with those of the world of dreams. I am aware of these 'fancies' only when I am on the very brink of sleep, with the consciousness that I am so."[20]

16. Zeki, *Inner Vision,* 68.

17. Massey, *Neural Imagination,* 43.

18. Tallis, *Aping Mankind.*

19. Poe, "Marginalia," *Introduction to Poe,* 536. I am obliged to Professor Robert Daly for the reference.

20. Loc. cit.

As though in anticipation of the very experiment of which I was later to be the subject, Poe speaks of trying to capture these moments for examination. "In experiments with this end in view, I have proceeded so far as, first, to control (when the bodily and mental health are good) the existence of the condition . . . and feel even the capacity of inducing or compelling it. . . . I have proceeded so far, secondly, as to prevent the lapse from *the point* of which I speak—the point of blending between wakefulness and sleep—as to prevent at will, I say, the lapse from this border ground into the dominion of sleep. . . . I can startle myself from the point into wakefulness."[21] Poe is here describing precisely what I was called upon to do during the hypnagogia experiment which is the main subject of this chapter: encouraging myself to fall asleep, but then interrupting the process just before it was completed. Poe goes on to speculate about the possibility that his experiences during hypnagogia may be universal. Be that as it may, "nothing can be more certain than that even a partial record of the impressions would startle the universal intellect of mankind, *by the supremeness of the novelty of the material. . . .* In a word—should I ever write a paper on this topic, the world will be compelled to acknowledge that, at last, I have done an original thing."[22] Since Poe left us no record of his "fancies," I am now obliged to write this "paper" on his behalf. It does not, however, attempt to deal with hypnagogia as a general state, which is what concerned Poe, but deals primarily with my experience of linguistic intrusions at sleep onset.

It may well be asked, What is the connection between neuroaesthetics and hypnagogic intrusions? The temptation would be obvious: might the intrusions not be poetic, therefore *ipso facto* aesthetic, emanations from the creative unconscious, manifestations of the imaginative powers latent in all of us? Unfortunately, they are not, but they do call for comparison with other, more clearly valuable "intrusions," and I will devote the later part of my chapter to an attempt to place them within a broader category of semiconscious utterances, certain of which clearly do have aesthetic importance.

It may well also be asked, since I am dealing with a phenomenon that shares a border with dream, How can I justify the omission of dream from this study? After all, if ever there was nonsense that is necessary for us in the most literal sense, it has to be dream; for, without dreaming sleep (and there is not

---

21. Ibid., 537.

22. Ibid. Another classic description of what happens as the mind slips into unconsciousness is provided by Robert Louis Stevenson, in *An Inland Voyage*, 78: "Something inside my mind, a part of my brain, a province of my proper being, had thrown off allegiance and set up for itself. . . . Thoughts presented themselves unbidden; they were not my thoughts, they were plainly someone else's."

much sleep that can be shown to be entirely devoid of dream), we eventually die. And we devote an enormous amount of our lives to this form of non-sense, the dream. It may be true that many dreams make sense, partial sense, or quasi sense. But the vast majority of dreams contain elements that cannot be fitted into any coherent scheme. If they are part of some economy that has an intelligible structure, it is an economy that is impenetrable to us, an occult economy of its own. What is clear is that, at least at the phenomenal level, we experience most dreams as nonsense; therefore, to us, nonsense they are.

Dreams are said to serve the purpose of consolidating or culling memories, but, if they do so, they carry out that function at a level inaccessible to our conscious awareness. One might even add, if they are performing that activity through means of which we are entirely unaware, why do they need us to stand around and observe the process in progress, since we don't understand it as such, anyway? In any case, I have previously made a concerted effort to address the problem of meaning, or of lack of meaning, in dreams,[23] and I will not try to recapitulate my arguments and observations there. Suffice it to say that I still find a core of untranslatability at the heart of every image, and our dreams make it obvious that images are essential to our survival. We have to be able to retreat into our private nonsense, our ultimate refuge, in order to continue with our lives. But many libraries have been devoted, with only limited success, to this question with reference to dreams. I will confine myself to that area of pure, unqualified nonsense on the border of dream, the hypnagogic intrusion.

Now, to address the experiment itself.[24] The technical description of the experiment can be found in the article "Intrusions of a Drowsy Mind: Neural Markers of Phenomenological Unpredictability."[25] To summarize: The experiment involved a subject (myself) wearing a high definition electroencephalography (HD-EEG) headset and equipped with voice recorder and timer with a button to press when there was something to report. The subject was placed in circumstances that encouraged drowsiness. When the subject experienced a verbal intrusion at sleep onset, he woke sufficiently to report and describe the event before drowsing off again. An attempt was made to correlate the spoken description of the event with any unusual electrical activity in the brain

---

23. Massey, *Find You the Virtue,* 20–30 and passim.

24. The full plan and background for the experiment can be found under the heading "A Study of Intrusive Language Episodes in Hypnagogic Sleep," at http://www.buffalo.edu/cas/english/faculty/emeritus-faculty.html under the link for Irving Massey. On the advantages of single-subject studies, see Hadhazy, "A Mind in Time," 18–20.

25. Noreika et al., "Intrusions of a Drowsy Mind."

immediately preceding the spoken report. A major problem with this experiment was that the time lapse between intrusion and report was highly variable, ranging from a few seconds to half a minute; this inconsistency increased the difficulty of finding the point on the EEG to connect to the intrusion. The specific aim was to find a signature for intrusions, but, since the behavior of the language system at sleep onset has not, to the best of my knowledge, been studied, it was hoped that our understanding of that general process would in any case be enriched. In the article cited above, Noreika et al. describe the signal that they have identified for the verbal intrusions reported by the subject.

It is not clear to me that the second, more general objective, that is, the clarification of the language system's behavior at sleep onset, has yet been attained. Some degree of spatial localization of the brain processes involved may still be achieved at a later stage of this investigation, by other, more specifically localizing, techniques than EEG, particularly functional near-infrared spectroscopy (fNIRS) and, possibly, magnetoencephalography (MEG). My hypothesis, still entirely speculative, is that intrusions originate in the subordinate hemisphere, which experiences some relief from the control of the left hemisphere at sleep onset, and that they are a consequence of dissociation, in which well-regulated, self-monitoring networks loosen with a decrease of consciousness. Another possibility is that there is a decrease of connectivity between language-serving networks of neurons and image/action or kinetic networks at sleep onset.

Localization, of course, even if achieved, always raises at least as many questions as it answers. As for the verbal reports of intrusions provided by the subject, they can be studied along various linguistic parameters, but content analysis in relation to neurological processes is apparently not yet within the scope of science. At this point, I will just give a couple of excerpts from the transcripts of my "babblings in the lab," to put some flesh on the bones of my description. The verbal element of the intrusion is given in bold type; the visual element is given in italics. There was an attempt on the part of the subject to guess at the sleep stage during which the intrusion occurred, on a scale of 1 to 7. The subject also attempted to score the degree of incongruity between the verbal and the visual materials, on a score of 1 to 5. There was an additional scoring of anomalous elements within the verbal and the visual experiences, which I have not given here.

Intrusion no. 126: '**Whether this monkey,**' that was a description of a *woman in a straw hat but really without a face, and really without hands, riding an old-fashioned motorcycle in a half circle.* Sleep stage: possibly 5. Incongruity scoring: 5.

Intrusion no. 129: **'Winter white man's coat,'** in the context *of putting a horse into a sort of violin case and zipping it up.* Sleep stage: possibly 4. Incongruity scoring: 5.

In intrusion no. 224: the verbal element consisted of my speaking about a **letter of recommendation** that I had to write about a student; the accompanying visual element had *an elderly couple sort of toddling or dancing backwards.* Sleep stage: possibly 3. Incongruity scoring: 5.

Intrusion no. 207 illustrates the not uncommon situation in which one part of the mind cannot, or refuses to, communicate its knowledge to another. I heard a word something like **rigoler** in the context of *trying to get out of a bolted door,* and thought at the time that it was a French word. Although I know German, I did not realize until I read the transcript that the word was based on the German word **Riegel**, which means "a bolt."

The last recorded intrusion of all, no. 227, is, after all my emphasis on language, just the word **'Image,'** in the context of *my own feet stretching out.* Sleep stage: not recorded. Incongruity score: possibly 4.

I could give numerous examples of intrusions to add to the above, as well as to the many in my project description, such as the one in which I was thinking about Unitarianism and the sentence "Indonesia is right on the road" emerged from somewhere. Once, I thought that something was being served up to me on a steel "chaotic," rather than on a steel tray. The one concerning a white man's clothing while a horse was getting into a guitar case was an image of which Salvador Dalí could have made good use—and Dalí did, in fact, have a method for capturing his hypnagogic images to employ in his pictures. Usually sitting upright in a chair, he would hold a key in his hand, with a plate on the floor beneath it. As he was falling asleep, he would lose his grip on the key, which would fall on the plate, waking him up—so that he could immediately record the images forming in his mind as he was losing consciousness.[26]

The other day, when falling asleep during a nap, I was thinking about a lady I had once met in a shoe store, when the word "Rector" presented itself clearly to my mind. It appeared to have nothing whatsoever to do with anything else that I was thinking at the time. This intrusion is of particular interest, as will shortly become apparent. It is possible, of course, that I had seen or heard that word somewhere recently, but, if so, what had brought it back to memory at that particular moment?

---

26. Dalí, *50 Secrets*, 36–37. Dalí specifies that these are hypnagogic rather than oniric images (38). He also insists that crucial problems in the elaboration of a work of art can be solved in sleep, "problems which in your state of waking consciousness you would never be humanly capable of solving" (33).

The same question lingers in the background of some relevant research at the University of Hertfordshire. Taking their cue from earlier work by George Mandler, Lia Kvavilashvili and her colleagues have been trying to identify the sources in memory of verbal intrusions during wakefulness. (They have been working at the behavioral, rather than the neurological, level.) They have found that, in a substantial proportion of cases, it is possible to trace intrusions to a "prompt" of some sort, sometimes recent, sometimes from the distant past. Initially, "someone's name (Niccolò Machiavelli), an image (of Twin Towers), or a familiar tune (America's National Anthem), pops into mind and amazes the person with its irrelevance," but upon closer examination "in almost 50% of reported mind-pops [sic] participants were able to ascertain that the actual or related contents of the mind-pop had recently been encountered in one's environment or internal thoughts."[27] These discoveries lend strong support to the theory proposed by Gottfried Leibniz three centuries ago, that our unnoticed peripheral perceptions (what he called, in the *Nouveaux essais sur l'entendement humain,* the "petites perceptions") play a very large role in our lives, although they are not apprehended consciously at the time. Wilder Penfield, of course, believed that he had succeeded in reviving these unconscious perceptions by direct stimulation of the brain,[28] although, I gather, there is still doubt in some quarters about the exact nature of the responses that he elicited. It should be noticed that there are quite a few forms of involuntary memory, each with its characteristic intrusion, that can be identified, and each, no doubt, with its own associated neurological pattern; the Hertfordshire team has succeeded in distinguishing among some of these. For that matter, though, the very distinction between voluntary and involuntary memories is not always clear. Lia Kvavilashvili and the other pioneering investigators of such intrusions have not yet determined why "mind-pops" occur when they do, or by what principle of selection these particular hidden memories (if that is what they are) are chosen for resurrection. After all, we have an infinite number of "petites perceptions" to choose from—why should one of those in particular become salient? I happened to be reading Barbara Pym's *Quartet in Autumn* recently, when I ran across the following passage: "Taking out a packet of jelly babies he [Norman] had a sudden and vivid picture of Letty, but why this should have materialized at this particular moment and with such intensity he could not have said. Surely nothing to do with jelly babies?"[29]

---

27. Elua et al., "From Mind-Pops to Hallucinations?" 165.

28. Penfield and Rasmussen, Chapter ix.

29. Pym, *Quartet in Autumn,* 98. Or, from a somewhat earlier source, Gissing's *Private Papers of Henry Ryecroft,* 130. Gissing wonders why unrelated sequences arise in the mind. He

The Hertfordshire investigators suggest that the occurrence of verbal intrusions during full consciousness may be associated with both a high degree of creativity and, alternatively, with a tendency to schizophrenia, in which, according to this theory, hallucinations would actually consist of a series of such involuntary semantic memories.[30]

At this point, in the course of writing this chapter, I encountered what seems to be a striking confirmation of the Hertfordshire group's claim that verbal intrusions are simply unnoticed memories. A few paragraphs ago I mentioned that the word "Rector" had sprung up in my mind during my hypnagogic encounter with a lady from a shoe store. A couple of days later, as I was glancing through the Elua et al. article on verbal intrusions, my eye fell on a line, "See Beck and Rector, 2003, for examples of such priming of hallucinations in their patients with schizophrenia."[31] I had, of course, not the faintest conscious memory of that reference, nor was there anything in the context to suggest a connection with ladies in shoe stores, unless perhaps "Rector" recalled "Beck" unconsciously, and I wanted to have ladies in shoe stores at my "beck" and call. But why, then, did the word "Rector" impose itself on the memory, whereas "Beck" did not?

Perhaps it would be better not to attempt such extreme forms of explanation. In any case, the results of the Hertfordshire investigation are an invaluable complement to our work, although they can go only so far in filling in gaps in the experiment in which we have been engaged: the emphasis in Hertfordshire is on the behavioral and psychological, whereas the Cambridge study is primarily neurological. Besides, intrusions during wakefulness are unusual phenomena, whereas verbal intrusions at sleep onset are, at least in my case, and in the case of some of my friends, normal, routine experiences. Waking intrusions might be accounted for by some unusual pressure forcing an unexpected association into consciousness at a particular juncture, perhaps in a momentary form of narcolepsy. On the other hand, when one is drifting off to sleep, the gradual disengagement of the language stream from the images and action of an approaching dream seems to be just an expression of the normal relaxation that accompanies the incipient sleep process. When we are falling asleep, we are, for once, relieved of the burden of relevance, and are no longer answerable to others for the words we think or speak. Whether it be Lev Vygotsky's self-directed speech of infancy that resumes control,[32] or

is talking with his gardener about soil conditions when "Of a sudden I found myself gazing at—the Bay of Avlona. Quite certainly my thoughts had not strayed in that direction."

30. Elua et al., 169.

31. Loc. cit.

32. Vygotsky, *Thought and Language*.

some other dialect of our internal language, "we have no difficulty in accepting our own language" (I quote myself). This is the ideal place where "the sounds we utter, whether privately or aloud, are coin of the realm. There we are ourselves, as we were to begin with."[33] It is a paradox: the one place where we are supremely confident that we are making sense, the one place where we are not in thrall to the approximations of a foreign language (the language of others), is the one place where we think in pure nonsense.

Clearly, we have a need for nonsense for its own sake, not only as an enhancer of sense.

Sometimes, what I have been calling "intrusions" are simply the consequence of the language stream's detaching itself from our other mental content and going its own way; sometimes, as in the case of the word "Rector" mentioned above, they cut inappropriately across whatever other language is running through the mind during the early stages of a dream. In either case, the answer to the question why the particular hypnagogic intrusions that occur do occur can at this stage be only a matter of imaginative speculation. Perhaps they are items at the head of a queue, waiting their turn for expression. Perhaps they are elements of fragmentary narratives that proceed below the level of consciousness, perhaps even below what we usually call "stream of consciousness," the literary form pioneered by Edouard Dujardin and Andrey Biely. Perhaps it is for us, as Zeman says of his patient Lucy, "as if some part of her were dreaming secretly all the time,"[34] and that these intrusions are, as Rodolfo Llinas has suggested, part of the continuous dream that accompanies us all our lives.[35] In this case, though, they would have to be understood as representing a dream process emerging from below, or behind, dream itself, since they often occur just as what we usually think of as the normal dream is getting under way. For me, they mark a threshold; they provide the guarantee that I am actually falling asleep. As such, as I have said above, they are accompanied by a grateful relaxation, the feeling that one has at last come under the domain of a more hospitable regime.

I should, by the way, make it clear that the "intrusions" I have been describing have nothing to do with "hearing voices," a phenomenon which

---

33. Massey, *Neural Imagination*, 84.

34. Zeman, *A Portrait of the Brain*, 104.

35. Llinas and Paré, "Of Dreaming and Wakefulness," 525. Cf. Merleau-Ponty, *Phenomenology of Perception*, 168: "That ever slumbering part of ourselves which we feel to be anterior to our representations, to that individual haze through which we perceive the world. There are here blurred outlines . . . which are in no way 'unconscious.'" In *Phénoménologie de la perception*, this reads: "Cette part de nous-mêmes toujours ensommeillée que nous sentons en deçà de nos représentations, de cette brume individuelle à travers laquelle nous percevons le monde. Il y a là des formes confuses . . . nullement inconscientes" (207).

in some cases may have pathological implications. My intrusions are not words actually heard, but simply presented to consciousness, unvoiced. In his interesting book on hearing voices, *Muses, Madness, and Prophets,* Daniel B. Smith quotes the automatic poet Sara Avio describing a related class of experiences while "hearing" her poetry: "These are voices, that separate themselves from the other voices of my thoughts; a sudden, different voice comes forward."[36]

## III. NONSENSE, NARRATIVE, INTRUSIONS, AND METAPHOR

Although the topic of "intrusions" may sound somewhat exotic, the bizarre verbal flotsam thrown up by the mind at sleep onset tends to be disappointing, because it is devoid of aesthetic content or flavor. Bizarre these bits of nonsense may be, but they are on the whole strikingly uninteresting, like undigested bits of food regurgitated. They seem to be sheer nonsense, entirely devoid of supportive context. Paradoxically, this very fact does lend them a certain interest, since pure nonsense is surprisingly hard to find. Our efforts to maintain our rationality appear to be more successful than we sometimes think. We have a natural tendency to find pattern or meaning in everything that we encounter, even in what may at first glance make no sense whatsoever, but these words and phrases during hypnagogia are products of a mechanical process, and there is nothing to be done with them. If this be the raw material of the stream of consciousness, or, rather, of one of our streams of consciousness, or of something beneath our streams of consciousness, it does indeed, *pace* William James, "appear to itself chopped up in bits"; one cannot say of it, as does James, "It is nothing jointed; it flows."[37] If one can call it a "flow," it is a halting, stuttering, stumbling flow; it seems to mark a hitch, or a breakdown, in the otherwise orderly progression of the stream of consciousness.

On the other hand, figuring out what these meaningless oddities are about might be compared to understanding the behavior of some erratic particle in physics that leads one to an understanding of many other, apparently more orderly, entities or processes. It is a little like what Gilles Deleuze said

---

36. Smith, *Muses, Madness, and Prophets,* 111.

37. James, *Principles of Psychology,* vol. 1, 239.

many years ago, in *Logique du sens*: that sense depends upon nonsense.[38] Or Nietzsche: "Im Anfang war der Unsinn" ("In the beginning was Nonsense").[39]

As prime examples of nonsense, without context and without apparent purpose, these intrusions force one into a confrontation with the larger, overarching aspects of nonsense, with its general role in language and in thought. Nonsense is, of course, a major subject in philosophy and linguistics, and has been treated in a highly technical fashion within those disciplines; as I have mentioned before (in Chapter 1), it appears as a topic in Frege, Carnap, Wittgenstein, and A. W. Moore, among others. In this chapter, I will allow myself again to use the term in a colloquial or naïve manner, in its various common acceptances, as it is generally understood.

The random accidents of mind are frequently a source of instruction, and not infrequently a source of pleasure. Who wants always to be tied to the procrustean bed of formal language? When we think of the wrong word for something—let's say "sailor's cap" instead of "hypothesis"—the farther the wrong word is from the right one, the more satisfying it is likely to be, especially if, as in this case, it involves a category mistake. The error benefits from its inappropriateness in the same way as a metaphor does. (I hope that I may be excused for returning to the topic of metaphor, which I had pretended to deal with conclusively in my first chapter; but the topic of intrusions is so closely related to the topic of metaphor that it is hard to keep them apart.) I always revert to an example from Coleridge: anyone can say "See the fingers of the birch twigs in the spring," but it took Coleridge to say "See the chocolate mist around the birch twigs in the spring!"[40]

Isidore Ducasse, the comte de Lautréamont, famously satirized the clichés of metaphor when he wrote that a young man was "as beautiful as the accidental meeting of an umbrella and a sewing machine on a dissecting table."[41] Lautréamont puts metaphor on the dissecting table with malicious satisfaction. T. S. Eliot also delivered a crippling blow to this universal trope with his evening "Like a patient etherized upon a table"[42] (once more, the surgical table!), and, for quite a while, especially around the 1980s, metaphor was

---

38. Deleuze, *Logique du sens*. "On Nonsense," is a systematic exposition of this principle. Deleuze's argument might be reformulated (imprecisely) as the assertion that the language series collides continually with a "Ding an sich" series of unspecifiables that obliges it to keep going.

39. Nietzsche, *Vermischte Meinungen und Sprüche, Nietzsches Werke: Klassiker-Ausgabe*, vol. 3, 438.

40. Coleridge, *Notebooks*, vol. 1, entry 1783.

41. Ducasse, *Œuvres complètes*, 322.

42. Eliot, "The Love Song of J. Alfred Prufrock," *Modern American Poetry*, 425, l. 3.

There was an Old Man of Thames Ditton,
Who called out for something to sit on :
    But they brought him a Hat,
    And said, " Sit upon that,
You abruptious Old Man of Thames Ditton ! "

There was an Old Man in a pew,
Whose waistcoat was spotted with blue ;
    But he tore it in pieces
    To give to his nieces,
That cheerful Old Man in a pew.

FIGURE 2. Edward Lear's illustrations of his
limericks "Old Man of Thames Ditton" (1872)
and "Old Man in a Pew" (1846).

more likely to be rejected than celebrated. Alain Robbe-Grillet claimed to have established a new genre, freed from metaphor, with his supposedly dead-pan novels, which instead are studded with intrusions, obsessive meaningless eruptions of asymbolic symbols, such as a stain on a wall or a seagull's eye.[43] Metaphor has fallen afoul of other literary fashions since then, but it seems

---

43. Robbe-Grillet, *Pour un nouveau roman.*

doubtful that it will lose the place assigned to it by Aristotle as the key to literary value. But every metaphor, in its element of incongruity or irrelevance, does have a nugget of a more or less nonsensical "intrusion" buried within it, as every eukaryotic cell depends on the alien ancestral bacterium encapsulated in its mitochondria. No matter how plausible, every metaphor retains something alien or unassimilable.

As Don McKay puts it, "The excitement of metaphor stems from the injection of wildness into language."[44] Rhyme and meter, although apparently expressions of regularity, are actually ways of soliciting this wildness, of teasing the unconscious to peek out of its lair—in other words, of purposefully soliciting "intrusions." With luck, what one then sometimes gets is a collaboration between the deliberate and the accidental, the volitional and the effortless. Edward Lear gives the unconscious, the stranger within, even bigger bait: he shows that he is willing to accept *anything* that it throws at him; he offers equally enthusiastic hospitality to the relevant and the irrelevant. There is no censorship here: the door stands wide open. And (*contra* George Orwell, in "Nonsense Poetry,"[45]) it is precisely in those passages in which Lear embraces total nonsense that the full depth of his genius becomes apparent.[46] This act of generosity, of totally unmotivated donation, is then ratified retroactively by the picture.

## IV. A BIT OF A DIGRESSION: EDWARD LEAR *VERSUS* METAPHOR

In his own way, Lear is more subversive than are the declared enemies of metaphor. Lear's nonsense, in the limericks, is not metaphoric. Metaphors are often mini-allegories awaiting interpretation. They invite us to translate them into a rational language. But Lear's limericks are short-circuited metaphors: whatever hopes we may have had that the old man of Thames Ditton's being forced to sit on a hat has a moral to it are dashed by the last line—"You abruptious old man of Thames Ditton!"[47] (And what of those noses!)

Lear's limericks are traps that lead us to expect the familiar devices of metaphors as they go about their business of mediating between dream and rationality, with a lifeline thrown toward the shore of our familiar world. But

---

44. Cook, *Field Marks*, xiii.

45. Orwell, "Nonsense Poetry," *How to Shoot an Elephant*, 190. "For myself, I must say that I find Lear funniest when he is least arbitrary."

46. Lear, *The Complete Nonsense of Edward Lear*, 38.

47. Ibid., 206.

Lear's poems do not end up where we think they will: they remain in unsafe, unsettled territory, such places as "the land where the Bong-tree grows,"[48] because they reject paraphrase into any neutral vocabulary. The Bong-tree cannot be anything but what it is: it is the most specific tree possible. It is not definable by anything other than itself. Let nonsense remain nonsense—and, as Verlaine said, "Tout le reste est littérature" ("All the rest is literature").[49] While working to undo the pretensions of metaphor, Lear creates a different reality, one that can stand on its own two feet—or, should it prefer, dance by the light of the moon.

It is (or was, at least in the 1990s) often argued that novelty in thought is itself dependent on a form of intrusion, on catachresis, that is, on metaphors that sometimes do not quite hit their mark, unexpectedly reformulating ideas in approximate or symbolic ways. So, for instance, my comparison of the search for a neurological signature of the hypnagogic "intrusion" with the search for something like the Higgs boson may be misleading, but Darwin's possibly having used the behavior of the stock market (with which he was preoccupied) as a basis for the concept of natural selection in biology proved quite consequential, whether he was entirely right or not. Nothing significant comes to light unless we strike the target off-center. It is fine to take a chance on being wrong if we turn out to be right in a major way (Cf. Hans Vaihinger's "Philosophy of 'As If'").

Nonsense is, of course, particularly important, not only for metaphor, but for poetry in general, and it is interesting to compare the genuine nonsense of hypnagogic intrusions with the seminonsense of nonsense poetry. For, what most nonsense poetry does is embed fragments of genuine nonsense in a semi-intentional frame or fabric, capturing real nonsense and exploiting it for highly intentional ends. If nonsense poetry were mere nonsense, no one would bother reading it. Nonsense poetry cannibalizes real nonsense and plays with it for its own purposes, teasing us with the feeling that we are at the margin of rationality and about to be released into blessed freedom, only to draw us back from the edge to cradle us in the security of a partial rationality.[50] We have been refreshed by the excursion into the unknown; we return laden with new because unspecified meaning, so all is not lost. Nonsense is where the wild things are, or the goblins; it is tempting, dangerous, yet in the end, reassuring. It is important to have gone over the margin. Nonsense poetry combines the

---

48. Ibid., "The Owl and the Pussy-Cat," 62.

49. Verlaine, "Art poétique," *Œuvres poétiques complètes*, 151.

50. This point has also been made by Jean-Jacques Lecercle, among others. See Williams and Bevis, "Introduction," *Edward Lear*, 1–15.

relaxation of self-abandonment, perhaps of sleep, with the relaxation provided by a reassembled, if slightly rearranged, securing frame.

A good example can be found in the paradigmatic example of nonsense poetry, "Jabberwocky." Jean-Jacques Lecercle points out that Humpty Dumpty's own explanations of Lewis Carroll's vocabulary in the poem are completely inadequate.[51] But the problem is not really that we have trouble in resolving the words into more familiar terms. The reason why we love the poem is not because we recognize another vocabulary beneath the bizarre language with which we are confronted. On the contrary, it is almost because we find it too easy to understand, far easier than it would be if it had been written in standard English. It is impossible to avoid being sucked into a literal reading of the so-called "nonsense" words: we automatically pick out the most relevant associations of the phonemes and connect them into a seamless web. In this situation, we are not even left with choices; we cannot stand back from the flow of associations and choose to overlook parts of the poem. That is why some of the "words" seem better than others, which only create bumps in the process of free association. We do not resolve "mimsy" into "flimsy," "mime," and "prim"; our minds go through the *whole* of English vocabulary and pick out the most relevant elements. That is why I say that most nonsense, even when apparently extreme, holds us within a frame, whether prosodic or semantic, that is more familiar than we initially realize. Much like Chaucer's "Rhyme of Sir Thopas," "Jabberwocky" provides us with an outline that says "fill in the blanks." In Chaucer's case, we are provided with the answers, but they consist of the meaningless jargon of chivalry; Carroll forces us to find meaning, whether there be any or not: he exploits our need to make sense of everything, as in the "Image Made by Chance" of Chapter 6 (see below).

Seen from another perspective, what Carroll does is show that one doesn't really need superficial coherence in order to make sense—that true sense and coherence lie at a deeper level. For all its seeming jovial humor, "Jabberwocky" makes us feel vaguely uneasy, as if we were being taken to some mysterious place underground. What has happened in this poem is that Carroll has restored us to true sense by going under the words to the sounds, forcing us into a world of genuine meaning, a world in which the atmosphere, or atmospherics, is the real meaning—the *whole* meaning.

But it would be dishonest of me, as well as self-contradictory, to deny that the nonsense of Lear's limericks, of Daniil Kharms's fables, possibly of parts of

---

51. Lecercle, *Philosophy of Nonsense*, 24. On the interplay of semantic stresses in language, see Hinchcliffe and Frey, "Shakespeare's Genius is Nonsense." On sound associations among words in Edward Lear's limericks, see Brown, "Being and Naughtiness," in Williams and Bevis, *Edward Lear*, 162–82.

Antonin Artaud's work, operate according to some other, perhaps even more daring or challenging principle, which I have not yet clarified for myself. Here, nonsense is not merely a poor relation of the rational (see above, footnote 45). To change the metaphor, these poets are not using the bait of nonsense just to give us the pleasure of knowing that we are in control after all. For, after all, nonsense does challenge us to let ourselves go entirely: the question is, Where will it take us if we do let go? Perhaps to a place where fragmented nonsense can be reassembled in another, and a better, pattern, rather than merely escorting us back to the solid, or stolid, fireside. After all, the Old Man in a Pew's nieces will clearly make wonderful use of the "pieces" of his "spotted" waistcoat ("spotted" intensifies the fragmentation of "pieces"). In fact, one of the nieces already seems to be using a piece of the poem/waistcoat as her ticket to the empyrean. Does not such a "nonsensical," "headless" poem, in its own way, like Rilke's torso of Apollo, also say "Du musst dein Leben ändern" ("You must change your life"—or, at the very least, rearrange it!)?[52]

Incidentally, I believe that the so-called language or sound poets, to the extent that I understand their work, are doing the wrong thing. I believe that some meaning clings to every sound when one is using language, and that it is not possible to divest sounds in speech or language of their associations. In playing with sound, one is necessarily playing with meaning. The Sami "Yoik" is another case in point.

I cannot bring myself to leave this topic without mentioning another, also entirely gratuitous, form of nonsense. It is what results when one repeats a word until it loses its meaning and becomes, or seems to become, only a sound.[53] I have used the word "nugget" occasionally, and it will serve as well as any other as an example. If one succeeds in detaching it from its meaning, the sounds remaining will still have some associations, but they will no longer be those of the word before it was driven back into its merely phonetic condition. But—and this is the important question—what has happened to the *meaning* of the word "nugget" once it has been deprived of its home in that word, of its body?

I can only say that it continues to exist, but off to one side, so to speak, because it has nowhere else to go. As a friend put it to me, it is held in abeyance. It cannot sink back into the dark, mysterious space of preverbal thought: once it has come out, assumed a body, it has forfeited its passport for the return trip. There is no way to detach its meaning from the noise to which it has become connected: it is committed to this world, and, conversely, there

---

52. Rilke, "Archaïscher Torso Apollos," *Selected Poetry*, 60.

53. See Lecercle, 23, for Carroll's own comments on the destruction of meaning through repetition.

is no way for this world to get rid of it. The bond between its sound and its meaning is indestructible. In other words, even if one repeats "nugget" until that sound loses all meaning, the word, and its meaning, must continue to exist somewhere. They can never be reduced to nonsense. For Lewis Carroll, not even a nonsense word can be reduced to nonsense. "My lord," he responded, when upbraided by the king in one of his juvenile dramas for creating a word, "rigol," just to fit in with the rhythm of a sentence, "the word is said, for it hath passed / My lips, and all the powers upon this earth / Can not unsay it."[54] Of course, "rigoler," in French, just happens to mean "to chortle."

But to return to the difference between hypnagogic intrusions and metaphors: metaphors, despite the element of randomness and irrelevance that is crucial to their nature, are the products of a self. There is always a self-perceived behind them: a person, and a personality. Hypnagogic intrusions, in contrast, are mechanical and impersonal. "Somebody" has produced them, but they could be anyone's.

## V. THE FRAME: GOOD AND BAD INTRUSIONS

I have been trying to bring the subject of this experiment, hypnagogic verbal intrusions, into relation with the broader topics of nonsense and metaphor. So far, though, I have succeeded primarily in creating what might be called a negative framework for these odd phenomena: they are *not* expressions of creative spontaneity, à la "Kubla Khan," and they occur in poetry mainly as something to be teased or played with, while we are on our way, galumphing back to the anchor of the poem, even if that poem be "Jabberwocky."

One of the things that these intrusions can do, though, as I have said, is help us to realize how different pure nonsense is from the aesthetic in any form. The aesthetic, no matter how confused it may seem, always has an element of order, or, at the very least, of purpose about it.

In an effort to get at this problem, the distinction between the products of the creative unconscious and mere nonsense, from another angle, I could cite a passage from Nathaniel Hawthorne on the transition from sleep to waking as a period "when the imagination is a mirror, imparting vividness to all ideas, without the power of selecting or controlling them."[55] Even more to the point

---

54. Quoted in Sutherland, *Language and Lewis Carroll,* 147. "Rigol" is an archaic word for "circlet," hence "crown."

55. Hawthorne, "The Haunted Mind," *Nathaniel Hawthorne's Tales,* 57. I am obliged to Professor Bob Daly for the reference.

is a well-known passage from John Dryden's preface to his play "The Rival Ladies." Here, Dryden speaks of the stage at which the play was still

> only a confus'd mass of Thoughts, tumbling over one another in the Dark. When the Fancy was yet in its first Work, moving the sleeping Images of things towards the Light, there to be Distinguish'd, and then either chosen or rejected by the Judgment.[56]

How are these "sleeping Images of things" different from my "intrusions"? And what makes some of those images—many presumably drawn from the memory—more valuable than others? Are the rejected ones similar to my "intrusions"? At least the valuable ones seem to have benefited by their passage through the sleeping or unconscious state, becoming material for metaphor. Metaphor is the physical face of thought, polished by sleep. To quote Shakespeare: when these, the valuable images of memory, fade (from consciousness), they become subject to a "sea-change / Into something rich and strange."[57] In sleep, they have become something better, more interesting than, different from, the merely representational conscious images that they were before their transmutation. They have undergone a process of digestion by the unconscious mind. Perhaps they belong to that part of the memory that, according to the *New Scientist*,[58] is meant for building the future rather than merely recalling the past.

Henry James has summed up the beneficent revisions of memory magisterially in another famous preface, the belated introduction to his novel *The American*. The idea for that work had come to James "abruptly," while he was riding in an "American horse-car":

> I was charmed with my idea, which would take, however, much working out; and precisely because it had so much to give, I think, must I have dropped it for the time into the deep well of unconscious cerebration: not without the hope, doubtless, that it might eventually emerge from that reservoir, as one

56. Dryden, "Epistle Dedicatory to 'The Rival Ladies,'" *Works of John Dryden*, 95. Nicholas Humphrey reminds me that Lewis also quotes this source in *The Poetic Image*, 69, among quotations from other authors to the same effect.

57. Shakespeare, *The Tempest*, 1.2.401–2.

58. Robson, "Memory," 33: "Memory researchers . . . believe that human memory didn't evolve so that we could remember but to allow us to imagine what might be." See also Schacter et al., "Remembering the Past," 657–61, and Dolgopolski, *The Open Past*.

had already known the buried treasure to come to light, with a firm irides-cent surface and a notable increase of weight."[59]

But what of the percepts that, so to speak, have never fallen asleep, and so have never been subject to this process? Although, in approaching the question of intrusions, I was sure that this was new territory for me, and that I had never thought about it before, I have been embarrassed to realize that I had actually once written about it, though in a totally different context (see below in this same section).

(I am, by the way, aware that I have begun to speak of imagistic and verbal intrusions almost as if they were interchangeable, but, in fact, all of these images do resolve into the verbal, or at any rate into a verbal account of them; even a metaphor is not a metaphor unless it has at least a verbal analogy. So, for the most part, when I have been dealing with images, I have dealt with them not in themselves, but with their spore print in words.)

I am assuming that my "intrusions" represent not the successes, but the failures, of memory: things that can't be forgotten because they haven't been properly assimilated, or, perhaps, have been filed in the wrong place, like Sibyl's leaves left undeciphered, blown by the wind into the trash pile—or, perhaps, into the neurological equivalent of a trash pile—of memory.

I last wrote about this subject in the "Orpheus and Eurydice" chapter of my book on literature and ethics, *Find You the Virtue*. There, I referred to such rejected images as "widowed" images, and I classed them with the images presented only as meaningless objects, common in works by Nikolai Gogol, Raymond Roussel, Albert Camus, Jean-Paul Sartre, and the previously mentioned Robbe-Grillet, among others, works in which the atmosphere of meaninglessness sometimes becomes so pervasive (e.g., in *L'Étranger*) that they seem to refer to a world that is already dead, or only alive enough to be able to suffer from its condition. The clearest description of such an object, and of its genesis, is given by Gerard Manley Hopkins, where he describes a piece of wood that, he tells us, he has seen *in a daydream*—in other words, it is an intrusion, and clearly defined as such. This is an object that he only later realizes was part of an outhouse. "I had seen it longer together and had that day been wondering what it was: in reality it is used to hold a little heap of cinders against the wall which keep from the frost a piece of earthenware pipe which there comes out and goes in again making a projection in the wall. It is just the things which produce dead impressions, which the mind, either because you cannot make them out or because they were perceived across other more

---

59. James, *The Art of the Novel*, 22–23. On the functions of gestation and the "cognitive unconscious," see Kandel, *Age of Insight*, 467–71.

engrossing thoughts, has made nothing of and brought into no scaping, that force themselves up in this way afterwards."[60]

This is almost the opposite of what Henry James refers to (a propos *The American*). I can think of no clearer description of an intrusion, of its source and of its arrested trajectory through the mind, so that it becomes a "revenant," an aimless, wandering ghost, never quite to be put to rest. Unlike those objects that, as Hopkins puts it, have been brought into a "scaping" by the mind, and so have been given a place and a meaning, it can never partake in an aesthetic experience.

Here, then, at last, we may have a partial framework for the topics of intrusions and of nonsense, at least in the context of the psychological and the aesthetic: there are two kinds of nonsense, then, the good (James's) and the bad (Hopkins's), which rest, respectively, on good and bad memories. The good intrusion is drawn from predigested memories (see above, Chapter 2 Section II.C), those, perhaps, with a Wordsworthian aura, memories, perfected, that can be used in metaphors, which I have elsewhere (in my subchapter on Miquelon, entitled "Metaphor as Double Vision") called the seeing of an imperfect image through a perfect one. The bad intrusion, whether verbal or visual, is inert; it has no flavor and no overtones; it has not been digested or understood. It does not even represent one of those tricks played on us by that shadowy other self, that poltergeist that lurks in us (memorably described by Vladimir Nabokov and by Danilo Kiš);[61] it is not even some device just intended to show us how little we know about ourselves, to make fools of us before dodging back to hide in our inner woodwork.

In the effort to find, or create, a frame for our "experiment," then, it has been possible to situate "intrusions" vis-à-vis the broad background of aesthetics, in relation to other forms of nonsense, in relation to metaphor; it may even be possible, eventually, to situate it in relation to some implicit narratives. As far as getting closer to the neurophysiological background from which verbal intrusions arise is concerned, though, the most we have been able to achieve so far is to identify the EEG signature of the intrusive event, as a first step towards understanding the neurology of free association.[62] Perhaps these events reflect a weakening of the "self-monitoring" system that usually accompanies speech (assuming a conceptual background for speech, rather

---

60. Cited in Massey, *Find You the Virtue*, 153–54.

61. Nabokov, *Speak, Memory*, 33; Kiš, *Hourglass*, 8, 145–50. See also Nooteboom, *Rituals*, 126, on sleep, "One of all the people you are is resting, the others remain awake."

62. On the mnemonic sources of free association during hypnagogia, see Stenstrom et al., "Mentation During Sleep Onset," 37–46, as well as Nielsen, "Describing and Modeling Hypnagogic Imagery," 75–94.

than Daniel Dennett's "pandemonium" model),[63] and have some affinity with Wernicke's, or "fluent," aphasia. Perhaps they are in fact like bits of the "word salad" heard in some cases of schizophrenia, or, when salient, like moments of Tourettism. One friend suggests that they may give us a glimpse of a sorting process going on somewhere in the brain, a possibility that has been developed at length by Sue Llewellyn.[64] Certainly, if our memories are what make up our dreams, as well as what happens during hypnagogia, they are memories that have been put through the shredder and reassembled according to principles into which we have, so far, little insight. A former colleague of mine has proposed—I do not know with what degree of plausibility—that intrusions may result from an overload of information in area V3A of the visual cortex during hypnagogia. Apparently V3A "receives input from all the sensory modalities" and behaves differently when the organism is in a state of heightened or reduced attention.[65] In any case, if we accept Dryden's metaphor from above, hypnagogic intrusions are among the least promising of the offerings on the conveyor belt of images and ideas ushered towards the light by Fancy. They seem voiced by what Shelley calls "the central stone / Of sullen lead,"[66] the very last among the confused streams of voices clamoring for articulation and recognition in our intentional life.

——◇——

Here we have encountered nonsense in its purest form. Hypnagogic intrusions, visual as well as verbal, conform to no known principle of sense. Even if their origins in some physiological processes were to be identified, they would remain opaque to our understanding.

---

63. Dennett, *Consciousness Explained*, 237–42.

64. Llewellyn, "Such Stuff as Dreams Are Made on," 589–607.

65. See Badgaiyan, "Nonconscious Perception, Conscious Awareness and Attention," 585, as well as id., "Nonconscious Processing and a Novel Target for Schizophrenia Research," 335–39.

66. *Prometheus Unbound*, 4.540–41.

# CHAPTER 6

# Perceptual Nonsense

## The "Image Made by Chance," Automaticity, and the Aesthetic Universal

## I. PATTERNS

### A. Perceptual Nonsense: The Image Made by Chance and Pattern Recognition

POLONIUS: My lord, the queen would speak with you, and presently.

HAMLET: Do you see yonder cloud that's almost in shape of a camel?

POLONIUS: By th'mass, and 'tis like a camel indeed.

HAMLET: Methinks it is like a weasel.

POLONIUS: It is backed like a weasel.

HAMLET: Or like a whale?

POLONIUS: Very like a whale.

HAMLET: Then I will come to my mother by and by.[1]

---

1. Shakespeare, *Hamlet,* 3.2:367–74. The initial impetus for this chapter was provided by a paper that was read at Cambridge by Rhodri Lewis of St. Hugh's College, Oxford, from which I have borrowed extensively. See "Shakespeare's Clouds and the Image Made by Chance," 1–24. I should also like to thank David Clarke, Jamie Currie, Ann Colley, and several Cambridge undergraduates, who kindly listened to an initial version of this paper, and provided invaluable advice. My colleague, Professor Carolyn Korsmeyer, kindly read a later draft, and offered searching criticisms to which I have responded only in part.

Arbitrary and pointless in the extreme, the scene seems to challenge us to find meaning in it, as one might seek to find shapes in a cloud. It hardly takes us beyond the pure nonsense of the hypnagogic intrusion, just discussed in Chapter 5. Turn it which way we can, it remains opaque to reason.[2] As evidence of Hamlet's insanity, or pretense of insanity, it is worse than useless; Hamlet is obviously in complete control, as he plays with the hapless Polonius.[3] It seems to have been thrown in as a practical demonstration of the hopelessness of making sense of anything. On the one hand, one can find meanings even in a cloud; on the other hand, these "meanings" don't mean anything, either. On the one hand, this is nonsense rampant: on the other hand, it reflects a body of behavior that is integral to human functioning.

## 1. Pattern Recognition

Pattern recognition is not optional, nor is it personal: it is the same for all of us. Even Polonius will see the same whale or camel that Hamlet sees, and Hamlet cannot help seeing the same whale or camel that Polonius sees. My topic will be the role of the aesthetic in this process, in the phenomenon of compulsory pattern recognition, but, before embarking on that enterprise, I would like to make some more general observations on the psychology of perception.

I had been working on my project for some time before I realized that two areas essential to my inquiry had already been well defined, and established as fully recognized domains of scientific investigation, by the time that I had begun to explore them. Both lie within the broader and familiar field of pattern recognition, of which I have just spoken, but each requires specific attention. They represent two particular strains in the process of aggregation and separation, respectively, or, conversely, of separation and aggregation, depending on which activity is regarded as fundamental.

---

2. I cannot resist passing on the following quotation from the unpublished correspondence of S. Foster Damon, which was sent to me by my friend, Professor David Ben-Merre. "Hamlet once met William Blake. / They chatted for politeness' sake. / Said Hamlet: 'Do you see that cloud?' / Said William: 'Yes, it is a crowd / Of Seraphim shouting "Glory! Hail!"' / Said Hamlet: 'No: It's like a whale.' / And so they parted, each one glad / That the other, and not he, was mad." The theme of shapes in clouds continues to crop up, sometimes in unexpected contexts. See the *New Yorker* cartoon, "What does that one look like to you?" (November 17, 2014, 57).

3. I have let the above reading of the scene stand, since it gives us a sense of how Polonius would have experienced the situation. In fact, the nonsense is so artfully deployed that I (with likewise failing faculties) had to be reminded that it is a completely rational rebuke of Polonius's sycophancy.

## 2. Pattern Separation

It is by no means clear how we separate one thing from another, or even, for that matter, how we separate that which is, presumably, ourselves from that which is not ourselves. That initial distinction, although obviously necessary for our survival, was held to be arbitrary by Johann Gottlieb Fichte.[4] To Novalis, the mere capacity for making such a distinction seemed so remarkable that he held it to be miraculous, even the founding miracle of our existence: "Die Möglichkeit der Selbstbegrenzung ist die Möglichkeit aller Synthesis, alles Wunders. Und ein Wunder hat die Welt angefangen" ("The possibility of self-limitation is the possibility of all synthesis, of all miracles. And a miracle inaugurated the world").[5]

There has been an attempt at finding a physiological correlate to the process by which we separate one thing from another in recent research on neurogenesis. Pattern completion—the aggregating function by which we fill in incomplete images to make a recognizable whole, as illustrated by the quotation from *Hamlet*—has to be balanced by pattern separation. The latter ability, "which appears to be linked to the production of new neurons," records our impressions "as unique, preventing them from blurring, one into the next."[6] When Hamlet asks Polonius to find a camel, a weasel, and a whale in the same cloud, he is simply making random demands, bullying Polonius by the incoherence of his questions, and ending with a startling non sequitur. But the fact remains that all those shapes *can* be seen in that cloud: coexistent, but distinct, and each one real in itself. What is more, the shapes not only can, but *must* be seen by any observer to whom they have been pointed out.

## 3. Pattern Completion

When I began considering this subject, I thought of pattern completion as an unusual and even somewhat unnatural event. After all, how often does one go around noticing shapes in clouds? Demanding that someone else find those same shapes in clouds must be an even rarer event. But I eventually realized that the completion of partial images is not only a constant, one might say, an incessant, activity, but that that tendency, sometimes in exaggerated form, has even become the subject of a specialty in psychology. Under the headings of "apophenia," "pareidolia," or just "patternicity," it has been studied intensively,

4. See, for instance, Léon, *La Philosophie de Fichte,* 25–26, 205.

5. Quoted in Benjamin, *Gesammelte Schrifte,* vol. 1, 35.

6. Kheirbek and Hen, "Add Neurons Subtract Anxiety," 64.

in both its normal forms and in those verging on the pathological.[7] A familiar example is the "rat" on Mars formed by a geologic formation.[8] An even more obvious, perhaps disagreeably obvious, case is the happy face (or frowning face), which can manage, even with a single eye-dot, to produce the desired expression. (This is not a modern peculiarity: a pebble with two dots above a horizontal line, now held in the Natural History Museum in London, was of sufficient interest to someone in the Upper Paleolithic to warrant his/her carrying it off to a distant cave for reinspection.) We need not go on into Gestalt-style observations about the ways in which we apprehend a cube.

No doubt, our inclination to complete patterns has an evolutionary basis: it is to our advantage to be highly conscious of the forms taking shape in our environment (see the work of Karl Friston on perceptual parsimony). I have recently become aware that this kind of activity can occur not only as the result of an act of attention, but even without our conscious awareness. I am one of those people who has music running continuously in his head, unless he is actually speaking.[9] If I am thinking, whether purposefully, or simply letting my mind drift, music is always there, and it does not interfere in any way with the thought process. One day, recently, I realized, as I was ruminating on the topic of this very chapter, while enduring a mildly obsessive tune that was playing in my head, that I was seeing a ram's head outside my window. It was shaped by a clump of leaves that I wasn't even aware I was looking at. The pattern had created or completed itself while my mind was entirely elsewhere, running on "idle," or in what is sometimes called the "default" mode. (Actually, that is often the time when the most intense concentration takes place.) In *My Struggle: Book Three: Boyhood,* Karl Ove Knausgaard gives one a good sense of just how pervasive this form of perception can be: "It was always a particular pleasure . . . to see the light in the hall come on, revealing the presence of all the familiar objects. The shoes with the grommets as eyes and the tongue as a forehead, the chilly gaze from the white two-holed electric sockets above the baseboard, the hat stand in the corner, with its back turned. And in my room: the pens and pencils assembled like a gang of schoolchildren in the pen stand, some insolently leaning against the edge."[10]

So much for the "rarity" of pattern completion. Perception itself depends on our ability to see, hear, etc., what isn't there; one might say that we have to depend on nonsense in order to construct reality. I will now allow myself

---

7. See, for example, Kazemzadeh, "Apophenoetics," 115–23. On patternicity, see also Shermer, *The Believing Brain,* 59–86.

8. See Powell, "Weirdlands of Mars," 58 and 60.

9. See Sacks, *Musicophilia.*

10. Knausgaard, *My Struggle: Book Three: Boyhood,* 144.

a digression, though one not entirely unrelated to the subject at hand. I have realized that, while engaged in thinking, if I direct my attention deliberately towards the music or the image that I have been unconsciously, or semiconsciously, experiencing, the thinking, the act of ratiocination, stops abruptly. Although unconscious, or semiconscious, perception is perfectly compatible with thought, the reverse is not true. There is no reciprocity. One can hear, and see, while thinking about something entirely unrelated to the objects of semiconscious perception, but one cannot ruminate on some unrelated subject while actively hearing or seeing.

I am not sure whether this observation points to anything significant: it may be just that, if you are listening or looking, you had better not be distracted by irrelevant thoughts. Whether there is some deeper puzzle behind this absence of reciprocity, in which thinking appears to be placed at a disadvantage, I cannot yet decide.[11]

To return to the question broached in the subsection entitled "Pattern Recognition" above, concerning a possible aesthetic element in pattern recognition, whether in Hamlet's cloud, or in other natural formations: is it possible to identify an element of automaticity, not only in pattern recognition as such, but in the aesthetic response to such patterns, and, if so, what are the implications of that possibility? After all, both Plato[12] and Aristotle[13] assumed that music had a direct, automatic effect on behavior and character; why should similar things not occur in the visual area? The topic of automaticity in some fields of aesthetics may be starting to come back into focus, as is suggested by the appearance of an article entitled "The Automatic Aesthetic Evolution of Different Art and Architectural Styles."[14]

The area of aesthetic automaticity with which I will be dealing is, however, sharply restricted. In this chapter, I will confine myself to three topics: one is the one that I have just broached, involving recognition of forms in natural shapes ("finding patterns"); another has to do with afterimages ("creating patterns"); the last is what Gerard Manley Hopkins calls "inscape," the pang

---

11. See Harris, "Let Your Mind Wander," 33: "A particular style of neural processing is suppressed when we pay direct attention to things, and it emerges when the brain switches to default mode. The daydreaming DMN [default mode network] activity processes personal memories and leads to identity formation."

12. Plato, *Republic*, 3.10–12: 398–403.

13. Aristotle, *Politics*, 8.1340a.40–1340b.5 and 8.1340b.10–13.

14. Bartoli et al., "The Automatic Aesthetic Evolution," 126–34.

of beauty that may seize one on encountering a striking landscape[15] ("appreciating patterns"). I will not attempt to deal with various related topics, such as E. T. A. Hoffmann's mechanical or semimechanical musical instruments,[16] Heinrich von Kleist's dancing marionettes,[17] or automatic writing (whether by Yeats or others). Incidentally, it should be remembered that "automatic" pattern recognition is not always aesthetically pleasant. Examples of a menacing effect can be found in literature, for instance, in La Motte-Fouqué's *Undine*, or in Goethe's "Erlkönig"; in real life, the shapes formed by the cracks in the ceiling over a hospital bed can feel more like the materials of a nightmare than entertainment.

## B. Perceptual Nonsense: Finding Patterns, and Automatic Recognition of the Aesthetic

### 1. The Image Made by Chance "Thought Experiment"

We usually assume that, when someone is confronted with a work of visual art, say, a drawing or a painting, and asked to express an opinion about it, that person will either find the work beautiful (positive reaction) or not beautiful (negative reaction), or will declare himself/herself to be indifferent to it. But there is presumably nothing automatic about any one of these responses: it represents a considered judgment, and is the outcome of a free choice.

When one sees a recognizable shape in nature—let's say, if not a camel or a whale, but a horse's head, or a human face, perhaps in a cloud—that experience may have two components:

(a) *The simple act of recognition.* Here we are still in the limited field of "pattern recognition," a capacity which, according to Simon Baron-Cohen, is especially developed in the autistic population, but which, as I have remarked, we employ routinely in daily life.[18] Since we do not see all of anything at any one time, we put together disparate details to form a coherent whole. An

---

15. Hopkins, *Journals and Papers*, 127. For a rare example of a sudden overwhelming response to beauty in literature rather than to visual beauty, see Keats, "On First Looking into Chapman's Homer," *Selected Letters and Poems*, 18.

16. E.g., Hoffmann, "Die Automate," *E. T. A. Hoffmans Werke*. vol. 2.

17. See Kleist, *Kleists Aufsatz über das Marionettentheater*, 9–16. For the English, see Kleist, "On the Theater of Marionettes," *Selected Prose of Heinrich von Kleist*.

18. Baron-Cohen, *The Science of Evil*, 115–16.

example given by Ramachandran is our ability to assemble the image of a Dalmatian dog out of an apparently random array of ink spots on a page.[19]

When we identify this Dalmatian dog, we are presumably seeing the same dog that everyone else sees, just as if it were the image of a real dog. In this situation, everyone's "imagination" produces the same result. The reaction is automatic and irresistible, as, for instance, when someone speaks a word, say, gold (Hughlings Jackson's example[20]), we cannot help but understand it. We do not "interpret" that dog one way or another: we simply see it.

(b) *Our aesthetic response to the imaginary form.* The second component of our reaction to an imaginary form in nature is the one that, in my view, presents a problem for aesthetics. That second component is our aesthetic response to the imaginary form. So, for instance, Hamlet and Polonius may have had aesthetic experiences vis-à-vis the animals in the cloud. They may have seen the camel as "grotesque." They could have seen the weasel as lithe and slender, or as "paradoxical in shape"—as at once slender and humped. The whale might have seemed "majestic and imposing" to them—or it might not.

As an object of aesthetic appreciation, the image made by chance is in an anomalous position. Such an object is not simply a landscape, or an element of a landscape that we admire, such as an irregular rock, falling snow, a waterfall, or what Plotinus might have reduced it to, a single star by night. Nor is it an animate, or semianimate, being whose beauty we may appreciate, such as an actual horse, an actual tree, or even an actual person. It is not a picture, a sculpture, or other deliberately composed work of art. It is not any of these, but it shares a border with all of them.

The image made by chance, then, may be experienced as having some aesthetic characteristics, although there can be no human intent behind its appearance. The shape of that appearance, we know, is identified automatically by the necessary process of pattern recognition. But if, say, the image in the cloud is seen by some as not merely recognizable but also as ugly or beautiful (and this is where the major question arises for me), is there an element of choice in that perception, or is everyone (of similar background) compelled to experience it as beautiful or otherwise, by a process as inevitable as the act of recognition itself? Faced with a similar problem, the third-century sophist, Philostratus the Athenian, found himself asking, "The things we see in the sky

---

19. Ramachandran and Hirstein, "The Science of Art," 15–51. For a sophisticated analysis of image recognition, see McMahon, "Perceptual Constraints on Pictorial Realism."

20. Hughlings Jackson, *Selected Writings*, vol. 2, 132. On the commercial exploitation of our impulse to form patterns, see Heaven, "The Obsessioneers," 38–41.

. . . how do you account for them? As the results of imitation, surely? . . . Then does god seem to be an artist?"[21]

Although Philostratus himself appears to reject this conclusion, perhaps it need not be dismissed out of hand. If it were indeed a god who was providing these images for us, then we would *have* to accept them as beautiful: we could not even be indifferent to them; we could not deny their beauty. That beauty would be inherent in the object, in the sight that is offered us; if not, as in Philostratus's conjecture, presented to us by a god, then, at least, for a number of Renaissance authors, by the "formative power" of nature itself.[22] Ambroise Paré says that "one sees in rocks and plants effigies of men and other animals, and there is no explanation for them, except to say that Nature is disporting herself (*se ioue*) in her creations."[23] For Zeno, there was a great power behind these "accidents": "What in the processes of our crafts is done by our hand is done with far more skillful craftsmanship by nature, that is to say by the craftsmanlike fire which is the teacher of the other crafts."[24] Such images are inherently beautiful, and we have no choice but to see them as such.

Of course, it is not only in Classical or in medieval sources that we find such views. In his studies of modern abstract art, Roger Caillois argued for a convergence between the forms already present in nature and the man-made. Recent attempts by artists to remove the traces of human intentionality from their works would, then, just be a somewhat perverse reaffirmation of the continuity between the natural and the human. Through his/her "démission des facultés" ("surrender of the faculties"), the artist tries to become the perfect voice of nature.[25] But "la nature dispose de plus de moyens, et plus puissants" ("nature possesses more, and more powerful, means"), and nature has always gotten there first.[26] It is interesting, with respect to the question I have raised concerning the possibility that the perception of beauty in the "image made by chance" may be compulsory and universal, that Caillois also asserts that "l'homme—partie intégrante de la même *nature*—aperçoit *nécessairement*

---

21. Jones, *Philostratus*, vol. 2, 4. One might add, as in the chorale, "What God does is done well" ("Was Gott tut, das ist wohlgetan").

22. Witmore, *Culture of Accidents*, 121. In the eighteenth century, nature is still "the mistress of all art." Price, *On the Picturesque*, 4.

23. Findlen, "Jokes of Nature," 292–331; 312–13.

24. Solmsen, "Nature as Craftsman," 496.

25. Caillois, *Cases d'un échiquier*, 194–96. One is reminded of the effort to reconcile intentionality with automatism in Kant's concept of biology. See Breitenbach, *Die Analogie von Vernunft und Natur*. Cf. Kleist, footnote 17, above.

26. Caillois, *Cases d'un échiquier*, 184.

l'harmonie et la beauté" ("man—an integral part of that selfsame nature—*necessarily* perceives harmony and beauty").[27]

But to return to my citations from earlier sources: Nostradamus also speaks of the "occult vaticinations inspired in us by that subtle spirit of fire which sometimes exercises our minds as we sit up nights contemplating the stars on high."[28] Or, as Nicholas of Cusa puts it, "the Samplar of all things shineth in the mind, as the truth in the image."[29] The beautiful image in nature has a powerful authority.

Perhaps the word "beauty" is too weak, or too general, to serve in this context. Here the wonderful example of the dramatically poised rider who seems part of the cloud, in the upper left-hand corner of Mantegna's *Saint Sebastian* (the Vienna version), can come to one's help.[30] It is highly specific, and it tells us that what we can see, or imagine we see, in a cloud can be kinetic and intense, fleshing out ideas of "beauty" with sinewy accuracy. I have elsewhere spoken of seeing part of a bush draped with withered leaves as a troop of Tartar horsemen galloping down a mountainside.[31]

Is there, then, a built-in capacity for the aesthetic response in everyone's perception, especially of imaginary forms? Do we suddenly, involuntarily, become aesthetes when we are confronted with beauty in an imagined shape, no matter how uncouth, how gross, how indifferent to all aesthetic qualities we may previously have been? Could there be a beauty in nature that not only comes out to meet us, but that may require us to pay homage to it?[32] The passage quoted above from Philostratus toys with the question, but shies away from it before having to face it squarely. And, if it must be answered in the affirmative—that is, that a certain form of aesthetic perception is compul-

---

27. Caillois, *Méduse et cie,* 53. Second emphasis is mine.

28. Quoted in Sieburth, "The Poetics of Futurity," 14. Cf. Gerard Manley Hopkins's belief that the divine is manifest in nature ("inscape") in "Nature is a Heraclitean Fire," *Gerard Manley Hopkins,* 180–81, where the fire of nature, when quenched, is restored and redeemed by the resurrection. Concerning the flame of nature behind human thought, see also p. 184, "To R. B.": "the strong / Spur, live and lancing like the blowpipe flame," (ll. 1–2), and "Sweet fire the sire of muse" (l. 9).

29. von Kues [Cusanus], *Philosophisch-Theologische Schriften,* vol. 3. On p. 499, we have "Namen strahlt in allen Namen auf seine Weise wider . . . so dass auf diese Weise jeder Name ein Abbild des genauen Namens ist" ("The Name shines back in its own way in all names . . . so that in this manner every name is a copy [reflection?] of the exact name"). On p. 498: "Ineffabile Nomen in omnibus nominibus suo modo relucet . . . ut sic omne nomen sit imago praecisi nominis." Dietlind and William Dupré translate "ineffabile" as "unaussgbar," i.e., "inexpressible."

30. Mantegna, *St. Sebastian (1457–1459),* painting.

31. Massey, "Two Types of Visual Metaphor," 287–88. See also Chapter 2, Section II.B.

32. Cf. Kant, *Critique of Judgment,* trans. Werner Pluhar, 90: "Beautiful is what without a concept is recognized as the object of a *necessary* liking."

FIGURE 3. Andrea Mantegna,
*Saint Sebastian* of Vienna, 1456–1459.

sory—does that detract from the value of the aesthetic, making it common-place, or does it, on the contrary, raise mankind to a higher power, to a level on which we are forced to recognize that all people have the capacity for the recognition of beauty, built into their perceptive equipment? If automaticity implies universality, is that a good or a bad thing? (I try to deal with this question more fully later in this chapter.)

### 2. A Hypothesis, or "Thought Experiment"

To recapitulate, then: if we are confronted with, say, a face in the bark of a tree, or recognize the Erl-King in a shred of mist, as in the Goethe-Schubert song, we do not simply recognize a neutral image: the face will probably appear interesting in some way, whether disturbing, malicious, sinister, grotesque, or possibly beautiful. The same will be true, say, of a landscape seen in agate: it may be irregular, stormy, peaceful, or serene. In other words, one will see some aesthetic feature in the image that one has "recognized." When we construct or perceive an "image made by chance," we perceive its formal and aesthetic features together with its "recognizable" features: the aesthetic aspects are integral to the percept, embedded in the object that we have constructed. We are as much committed to them as we are to any of the representational characteristics that we bestow on our "discovery." It may be that we ourselves have fashioned these idiosyncrasies, but they are for us just as much part of the event as are its recognizable details. To repeat: the aesthetic features of the image made by chance are no more, and no less, a part of the constructed percept than is the face or the landscape itself. (The indissoluble unity of affect and percept is obvious in the olfactory sense: it is strikingly expressed in Christopher Smart's "There is no rose to minds in grief, / There is no lily for despair."[33])

Everyone, then, who sees this same "image made by chance" has been obliged to repeat the process of constructing the same aesthetic features that I had constructed in building up the recognition. It is a matter of "love me, love my dog"—if you recognize the image, you must recognize all the emotional/aesthetic attributes that accompany it—even if my "dog" be only a landscape sketched in a pebble, or an arm seen in a drooping branch. This process is quite different from what happens if I look at, say, a picture. In the case of the picture, the image itself has already been provided for me—I am not creating it—all I am being asked to do is judge its aesthetic component. In the case of the image made by chance, though, it is I who am creating the aesthetic characteristics of the image along with the image itself.

---

33. Smart, *Abimelech, an Oratorio*, 190.

It is, then, not entirely illogical to ask whether others may not share one's subjective response to an image made by chance.

## C. Creating Patterns: Automatic Production of the Aesthetic

Another version of aesthetic automaticity, on a par with the automatic, so to speak, involuntary, experience of the aesthetic described above, is the production of art "objects" unconsciously, by some inner process as unintentional as seeing itself. This is not a matter of creative forces welling up from the unconscious, or of some tempestuous urge carrying one away like the proverbial West Wind. I have tried to deal with this aspect of the problem in another chapter of *Find You the Virtue*.[34] To summarize: I had been picking blueberries during the day; when I closed my eyes that night, the blueberries came back, of course, but this time with jewel-like intensity, more beautiful and more vivid than the actual blueberries that I had been picking, and arranged in wonderful patterns. These patterns were not mere geometrical forms, but aesthetically rich and satisfying panoplies of detail. They were undeniably works of art, but created automatically by some entirely unconscious mechanism in me. I quote: they were "well-planned configurations of visual material that I myself was forced to admire."[35]

What was even more extraordinary was that sometimes, when I would step out onto the roofless porch of the house in the wilderness, amid the total darkness of a starless night, with my eyes wide open, these patterns would appear before me with all their power, just as they would do when I closed my eyes in bed. At times, they would even appear "highlighted with an intensity that approached the painful."[36] I have had the same experience more recently with blackberries: although the patterns formed were more random, they also created a strong, vivid aesthetic effect. (Whether any relation could be established between such aesthetic afterimages and the illusory patterns produced by hallucinogens is a question that psychopharmacologists might wish to explore.) Here we have "the image made by chance" produced entirely by the brain, rather than, as in the case of Hamlet's cloud, "the image made by chance" produced by nature.

The conclusion, although counterintuitive, seems difficult to avoid: perhaps I had been trying to see enhanced blueberries all day long, but they had been suppressed by my conscious seeing of the real objects around me. What

---

34. Massey, *Find You the Virtue*, 118–19.
35. Ibid., 119.
36. Ibid., 118.

was the status of the blueberries *before* I closed my eyes? It was as if there were a different visual system behind the usual one, a separate system of which I could not be aware. Could it be that the conscious system operated as a kind of flickering screen saver, with shifting images of ordinary objects perhaps masking or suppressing pictures of the berries waiting to take form underneath? (I believe that there is also evidence of a separate language system underlying the familiar one, which is revealed at certain transitional moments, in semiconscious states; it is also autonomous, but it does not necessarily display any aesthetic proclivities.)[37]

There is one description of such an experience in literature so striking that I cannot help quoting it in its entirety. Although the author does not refer to what she saw specifically as an aesthetic experience, the description itself is so graphic and intense that it is impossible to see it otherwise. As a child, the nineteenth-century Russian mathematician Sofya Kovalevskaya would go picking mushrooms in the forest, and later,

> Between sleep and waking, I could still see the forest before my eyes. If anything, I saw it more clearly. . . . Many ephemeral impressions, which at the time merely glided past me without coming directly into consciousness, now returned, vividly and insistently. Here was an enormous anthill looming up out of the darkness; each fir needle on it projected in such graphic relief that I felt as if I could pick it up. The ants dragged their white eggs behind them quickly and busily until, suddenly, all of them vanished somewhere together with the anthill. And in their place appeared a soft white lump like a big clump of snow.
>
> Now I could see that the whole thing was made of tiny gossamer spiderwebs, and in its very center was a little dark speck. I wanted to grasp that clump in my hand, but the thought had no time to take form before the black speck in the center spun into rapid motion, and black dots spilled out of it in all directions like radii from a center to a circumference. Only they weren't dots, they were tiny black baby spiders, all of which ran and scurried about.
>
> This morning, in fact, I really had discovered a strange clump like this one, but I hardly noticed it then. And now I could see it so vividly, as if it were real.[38]

---

37. See above, Chapter 5, as well as Massey, *Neural Imagination*, 64–67.

38. Kovalevskaya, *A Russian Childhood*, 93–94.

Here Leibniz's peripheral "petites perceptions"[39] have come back with a bang, not to mention the details of subjects' lives elicited by Wilder Penfield through direct stimulation of the brain.[40]

As in the case of my own afterimages of berries, these too are described as more intense, more vivid, more detailed, more exciting than the original experiences. There is also a sense of aesthetic order emerging from the randomness as the black center begins to spin, and the little spiders race down the sides of the dome-like object "like radii from a center to a circumference." One senses the later mathematician *in nuce* here.

Seeing something as that which it is not is the basic procedure of metaphor. As such, it provides a powerful springboard for the aesthetic. Jeffrey Gray argues that "unconscious processing possesses most of the hallmarks of fully-fledged intentionality."[41] Such unconscious intentionality can serve aesthetic as well as practical functions.[42] Our inborn need to extract something recognizable from the random array of our surroundings makes us unconsciously see the arm in the branch, the sweep of the willow; seeing them as beautiful is also an unconscious intentional act, but one that goes beyond the utilitarian task of enhancing our safety.

It is often observed that a process of gestation which happens unconsciously may enrich or perfect our conscious thinking. Thus, Henry James had famously consigned the germ of his novel, *The American*, to some unknown chamber of his mind for an extended period before it reappeared to him, fully fledged, in December 1875. I have used this example before, but I will repeat it, because it is relevant to the present context. "I [must] have dropped it for the time into the deep well of unconscious cerebration: not without the hope, doubtless, that it might eventually emerge from that reservoir . . . with a firm iridescent surface and a notable increase of weight."[43] What James describes has some relation to my own experience with the blueberries and to Kovalevskaya's with her anthill, but with one notable difference: neither Kovalevskaya nor I had made the least effort to shape any part of our perceptions, much less to "drop it into the deep well of unconscious cerebration." Each whole event took place without a trace of intentionality, and with no conscious participation whatsoever on our part. We could not have dropped anything into the

---

39. Leibniz, *Œuvres philosophiques*, vol. 1, 80. Another striking example of the "petites perceptions" recurrence during the hypnagogic state can be found in Platonov, *Soul*, 75–76.

40. Penfield and Rasmussen, *Cerebral Cortex of Man*. I am aware that the significance of Penfield's findings has been contested.

41. Gray, *Consciousness*, 46. See also Issa and Rosenberg, "Peripheral Mechanisms," 108–22.

42. Chatterjee, "Where There Be Dragons." Cf. Chatterjee below in Section II.F.

43. James, *Art of the Novel*, 23.

reservoir of the unconscious because there was nothing to which we had given even a fledgling shape; nothing, so to speak, to drop.

But the two questions I was asking before the above digression, one about forms that we recognize in nature, the second about afterimages, though closely related, are not exactly the same. I will, for the moment, return to the first subject, and ask once more, can there be an element of automaticity in our discovery of beauty in the images formed by the natural world?

## D. Valuing Patterns: Automatic Response to the Aesthetic

Here again I find myself constrained to use examples from *The Neural Imagination*.[44] In that book, I was at pains to show that aesthetic experience is not subject to scientific explanation, and surely not according to the scientific categories now available. At the same time, I could not deny that certain aspects of aesthetic experiences had an apparently automatic quality about them that could not be gainsaid. Perhaps they were products of our nervous system operating on its own, so to speak, and therefore, after all, open to scientific description?

I had been walking in the Alabama swamp near Buffalo, a landscape not at all conducive to imaginative projections, when, without transition or warning, "suddenly I noticed a few black teasels high on a bush, then a small tuft of purple-sepia grass reaching out across the snow, and at the back of the little field a mass of yellow reeds like a snowman made out of corn husks. Each of these details was as vivid as if an ophthalmologist had slipped exactly the right lens into the heavy apparatus on the bridge of my nose." I called out to my wife, "I am being assaulted by inscapes!" The same occurred a few more times, "in flashing glimpses," on the return trip, "as though something in me chose to slip the inscape lens into place a few last times before my giving up and going back to the city."[45]

"Inscape," Gerard Manley Hopkins's term for the vivid perception of something in one's surroundings, or for the visualization of something in those surroundings as striking, is the essential aesthetic experience. If that can happen in a way that seems automatic, having nothing to do with one's conscious purposes, then the aesthetic is, so to speak, up for grabs. It is not that everyone will have the same intensity of experience as Hopkins, or be able to record it with his magnificence of style, but that is not the point. It is rather

---

44. Massey, *Neural Imagination*, 4–5.
45. Ibid., 5.

that, if everyone *has* to see, even if only occasionally, a beautiful image—in fact, an *identical* beautiful image, the same one that everyone else sees, in the natural world—then everyone is equally dowered with a certain capacity for seeing beauty, as well as being required to have a universally shared specific aesthetic experience (see above, Section I.B.1). To be sure, as Dante's Piccarda would explain,[46] the vividness of that vision would vary with the individual's ability to receive it. What was most striking about the experience that I underwent was not the strength or the content of the "visions" that I had, but the discrepancy between the richness and specificity of those visions and the quasi-mechanical way in which they arrived, as if out of nowhere: one might say, imposed on me. Was there a switch that turned on a certain way of seeing in my brain, rather as there is a switch that enables one to fall asleep? Here again we seem to be dealing with "the image made by chance" structured in a crucial way by the brain, rather than (as in the case of images in clouds) the "image made by chance" just produced by nature (see above, Section I.A.3).

To return to the main questions with which I began, though: is our response to the imaginary forms that we perceive in nature simply part of the way we orient ourselves to our surroundings, as automatic and instinctive as proprioception itself?[47] And, if so (as I ask elsewhere), is this democratization of the imagination something that we should celebrate, or that some might deplore? In any case, it does raise the possibility that Hamlet was premature in mocking Polonius for his presumed inability to see something of interest in a cloud, but we will never know.

In a parody of his own earlier parody of Polonius's lack of wit, Hamlet, far more alert than Polonius to ambiguities in his environment, chooses to demonstrate his superior powers of imagination by interpreting a sound, and a stirring in the arras, as the movement of a rat (3.4.23). Hamlet's later apparent failure to distinguish a bated foil from a poisoned rapier in the hand of Polonius's son carries an echo from this scene, lending a certain aura of retributive justice to the ending (5.2).

## E. A Digression: The Secret Life of Sentences

Since I have been talking about semiconscious or unconscious mental processes, I will take the liberty of examining another aspect of thought that is difficult to pin down or define in standard terms.

---

46. Dante, *Paradiso*, 3.85.

47. Montero, "Proprioception as an Aesthetic Sense," 231–42.

A cloud has a useful purpose: it provides rain. It can also provide diversion, by means of assuming various shapes for the interest and entertainment of the viewer.

A sentence may also be useful. In certain contexts, it can tell one what to do. One listens, and one acts according to its instructions, or in a manner consistent with the information that it makes available.

A sentence also functions in different ways: it can provide entertainment; it can change one's mood; and it can create subtle changes in one's mental environment that are hard to specify. Sometimes a sentence may also appear to be good: often it is plainly bad, or indifferent. It is this less clearly practical set of functions and effects that I will try to consider.

One of the striking things that happens when one is reading poetry is that one decides whether a line is good before one has understood it. In part, this is simply because the mind acts more rapidly than we realize: a first grasp of meaning takes place when we encounter any sentence, whether in poetry or elsewhere; then we "work at" understanding the sentence, and arrive at a second, more considered understanding. But, in the reading of poetry, that second stage of understanding is never arrived at, or is suppressed. We remain with our "first impression"; especially if the line is a good line, we are, so to speak, stuck with that impression, and never arrive at what we might call a full understanding. In fact, if the line is really good, I would venture to say that we will never understand it. We can begin to grasp what Henry David Thoreau meant when he said, "Give me a sentence which no intelligence can understand. There must be a kind of life and palpitation to it, and under its words a kind of blood must circulate forever."[48] Instead of "understanding" in the ordinary sense of the word, we are left with something more like a bruise, from the impact of the line.

The quality, then, both in the sense of the value and of the flavor, texture, or other constituents of the effect, is what remains. That is the aesthetic element of the sentence.

All of the above has been set forth more fully in my *Find You the Virtue*,[49] but I would like to add another stroke to this picture.

What if every sentence, except one used in a strictly scientific context, has such an aesthetic element in it? By this I do not mean that it is beautiful or ugly. What I mean is that perhaps every sentence in ordinary language has such a fluid "je ne sais quoi" level or component in it, and that is the really operative element in that sentence. This is where the real life of the sentence

---

48. Thoreau, *A Week on the Concord*, 122.

49. Massey, *Find You the Virtue*. Regarding sentences, see pp. 12–17; for the afterimages of berries, pp. 118–19.

goes on. That ineffable quality may be part of what the "affect theorists," such as Teresa Brennan, have been trying to convey.[50] I don't mean that language consists only of speech acts, that its meaning is inflected by tone of voice (which, of course, it is), or that it simply produces emotional responses of one kind or another. I am suggesting that, except in certain very clearly circumscribed forms of discourse, the indefinable defines the sentence, and that what we respond to is that occulted, oblique, or aesthetic meaning, not its explicit, paraphrasable content. What, then, if the play of discourse proceeds at a subtler level than we recognize?

We tend to accept the assumption that what can't be defined (which means, increasingly, what can't be measured) doesn't exist: or, at least, requires that we maintain a decent Wittgensteinian silence about it, on pain of being relegated to the ranks of the practitioners of nonsense. On the other hand, the occlusion of paraphrasable content that takes place in the experience of poetry is a recognizable fact, all the more striking because words in poetry are chosen specifically for their precision. May not some of that same forcing underground, or detouring, of meaning, apply to language in many other situations?

## II. KANT AND THE *CRITIQUE OF JUDGMENT*

### A. *The* Critique of Judgment

It will be obvious to anyone who has even glanced at the *Critique of Judgment* that many of the problems I have raised, and will raise, are central issues in Kant. The universality of the aesthetic response, and the demand for universal agreement about art, are such pervasive considerations in Kant's "system" that they even, arguably, subsume the ethical. In fact, these issues, maddeningly irresolvable yet inescapable, produce a kind of contagious fever for anyone who begins to explore them, and can rapidly turn into obsessions. If there be any cause other than my own incompetence for the redundant character of the following pages, it is that I have been trapped in the whirlpool created by Kant's improbable yet apodictic assertion in the third *Critique*: that we are all morally obliged to agree about art.

Although Kant's *Critique of Judgment* does not deal systematically with the image made by chance (and it is in fact hard to tell exactly where it fits in the Kantian scheme), there are abundant hints that he did devote a good deal of thought to that phenomenon. In chapter 42 of the *Critique of Judg-*

---

50. Brennan, *The Transmission of Affect.*

*ment,* Kant speaks of "die Bewunderung der Natur, die sich an ihren schönen Produkten als Kunst, nicht bloss durch Zufall, sondern gleichsam absichtlich, nach gesetzmässiger Anordnung und als Zweckmässigkeit ohne Zweck, zeigt" ("the admiration of nature, which reveals itself through its beautiful productions as art, not only accidentally, but at the same time deliberately, according to a regularized organization and as purposiveness without purpose").[51] Kant's wording here is surprisingly similar to the language of Philostratus or of Ambroise Paré in describing such images (see below, Section II.B.1). In fact, Kant's talk of the "Chiffreschrift" ("language of symbols") through which nature speaks to us "figürlich" ("through symbols," p 226) via its beautiful forms, and the accompanying list of "correspondences" which he provides (pp. 227–28) is altogether astonishingly old-fashioned. It is only a step back from such thinking to the Abbé de Chesneau's pigeon, cited in Chapter 3 Section II.

Quite apart from the question of the image made by chance, though, there is much in Kant's work that overlaps with my description of automaticity in aesthetic experience. As I have suggested that when one person sees an illusion in nature which he/she regards as beautiful, everyone else will also have to experience it as beautiful, so Kant, too, insists that judgments of taste have "universal validity."[52] Since genuine works of art are produced by genius, and genius makes nature available to us through art,[53] for Kant, the universally applicable judgments of taste should be valid for such beautiful objects in nature as well as for works of art.

There is, however, a restrictive clause in Kant's democratization of aesthetics; he claims that "this direct interest in the beautiful" is found only in those "whose way of thinking is already trained to the good or exceptionally receptive to this training."[54] To extrapolate from Kant's argument, one might presume that a cultivated taste could serve as a universal standard, to which all should aspire. Ann Colley has pointed out to me a passage in Hopkins which

---

51. Kant, *Kritik der Urteilskraft,* 226; *Critique of Judgment,* trans. J. H. Bernard, 143–44. This is the view that Kant himself had earlier ridiculed (as had Goethe): see Bostridge in *Schubert's Winter Journey,* 256–57. Bostridge traces this theme, and its implications, on through Schopenhauer and up to the present (244–62).

52. Kant, *Critique of Judgment,* trans. Werner Pluhar, 154. There are other passages in Kant that make an implied reference to the image made by chance: for instance, where Kant says that bird songs seem to express "joyfulness and satisfaction" ("Fröhlichkeit und Zufriedenheit," 228), or where he says that nature, in its beautiful forms, speaks to us figuratively (loc. cit.). I cannot here go into the issue of Kant's relation to Baumgarten with respect to the judgment of taste, though it would be important for an understanding of the background.

53. Ibid., 174–76. On the equivalence of nature and art, see also ibid., 31.

54. Ibid., 168. Even the radically egalitarian Jacques Rancière tends to look to "a handful of exceptional worker-artists" for evidence of aesthetic taste among the uninstructed. See Davis, *Jacques Rancière,* 133.

is very much to the point: like Kant, Hopkins assumes that "simple people" are unable to perceive beauty in natural forms (in this case, the architecture of a barn), but he also stresses its potential availability to everyone. "I thought how sadly beauty of inscape was unknown and buried away from simple people and yet how near at hand it was if they had eyes to see it and it could be called out everywhere again."[55] Philostratus (see above, Section I.B.1) also concedes the power of imagination "to all men, artists and nonartists alike,"[56] much as his conception of imagination may differ from that of Hopkins.

With my hypothetical case, concerning the beautiful image in the cloud, what I am trying to do is create a trap, to show Everyman, whether cultivated or ignorant, actually caught in the act of testifying to the universality of beauty, captured in a kind of aesthetic flagrante delicto (see also below, Section II.B). I would evoke from all observers, no matter how "simple," a concurrence or agreement which would prove, once and for all, that we all share the same experience of beauty: that, to quote Hopkins once more, "it could be called out everywhere again."

Even if we were to acknowledge that there may be disagreement among persons about the beauty of a particular natural scene, or that the same person may experience that scene at one time as beautiful and another time as insignificant or neutral, Kant could still provide us with a ready explanation. All we would have to do is refer to the passage in which he declares flatly that "what counts in judging beauty is not what nature is, nor even what purpose it [has] for us, but how we receive it."[57] As Hopkins says of an autumn landscape:

These things, these things were here and but the beholder
Wanting; which two when they once meet,
The heart rears wings bolder and bolder
And hurls for him, O half hurls earth for him off under his feet.[58]

". . . but the beholder / Wanting." There are no ready-made beauties in nature independent of ourselves; there isn't an array of objects out there to be plucked, so to speak, and put in our buttonhole. There are only moments of contact between something in nature and something in ourselves, under

---

55. Hopkins, *Major Works,* 211.

56. Quoted in Janson, "The 'Image Made by Chance' in Renaissance Thought," 254–66, 257–58.

57. Kant, *Critique of Judgment,* trans. Werner Pluhar, 224. I prefer "how we take it" to Pluhar's "how we receive it." For the original, see Kant, *Kants Werke: Akademie-Textausgabe,* vol. 5, 350, where the phrase is "wie wir sie aufnehmen." The experience of beauty ultimately depends on our being in the appropriate state of mind when we confront/receive the natural object.

58. Phillips, ed., *Gerard Manley Hopkins,* 134. "Hurrahing in Harvest," 11–14.

the aegis (at least for Hopkins) of divinity, in which a beauty is created that becomes permanent once it has been experienced. There are no fixed things to admire; there are only encounters that give fixity and body to the things that we then admire. Once this happens, once one has seen, say, the beautiful forms in the snow-laden spruce boughs, we realize that their beauty is an intrinsic part of their shape. Beauty is not something added to form: it is not a supplement.

This approach, emphasizing the crucial role of the "how we take it," stressed by both Kant and Hopkins, seems to me to provide an adequate explanation for any differences of opinion or of experience in relation to a particular natural scene; but we are not always tolerant of dissent. Although I myself had not introduced any imperative or normative element into my scheme, it has been pointed out to me that there is in it a tacit demand that others share my enjoyment of beautiful illusions, and a probability of puzzlement, disappointment, or perhaps even disapproval, if they should fail to do so. Although I have attempted to resist this suggestion, I have finally been forced to admit that it is fair, and then I fall back into lockstep with Kant: "He who declares something to be beautiful holds that everyone *ought* to give his approval to the object at hand and that he too should declare it beautiful." This is "the *ought* in an aesthetic judgment."[59]

Kant, of course, grounds the experience of aesthetic beauty in the moral sense,[60] which would account for its claim to universal assent at a stroke. If beauty is the morally true, how can we dispute it? Whereas I am somewhat inclined to agree, a reasoned rather than a perfunctory act of agreement with this argument would require a greater effort than I am now in a position to exert.[61] But there is also another, possibly major, difficulty about my accepting without reservation Kant's linking of the aesthetic with the moral sense. For Kant, if the aesthetic is founded in morality, there has to be a freely willed moral choice involved,[62] whereas what I am trying to show is precisely the opposite: that the aesthetic response, whether moral or other, can in some circumstances actually be involuntary. In this respect, by making the aesthetic virtually compulsory, I grant that I come perilously close to classing it with

---

59. Kant, *Critique of Judgment*, trans. Werner Pluhar, 86. Richard Moran rejects Kant's demand for universal agreement in aesthetic judgment. See "Kant, Proust, and the Appeal of Beauty," 321. For an approach to the problem of universality vs. individuality in aesthetic response through cognitive psychology, see Hogan, *Beauty and Sublimity*, Chapter 2.

60. Kant, *Critique of Judgment*, trans. Werner Pluhar, 228.

61. Quentin Meillassoux has made a determined attempt to develop an independent approach to the relations among nature, morality, beauty, and the universal. See Harman, *Quentin Meillassoux*.

62. Kant, *Critique of Judgment*, trans. Werner Pluhar, 229.

those phenomena that are, as Kant puts it, "subject to empirical principles,"[63] rather than depending primarily on "how we receive it [nature],"[64] though, as I have attempted to show, such a reclassification would not necessarily imply a degrading of the aesthetic.

One of the distressing things about Kant's claims concerning the universality of aesthetic judgment is that they are so obviously right and wrong at the same time, as Kant himself points out, if not in exactly those words.[65] On the one hand, "De gustibus non est disputandum" seems intuitively reasonable, but, on the other, I may feel that there is something vaguely wrong with anyone who does not share my enthusiasms: say, if I were a Wagner fan (which I am not), for Wagner's music. Perhaps (and here again I might fall back on Kant), that misguided person (in this case, myself) is even guilty of some sort of moral failing for not appreciating Wagner! In a moral context, the escape clause that I invoked with respect to natural beauty is not so readily available to us: morality is not such a subjective matter. We cannot use the excuse that Wagner's music is not required to produce a uniform response in everyone because it is only something that has been produced by ourselves in a moment of inspired contact with nature.

## B. A Digression: "Inscape," or Escapism?

There is another set of alternatives (I will not dignify them with the term "antinomies") that asks to be explored. This duality, or paradox, is even more disturbing in its implications than the one between the individual and universal standards of judgment in aesthetics. What if the privileged contact with nature, resulting in phenomena such as Hopkins's "inscape," were merely an illusion rather than a moment of inspiration? What if it were a self-deluded, not to say narcissistic, exercise? An avoidance of, rather than an engagement with, nature: an escape rather than an "inscape"? This question cannot be ignored; at the same time, it creates a diversion from the main themes of this chapter, and may be skipped by anyone who does not enjoy intricacy.

When we are in love, or fancy ourselves in a state of emotional security, an anthropomorphic impulse is unleashed in us that drives us to read our surroundings as a reflection and expression of ourselves—as a very dictionary of our desires and feelings. But, in fact, in and of itself, the world around us is nothing of the sort, and, as Alain Robbe-Grillet reminds us in his essays

---

63. Ibid., 224.
64. Loc. cit.
65. Ibid., 210.

attacking the metaphoric position, there is no possibility of collusion between ourselves and nature; not even the Kantian kind of collusion, by which nature asks us to respond to it.[66] Nature is patently indifferent to us. Some see that indifference as an active ill will or repudiation—for instance, Leopardi in "La Ginestra":

> Madre è di parto e di voler matrigna.
> (She is the one that bore us, but she treats us like a stepmother.)[67]

For Alfred de Vigny, in "La Maison du berger," there is always an active menace embedded in Nature:

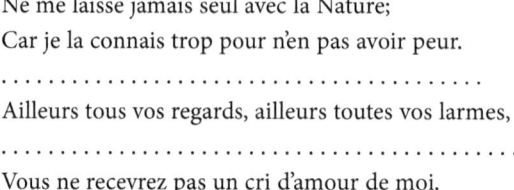

> Ne me laisse jamais seul avec la Nature;
> Car je la connais trop pour n'en pas avoir peur.
> . . . . . . . . . . . . . . . . . . . . . . . . . . . . . . . . . . . .
> Ailleurs tous vos regards, ailleurs toutes vos larmes,
> . . . . . . . . . . . . . . . . . . . . . . . . . . . . . . . . . . . .
> Vous ne recevrez pas un cri d'amour de moi.

> (Never leave me alone with Nature; / I know her too well not to be afraid of her. / . . . / Turn your gaze elsewhere, weep for other things, / . . . / Never will you get a cry of love from me.)[68]

Here we seem far away from those poets who celebrate our kinship with Nature, from a Hopkins, a Wordsworth, a Lamartine. And, on the face of it, the argument against plundering the forms of Nature to decorate our bower seems irresistible. One has only to find oneself confronted with an immediate threat to one's existence from a natural source (from water, from earthquake, from the heavens above) to recognize its force. Nature is not ours for the taking. (Here, musical inspiration has an advantage, since it does not depend on the external world for ratification). So, what are we to do, faced with such an apparently alien scene? We need the embodied, in order to have something to be conscious of, yet we complain of the consequence, that it is unlike ourselves.

We might begin by reminding ourselves that we too, despite the pettiness of all our desires and preoccupations, are products of the universe, just

---

66. Kant, *Critique of Judgment,* section 67.

67. Leopardi, "La Ginestra—Il fiore del deserto," *Canti,* 135–43. The line I quote here is on p. 138.

68. De Vigny, "La Maison du berger: Lettre à Éva," *Œuvres complètes,* vol. 1, 173–82. The passages I quote are on pages 180–81.

as surely as the water and the rocks, the sticks and stones, that surround us. Consciousness itself is as incontrovertibly real as any flood, avalanche, or hurricane, as any stick or stone. And, given that fact, it is only natural and appropriate for us to create or find some connectivity between ourselves and our surroundings, to look for a common footing with these apparent strangers. Metaphors are our means of asserting our connection to and our continuity with the world that faces us. In some way or other, we are in it together.[69]

As for those metaphors, though, one might add: a metaphor, however it may have been formed, once created, acquires a reality of its own, that cannot be withdrawn by all the power in the universe. (Can something analogous even be said of meaning, in general?) What would it mean to say, of the lines in Keats's "To Homer":

> Aye, on the shores of darkness there is light,
> And precipices show untrodden green[70]

that they just represent an illusion? Or that the whole of *King Lear* (or, for that matter, Beethoven Opus 111) is just an illusion? The mind is not out of place in this world, even though the world may sometimes seem out of place within it.

The subjective domain as a whole acquires, in its activity, whether as thought or as experience, a value and a reality of its own. Think of memory, for instance.[71] Besides, we already create some intermediate structures between thought and object—even a philosophical system has objective structural features. Peter McKellar goes so far as to say that "those thought products which we call scientific theories are not wholly unlike those we call works of architecture."[72] The wall between the mental and the physical is not entirely impermeable. Even Robbe-Grillet, for all his insistence on the autonomy of nature and of the object, acknowledges, "C'est la matière elle-même qui est à la fois solide et instable, à la fois présente et rêvée, étrangère à l'homme et sans

---

69. When Flaubert declares that his feeling of identification with objects is as strong as his identification with humans, Jacques Rancière comments, "Behind the masquerade of fraternity there is the sympathy that links together the fibers of the universe." Rancière, *The Flesh of Words*, 158. My own excursion into hylozoism here follows from the trajectory of my argument, though it may appear as merely another step on the well-traveled ground mapped by Spinoza, on via Shelley (conclusion of "Prometheus Unbound"), more recently by Michel Serres, Bruno Latour, Bill Brown, and Jane Bennett.

70. Keats, *Selected Poems and Letters*, 157, ll. 9–10.

71. Massey, "Shelley's 'Music,'" 430–38. See also my remark regarding the Christopher Smart quotation above in Section I.B.2 of this same chapter, that in the olfactory sense, the subjective is indivisible from the percept as such.

72. Mavromatis, *Hypnagogia*, xv.

cesse en train de s'inventer dans l'esprit des hommes" ("It is matter itself that is simultaneously solid and unstable, both present and dreamt, alien to man yet at the same time constantly busy inventing itself in the mind of men").[73] Even the image, for all its disputed status in reality, is granted, however grudgingly, an affirmative dimension. "L'image ainsi traitée . . . empêche de croire en même temps qu'elle affirme"[74] ("The image, dealt with in this way . . . undermines belief in the very act of affirmation"). For that matter, for all of Robbe-Grillet's supposed attempts to expunge metaphor from his novels, they remain irresistibly metaphoric. Reality itself forces poetry on us.

There may be some who will find my effort to deal with the objections to the metaphoric stance inadequate. Short of undertaking to draw up a treatise on the subject, I can only ask: is there anyone who is prepared to dismiss the whole of poetry as nonsense? At the very least, if it be nonsense, it can be nothing less than necessary nonsense.

## C. The Object in Aesthetic Theory

These references to Robbe-Grillet summon recollections going back at least as far as "Die neue Sachlichkeit," with its emphasis on the value of objects as such. Robbe-Grillet might be considered a crucial presence in the literary wing of what might be called the objectivist movement, most strikingly exemplified by the writings of Albert Camus (or, at least, by the branch of existentialism which was identified with Camus), and culminating in Meillassoux's and Harman's "speculative realism." This movement, as a whole, tends towards the suppression of subjectivity and the glorification of, or, at least, the rehabilitation, of the object. (The direction of this drift in the arts and humanities is, of course, precisely contrary to that in physics, which has led to the virtual elimination of notions such as materiality or solidity.) In Camus's *L'Étranger*, Meursault's refusal to show emotion, and Camus's general insistence on letting the visible object or situation speak for itself, instead of trying to find depth or "meaning" in it, marks a critical moment in twentieth-century

---

73. Robbe-Grillet, *Pour un nouveau roman*, 160–61. In a brilliant page in *The Flesh of Words*, Jacques Rancière shows that it was Kant himself (though perhaps anticipated by Karl Philipp Moritz) who created the conditions for the most extreme version of the man/environment amalgam, by requiring that the response to natural beauty be without conceptual content (18). Once purged of its conceptual limitations, the experience of beauty could become a site for the Wordsworthian trancelike state in which mind, nature, and idealized community blend into one. (It will be remembered that Kant, like the early Wordsworth, was a supporter of the French Revolution.)

74. Ibid., 163.

thought and beyond. It prepares the ground, for instance, for Meillassoux's attempt to restore some body to Kant's amorphous and indefinable "Ding an sich,"[75] as well as for the assertion that there is an inherent beauty in objects that does not require an observer.[76] This turn away from the human perspective in aesthetics, so that the aesthetic emanates from the object rather than from the observer, has become one of the hallmarks of speculative realism. (It should not be confused with the "no ideas but in things" of the earlier phenomenological movement.) My own interest in the "image made by chance" shares a facet with this idea, since the beautiful shapes provided by nature, to which I draw attention, do not involve human intervention. In fact, if we follow through on Roger Caillois's assertion that nature always "got there first" (see above, Section I.B.1), and is the storehouse of beautiful forms from which we merely borrow, as I am inclined to put it, at this "ground level" of aesthetics, the object does really reign supreme.

## D. "Critical Judgment" As Such

I will later attempt to explain why I think that we are not in all circumstances required to have the same opinion about works of art, at least, not about those produced by artists (see also Chapter 6); right now, I wish to argue that we overrate the role of critical opinion in the first place.

The point is that we should not have exaggerated the role or the importance of criticism to begin with. Art does not arrive in our domain in order for someone to have an opinion about it, or as a result of someone's having had an opinion about it. Judgments of taste may or may not have a moral ground, but the artist himself/herself is mercifully spared the necessity of deciding that issue. (The morality of art, and of artists themselves, broadly speaking, is an entirely different matter. Kant does also try to deal with this problem, but, as far as I can see, with no more success than anyone else.)[77] It is true that evaluation is fundamental to criticism, but it is not fundamental to the work of artists themselves, who are, again, all in the position of Dante's Piccarda: they just do the best they can, and let the critics argue about the rest. Variously inspired (or uninspired), they have to do what they are doing; the translation of their activity into the vocabulary of critical opinion is another matter. This is as true of artists who seek popularity, of a Rubens, as it is of a Rimbaud or

---

75. Meillassoux, *After Finitude,* 27; Harman, *Philosophy in the Making,* 120–21.

76. Muecke, "What if Objects Were Beautiful?" *Aesthetics after Finitude* (October 18, 2013), aestheticsafterfinitude.blogspot.com.

77. Kant, *Kritik der Urteilskraft,* 221–22.

a Dickinson. From the point of view of the production of art, the question whether there will be different opinions about the value of specific works or whether everyone will judge them the same way is simply of no interest. It is in another domain; it is not the artist's business. There have been attempts at various times (I think of Friedrich Schlegel,[78] of Oscar Wilde,[79] or of Giorgio Agamben[80]) to place criticism and art on the same footing, but they do not alter the terms of the equation or the equation itself: art and criticism, especially evaluative criticism, are not interchangeable; though they may intersect, overlap, or run parallel for a while, they are two different practices.

It is the work itself, beauty in the work itself, that imposes assent: not someone else's judgment. It may be this realization that accounts for Kant's never having engaged in the futile exercise of ranking works of art in order of greatness, or, indeed, of comparing them at all.[81]

### E. The Aesthetic Universal and the "Automatic" Genius: Beauty and the Everyday

#### 1. The "Automatic" Genius

If a large part of the underlying aim of my original project was to establish the universality of the aesthetic, a purpose which seems to be increasingly apparent, then strengthening the evidence for that universality by additional means would not seem to be irrelevant or unreasonable.

The question of universality, as either desirable or, possibly, disqualifying the aesthetic, arises in a striking form at the beginning of the twentieth century. An example is the case of the dancer "Magdeleine G.," who was able to perform at a professional level under hypnosis; it was thought that she might be transforming "the sound vibrations of musical instruments into electric vibrations that her nervous system directly processed."[82] Was Magdeleine just "channeling" the hypnotist's subliminal instructions, "[o]r was she proof of

---

78. Schlegel, *Schriften zur Literatur*, 22.

79. Wilde, "The Critic as Artist," 754–60.

80. See Watkin, *The Literary Agamben*, 119; 196.

81. See Crawford, "Comparative Aesthetic Judgments," 289–305. I am grateful to Professor Arthur Efron for referring me to this interesting article.

82. LaCoss, "Our Lady of Darkness," 52–73; 61. A similar case, involving a singer rather than a dancer, had been presented with uncanny foresight a decade earlier by George du Maurier in the novel *Trilby* (1894). Alison Winter has explored the background for such phenomena in *Mesmerized*, including the case in which a hypnotized subject was able to repeat Jenny Lind's vocal acrobatics (118).

some greater, universal condition in humans, an example of how there was a murky, submerged reservoir of artistic talent within all individuals that could be tapped under hypnotic conditions that would make anyone a creative genius?"[83] The Symbolist belletrist Otto-Julius Bierbaum, in a review of 1904, wrote, concerning Magdeleine G., that "Beauty is not an invention of some privileged artists, but [that] it is something immanent within human nature itself."[84] André Breton spoke approvingly of Magdeleine G. in "Le Message automatique" of 1933,[85] and she was a subject of interest to no less a psychologist than Theodor Lipps, not to mention Theodore Flournoy.[86] However, if this issue could be settled simply by quoting authority, one could cite Hume himself, who ventured, if with some qualifications, the assertion that beauty may be "fitted to give a pleasure and satisfaction to the soul" because it follows from "the *primary constitution* of our nature."[87]

## 2. Beauty and the Everyday

One obvious support for the claim that aesthetic experience is universal can be found in the numerous anecdotes in which persons who were thought devoid of aesthetic appreciation unexpectedly revealed strong sensitivities in this domain. These are usually the individuals whom Hopkins refers to as "simple people" (see above, Section II.A). I myself can call to mind many cases, all happening to involve people in subsistence farming, and all of whom I knew well. The first was someone who was entirely illiterate, and who had never shown any interest whatsoever in the visual arts. One day, catching sight of a perfunctory sketch I had made of some Brahmin cattle, he exclaimed (in his terms) at the vitality and accuracy of the drawing; foolishly, I had never thought for a moment that he would pay any attention to a drawing of any kind. Another friend of mine who had undergone the worst indignities and extreme hardships of rural poverty, and whom I would have expected to regard "landscape" as nothing but a source of suffering, to my astonishment one day remarked on the particular beauty of a view at a bend in the road about forty miles from his home. Again, we tend to assume that people who do not read cannot speak well, but I have been repeatedly struck by the beauty and precision of phrase that flashes through the conversation of uneducated

83. LaCoss, "Our Lady of Darkness," 55.
84. Ibid., 67.
85. Ibid., 70.
86. Loc. cit.
87. Hume, *A Treatise of Human Nature,* 299.

people in remote rural areas. Some (such as a butcher whom I knew) clearly have a special gift for language, though I have not noticed that those around them pay any attention to it. In other cases, equally unremarked, ordinary talk can take a powerful dramatic turn. Another friend was telling of an auto accident that had taken place the day before, in which a sixteen-year-old girl had been killed. Her father was among the first on the scene, and had lifted her out of the car. Apparently, it was hard for her father to believe that she was dead. Lear: "Look, her lips, / Look there, look there!"[88] Bill Aikens: "She was right soft." Shakespeare could have said no less.

———

I have watched public open-air readings from the *Mahabharata* in Nepal, and public storytelling is not yet an entirely lost art elsewhere. The ballad tradition (both the production of ballads and the universal audience for them), still very much alive within my memory, attests strongly, on the societal level, to the universality of the aesthetic. Music, obviously, is everywhere; at all times, everywhere. An unforgettable moment for me was seeing the transfiguration (I might almost say "beatification") of a hard, tough Quebec farmer when his fiddle touched his jaw, his face abruptly showing that he had crossed the threshold of a sacred precinct. (Or realizing that my uncle, an equally tough, unsophisticated, and unsentimental businessman, would listen with rapt pleasure to classical music on the radio late at night, when everyone thought he was sleeping.) Some groups have required the production of a song or poem, a vision, as the price for full admission to adult society, as, of course, in a highly sophisticated context, the Chinese courts required a poem to be written as part of the civil service examinations for the bureaucracy. For that matter, could one say that the general European population had no relation to, or made no contribution to, the conception of the cathedrals?

Could one question that love itself involves the seeing of beauty in another person? Or is there such a thing as an entirely unaesthetic love?

A renewed recognition of the role of the aesthetic as it permeates everyday life is illustrated by a recent article in the journal *Psychology of Aesthetics, Creativity, and the Arts* entitled "Mundane Aesthetics,"[89] and its omnipresence is the underlying principle of the collection entitled *Neuroaesthetics* edited by Martin Skov and Oshin Vartanian.[90] Of course, this omnipresence has been pointed out by many, and I reemphasize it not so much because I have some-

88. Shakespeare, *King Lear*, 5.3.310–11.

89. Whitfield and de Destefani, "Mundane Aesthetics," 291–99.

90. Skov and Vartanian, ed., *Neuroaesthetics*. See also Porter, *Origins of Aesthetic Thought in Ancient Greece*, 528–29.

thing original to say about it, but rather because it is an essential stage in the trajectory of this chapter. My point is not so much the one cogently argued by Ellen Dissanayake, in books such as *Homo Aestheticus: Where Art Comes from and Why*: namely, that the aesthetic faculty is invaluable (nor, in Dennis Dutton's version, that it provides Darwinian survival value).[91] My emphasis is rather on its commonplaceness, on its mere ubiquity, on the fact that the aesthetic is simply inherent in human experience (not to mention animal experience).[92] After all, we always like or dislike things in our physical surroundings, and in that sense we are continuously making aesthetic judgments. Granting, then, at least provisionally, on the basis of the various examples given above, that the aesthetic is a universal attribute of human psychology, would that fact (as I have asked perhaps too often) reduce the value of the aesthetic? For that matter, even if it could be translated into physiological terms, would that eliminate its value?[93] We generally continue to attribute value to love, despite its universality (Shelley—"Common as light is love"[94]), and despite numerous attempts to reduce it to a physical condition, so why not do the same for the aesthetic? I do not believe that the aesthetic is seriously threatened from that quarter.

On the other hand, it might be argued that the putative universality of the aesthetic, which would seem to remove it from the roster of strictly voluntary functions, does suggest at least some physiological element involved in its occurrence. I will return to the question of physiological determinism, but let me make the preliminary observation, at this point, that neither universality nor automatism is the same as determinism. The aesthetic is not something that is forced on us; it is still we who have to make the determination that something affects us aesthetically, or that it does not. Universal agreement on an aesthetic experience still requires conscious concurrence. We may be taught to like something, but we cannot be forced to like something. Even the beauty (or ugliness) of an object made by chance has to be ratified by consciousness; and, unlike the action of (say) a pheromone, it always involves a judgment or an evaluation.

This is the important observation to be made about what is in some respects the test case for the automaticity of the aesthetic, (yes, still again!) my experience in the Alabama swamp near Buffalo, New York, that I have described in Section I.D. In that event, the aesthetic was something that could

91. Dissanayake, *Homo Aestheticus*; Dutton, *The Art Instinct*.
92. Rothenberg, *Survival of the Beautiful*.
93. Dutton, *The Art Instinct*, 9.
94. Shelley, "Prometheus Unbound," *Selected Poetry*, 99. See 2.5.40–41: "Common as light is love / And its familiar voice wearies not ever."

be said to have been "sprung" on me—without my participation, as far as I could tell, without will or effort on my part. The aesthetic event was delivered like a package on my doorstep, ready-made. But that does not mean that it was simply a physiological event that one could have triggered by setting up the right neurochemical conditions in my brain. Clearly, there was something in me that needed such an event to happen, that created the conditions for it to happen, or it would not have happened. And the richness, the flavor of the experience itself, its content as an internal work of art, was not something that was imposed on me. We are participants in the aesthetic; we cannot be its victims.

Even in the case of my experience with the afterimages of berries (see above, Section I.C), I could still not be said to be their "victim," because I liked what had happened, although I was apparently more their subject than their originator. To repeat, though: we cannot conclude that an aesthetic impulse is nothing more than a mechanical function, like a reflex, simply because it is built into our system, because it is in some sense "automatic."[95] After all, it is finally I who decide even that the pattern of berries that I am seeing is beautiful, and in what way it is beautiful; that decision cannot be made for me.

## F. The Neuroscientific Connection

As I have said once before, the initial impetus for this chapter was provided by my hearing a lecture at Cambridge on the perception of imaginary shapes in Shakespeare. Dr. Lewis's talk set me in mind of my own enduring perplexity about the imaginary situation I have described repeatedly, in which an observer is asked to ratify (or reject) one's perception of beauty in a natural image. I realized gradually, though, that my obsession with this fanciful question in aesthetics concealed other preoccupations, one of them being, as I have said above, the universality of the aesthetic; but there was another.

I had written a book, *The Neural Imagination*, in which I had been at pains to show that recent discoveries in neuroscience did not undermine the autonomy of the arts. At the same time, I described some situations, among them some that I have mentioned several times (such as the one in Section I.D above), in which a fair-minded critic might find cause to think that something strictly mechanical might after all be at work in aesthetics: in other words, something that might, therefore, be subject to neurological description (as

---

95. On the difficulty in distinguishing automatic from consciously controlled systems in biology, see Carey, "Decoding the Brain's Cacophony," 4. See also Kahneman, *Thinking, Fast and Slow*, 9–30.

described earlier in this chapter, in Section I.D); perhaps, then, not so much mechanical as instinctual.[96]

It is in an attempt to take the bull by the horns, and to settle once and for all this lingering question, that is, whether these aspects of aesthetic experience make it vulnerable to mechanistic explanation, that I have been moved to pursue this inquiry beyond its initial phase. I believe that a hint of the uncertainties created by this concern can be found even in Kant, despite the confidence with which he elsewhere asserts the freedom of aesthetic judgment. What does he mean (with even less than his usual perspicuity) when he says "Aber das Geschmacksurteil macht auch nur Anspruch, *wie jedes andere empirische Urteil* [italics mine], für jedermann zu gelten, welches, ungeachtet der innere Zufälligkeit desselben, immer möglich ist" ("But the judgment of taste also only claims, *like any other empirical judgment,* to be valid for everyone, which, in spite of the inner contingency thereof, is always possible").[97] A dedicated Kantian would certainly find a means to explain away the implications of "wie jedes andere empirische Urteil" ("like any other empirical decision"), but, to the casual reader, it looks as if Kant is lumping the aesthetic response with all other perceptions, as just one more physiological response, as automatic and mechanical as perception itself.

Someone intent on proving that the aesthetic is, in fact, "just one more physiological response," and (in my words) "vulnerable to mechanistic explanation," might attempt an extreme maneuver. Such a person might ask whether, in the situation involving afterimages, it might not be possible to subtract the merely reproductive element of the afterimage from its aesthetic component, isolating the latter, in its pure form, so that it might potentially be subject to investigation as such. Might there be some way of determining whether the representational part of a response to a natural form of beauty (as, say, of Shakespeare's "Towered citadel" in a cloud[98]) could be detached from its aesthetic element, perhaps by identifying individuals who perceive these shapes but evince no response to them, and by comparing their reaction with that of more responsive individuals? And, again, in the latter case, might one study the difference, perhaps in physiological terms? This is not only idle speculation. Martin Skov, for instance, envisages the possibility of distinguishing between the neural processes that underlie ordinary language from those

---

96. See above in Section I.D, and in Dutton, *The Art Instinct,* 9.

97. Kant, *Kritik der Urteilskraft,* 51.

98. Shakespeare, *Antony and Cleopatra,* 4.14.4.

involved in poetry.[99] Chatterjee points out that evaluation systems operate side by side with classification systems in visual perception.

It is hard either to confront this problem head-on or to dismiss it: it has, obviously, implications too serious to be ignored, but to implement a program for investigating it presents great difficulties. The attempt to triangulate the aesthetic process neurologically has not had great success in the laboratory.[100] This is not to say that a project to separate the aesthetic from the rest of a perceptual response, no matter how difficult technically, should not be undertaken, or that it might not produce interesting findings: one just should not assume that such findings would be self-interpreting, or that they could "reduce" the aesthetic to a fixed set of physiological equivalents.

If, with appropriately limited aims, one chose to continue exploring the scientific implications of the model, one might propose a more pragmatic way to approach the experiment, by using an inkblot method, à la Alexander Cozens,[101] the game "Blotto" (known, in nineteenth German art, as "Klecksographien"), or even Rorschach (a technique exploited by Andy Warhol); if that were not sufficiently "scientific," one could employ for observation clouds generated randomly by a computer and ask for responses to their aesthetic features, thereby providing at least some degree of statistical objectivity.

Here we inch back towards the "empirical aesthetics" of Gustav Fechner,[102] which had its faint echoes in the work of I. A. Richards,[103] and in later gestures towards the quantifying, or the demystifying, of aesthetics. But, as can be understood, for instance, from the work of I. C. McManus and Ben Wu,[104] the results obtained from investigations of this sort are limited, at best.[105] As I have tried to show in *The Neural Imagination* (182–84), no attempts to set such investigations on a scientifically respectable footing can *in principle* bring them any closer to the spirit, or, for that matter, to the reality of the arts. This is the conclusion that I find myself, after all, obliged to repeat. For, without subjectivity there is no art. It is hard to say whether an attempt to manipulate

99. Skov, "Neuroaesthetic Problems," 9–26. See also Chatterjee, "Where There Be Dragons," 4–6.

100. Massey, *Neural Imagination*, 8–9.

101. Sloan, *Alexander and John Robert Cozens*. See particularly p. 30, regarding the two-page 1759 prelude to *New Method of Assisting with Intervention in Drawing Original Compositions of Landscape*.

102. Phillips et al., "Fechner's Aesthetics Revisited," 263–71. Francis Hutcheson, in the eighteenth century, held a similar view of the intrinsic aesthetic qualities in geometrical forms.

103. Richards, *Practical Criticism*.

104. McManus and Wu, "The Square is . . ." 130–39.

105. For some relevant recent bibliography, see Benzon's post on September 8, 2013, "Neuroaesthetics." new-savanna.blogspot.in/2013/04/neuroaesthetics.html.

a brain by mechanical means to produce the *Duino Elegies* (Rilke) would be more futile or more ridiculous. One could ask the same concerning Federico Garcia Lorca's "Romance del Emplazado," where the bulls charge the boys bathing happily "in the moons of their curving horns." Perhaps the horns that I set out to grasp (above) were not so dangerous after all.

As for the relation of the universal in aesthetics to the psychological: first of all, if the aesthetic is universal in our experience, it leads not away from but towards something of the highest value: what one might call the universally unique. Second, the universality of the aesthetic, its pervasiveness in our psychological processes, makes it even less subject to a reductionist interpretation than if it were a peripheral attribute. It seems to be involved with the very basis of our being: it may continue to function even in the case of massive loss of a process as crucial as memory, as happened to the illustrator Lonni Sue Johnson,[106] who continued painting despite major damage to her hippocampus. In a word, we are no closer than we were to hauling the Muse out, in a swirl of wiring, from her lair in the orbito-frontal cortex, though subtler facets of the problem have perhaps been revealed during the course of this inquiry.

My first, simple idea, about shapes in clouds, had some appeal, even if that appeal lay only in its simplicity. It did not rely on elaborate philosophical justifications. Like the play "The Mousetrap" in *Hamlet* (3.2), it was intended to make the subject of the experiment "squeal"; it would catch the unsuspecting observer in the very instant of committing an aesthetic act, and of having to confess to that act. In Platonic terms, this approach might be called "maieutics," or midwifery: forcing someone to reveal a prior knowledge that, though universal, had at that point been only latent in the mind. At the same time, it could serve the purpose of a "Gedankenexperiment": although in itself not practical, it could force one to consider other things that might lead to more fruitful thought.

## III. SOME CONCLUSIONS

### A. Automaticity (A Review)

Perhaps it is time to group some of these issues in retrospect. There is a danger of confusing categories. First of all, it is obvious that mere spontaneity need not be classified as automatic: if it were, a great deal of poetry would be considered "automatic." Neither is the involuntary necessarily automatic: we

---

106. Rabin, "A Few Strokes of the Past," 4.

do not think of our immediate, uncontrolled responses in love or in anger as mere reflexes. The unconscious itself is far from automatic: that part of us that is capable of plotting a complicated dream with an entirely unforeseen conclusion is clearly possessed of deliberation and intentionality. Intuition, in turn, operates more by a higher reason than by automatic mechanisms.[107] The surrealist writers and artists of the 1920s and '30s used automaticity as a conscious strategy for escaping the top-down conventions of traditional form, in order to allow for associative and emotional processes to function: automaticity was not just an end in itself.[108] Of course, such artists ran the danger of being caught between two stools: on the one hand, their work had to be understood as being "out of their control" in order to be considered valid; on the other hand, if it were too far out of their control, it might immediately be classified as merely mechanical—that is, as the opposite of creative, or of being enriched by unconscious processes. But, to return to what might be called the deliberate search for spontaneity: Arthur Rimbaud purposefully sought for what he called the "dérèglement de tous les sens" ("disorder of all the senses"),[109] presumably in order to free his imagination: but the product of this strategy was a highly ordered, almost rationalistic form of poetry, as is apparent in the *Illuminations*. So much for the merely mechanical nature and products of automaticity.

To classify briefly the *forms* of aesthetic automaticity with which I have been dealing: there is automaticity (1) as a universal response to natural aesthetic objects (such as shapes in clouds); (2) as the spontaneous generation of aesthetic images by the mind (as in the case of my afterimages of berries); and (3) as a possibly automatic component in those quasi-spasmodic responses to landscape that are associated with the Hopkinsian concept of "inscape." At least in the last case, they might at one time have been described simply as moments of inspiration.

## B. *Coda* and *Postscript*

In abandoning the simple formulation of these problems as an experiment in looking at a cloud, the notion with which I began, I console myself with the thought that, since antiquity, groups of people have been standing around wondering about clouds, without any remotely satisfactory results. Even a modern meteorologist who set out "to crack the code of clouds" was soon

---

107. See Eysenck, *Genius*, 170–201.

108. See Clinton, "André Breton's Skeleton Key," 108.

109. Rimbaud, *Œuvres complètes*, 270.

FIGURE 4. Nicholas Hilliard, *Unknown Man
Clasping a Hand from a Cloud*, 1588.
Courtesy of the Victoria and Albert Museum.

frustrated: "But clouds, wandering and capricious, had foiled his efforts."[110] As for Aristophanes's *Clouds*,[111] in that play the shapes in the heavens end up parodying or satirizing their investigators themselves. The passage from Philostratus about the image made by chance, as quoted by Janson,[112] cites numerous such examples of bewilderment among the observers of clouds, and Janson's footnotes lead us into a further wilderness of quotations from Classical and Renaissance authors (Leonardo among them),[113] all preoccupied with imaginary shapes, their appraisal, even their attempted capture. Maybe what we need is a helping hand from the clouds themselves (see illustration).

<hr />

110. Ferris, "Gleaning Clues," F7.

111. Oates and O'Neill Jr., ed., *Complete Greek Drama,* vol. 2, 541–99. The passage in which Aristophanes and the clouds mock the observers occurs on p. 555, ll. 346–64.

112. Janson, "The 'Image Made by Chance' in Renaissance Thought," 257–58.

113. Kemp and Walker, eds., *Leonardo on Painting,* 222.

These attempts to deal with the image made by chance derive from a strong underground theme in the history of aesthetics. Not only I, but even Kant, can only claim to be inheritors of a basic problem: something that is out there is also in here, and we make it again into something out there. But then it is real.

## C. Post-postscript

This postscript was precipitated by a passage in the article by Richard Moran cited above,[114] in which Moran questions the necessity for universal agreement on the value of the aesthetic object. I will begin by transcribing my notes, in their raw form.

"Why *should* there be universal agreement about the quality or value of a work of art? Because, without such an agreement, the aesthetic object ceases to exist. What remains is some individual's nameless response to something—to god-knows-what. Agreement is what *constitutes* an aesthetic object; at least, an implicit agreement. The category of the aesthetic rests on that implicit agreement, on the assumption that somewhere, somehow, our opinions can coincide. The real issue behind the expectation of agreement is that, trusting each other to come out in the same place, we affirm our humanity. The possibility of the coincidence of our aesthetic judgment is the proof of our humanity, for the aesthetic is what makes us all human.

"This is also why the aesthetic, as Kant requires, must lie beyond self-interest. The fact that it is not self-interested explains the linkage between the aesthetic and the ethical.

"It may be argued, with some justification, that there are many situations other than the aesthetic in which we find it difficult to understand why others do not share our tastes. But in no other case (not even in the case of such a fundamental cultural marker as a taste in bread) does someone's very humanity depend on taste: nowhere, other than in the aesthetic, do we conceive of a commonalty of taste as being a common denominator for humanity as a whole."

That is what finally became apparent to me as I meditated on this unlikely topic, this "nonsense" about clouds, or clods. Why, at this primordial level of "art," at a level at which it is still barely distinguishable from the shapeless world, should I not only have wanted, but actually expected, others to have exactly the same feelings as myself about these discoveries of forms in nature?

---

114. Moran, "Kant, Proust, and the Appeal of Beauty," 321–23.

I believe, as I have said above, that it was because I wanted reassurance that humanity exists. That is what is at stake. The aesthetic is the unconscious contract that makes the whole world kin. It is the field where we recognize a common horizon. By recognizing my response, and by participating in my response, the "other" becomes less other, and ratifies my humanity, precisely at this, almost literally, ground level (or cloud level) of the image made by chance. It is not approval of my opinion that I desire, but proof that the contract holds. It does not matter that we may disagree about individual examples of art: we still agree that there is such a thing as art, separate from us as individuals, something that goes beyond our individual needs and desires; something that confirms our solidarity at a level deeper than the local, the tribal, or the national. The fact that art is disinterested (as Kant insists) is merely a by-product of the fact that it is universal.

This demand for universal assent in aesthetics, whether in Kant or elsewhere, is not, then, an authoritarian maneuver, an attempt to force others to submit to our arbitrary opinion, or to an opinion merely identifiable with, say, economic class. It is, on the contrary, an appeal for confirmation of our identity, which is a product of our sociality, of which art is the evidence. That is why Professor Miranda's attempt to prove that each of us hears a different Beethoven is hopelessly wrong-headed.[115] The totally private work of art is an oxymoron, even less plausible than a totally private language.

I believe, then, that the call for a universal response to a work of art is really a "cri de cœur"; we do not want to be alone in the universe, pleading in vain (like Tennyson in "In Memoriam" or "Break, Break, Break"[116]) for the sound of a beloved voice. We expect consensus because we cannot imagine a world void of the aesthetic; the aesthetic is the physical evidence of our commonalty. It is the proof that we are all in it, all here, together, as our thoughts are brought together, to our collective benefit, whether by a shape in a cloud, by a suffering Saint Sebastian, or by Rilke's torso of Apollo, which, lacking a head, has become all eyes:

> . . . denn da ist keine Stelle
>     Die dich nicht sieht. Du musst dein Leben ändern.
> (. . . For there is no part of this
>     That doesn't see you. You must change your life.)[117]

---

115. BBC, December 20, 2012, "Music and the Brain."

116. Tennyson, *Selections*, 96, ll. 11–12: "But O for the touch of a vanish'd hand, / And the sound of a voice that is still!"

117. Rilke, "Archaïscher Torso Apollos," in Norton, 180.

All art is an accusation. Art is the place where, of necessity, we see and are seen. It is also the place where we have to see ourselves, as well as each other, as we should be.

———<>———

Moving from chapter to chapter, one cannot help but find that complexities accumulate, and it becomes harder to find grounds for a summary. Still, this chapter may be aligned, approximately, with one of the three general categories or situations that underlie this study: (1) situations in which the distinction between sense and nonsense is challenged; (2) those in which nonsense is seen as transcending sense; and (3) those in which we encounter nonsense in its purest form. Of these three, the second category comes closest to describing the "image made by chance." As Hamlet makes clear, for him the images in clouds are mere nonsense. Yet, the more closely we examine the phenomenon, the more fully we realize that it is not trivial. First of all, these images are necessary: we cannot choose not to see them; in fact, we could not get rid of them if we wanted to. Secondly, they are closely related to fundamental functions of our imagination, creative as well as simply "reproductive"; whether we consider them nonsensical or otherwise, they are ground-level art: for some, God's own art. They cause the material to levitate.

# CHAPTER 7

# Assorted Nonsense

This chapter is an attempt to deal with a few topics that have not yet been, or have been inadequately, addressed.

## I. NONSENSE *VERSUS* SENSE IN E. T. A. HOFFMANN (AND KANT'S SOLUTION)

Hell is more exciting than heaven, yet most of us try to get from the first to the last. The same principle will apply in the final chapter of this book. It would have been more effective rhetorically for me to have ended with Nathanael whirling around his tower, as in one of the following paragraphs; but the sobering precepts of Kant have been allowed to prevail. Nonsense itself, perhaps, will have to play the role of purgatory, an inescapable place of passage, with all the uncertainties of the transition to a resolution crowded into it.

    E. T. A. Hoffmann's "The Sandman" has haunted minds since it was written in 1816. It was a touchstone for Freud; in my own overextended lifetime, it has reappeared, as it were unbidden, in several different contexts in what I have written. It seems that it will just not go away: it has the same kind of unmitigated urgency as *Jekyll and Hyde*: "Look at this: this is for you." Of course, one can also try to dismiss its events as mere literature. "The professor of poetry and rhetoric took a pinch of snuff, snapped his snuff-box shut, cleared his throat, and solemnly declared, 'Ladies and gentlemen, do you not see the point of it all? The whole thing is an allegory—an extended metaphor! You understand what I mean! *Sapienti sat!*'"[1]

The irreconcilable rift between a mechanistic approach to art (which, at the limit, would reduce art to useless nonsense) and the insistence that art cannot be reduced to neurological or other physical principles, has been a recurrent issue in this book. It appears in many forms. In any discussion of metaphor, it is likely to come up as the distinction (in Coleridge's terms, plagiarized verbatim from Kant) between fancy (a mechanical function) and imagination. In my chapter on the Baroque, it appears as the dominance of the artificial over the real (such as it, the real, may be: for Kant, of course, the "real," the "Ding an sich," remains inaccessible and indefinable). In the context of Keats's poetry, it lies in the difference between true and false inspiration (both, if in very different ways, related to madness). In my chapter on neuroscience and the arts, it is expressed as the abovementioned difference between a neurological and what (to fall back, once more, on an unsatisfactory term) one might call a humanistic view of the arts. And, in the chapter on the image made by chance, it is expressed as the choice between aesthetic response as an automatic, compulsory reaction to a stimulus, on the one hand, and a decision arrived at freely about that stimulus, on the other.

But nowhere has this opposition been displayed with such raw violence as in "The Sandman." This abstruse issue in aesthetics here assumes the dynamic, or demonic, force of events in an all-too-persuasive life. The most relevant analogy, albeit on a historical scale, is probably to be found in the wars over iconoclasm—i.e., over pictures—that have punctuated history, and remain an engine of apocalyptic destruction in our own time. Kant himself, assuming a tone of almost messianic certainty, takes up the cudgels on behalf of pure abstraction, against the wooden dolls or graven images of popular—or Papist—religion.[2] It is as though neither Hoffmann nor Kant (whose lives, incidentally, overlapped substantially) could let the problem remain as an issue in philosophy, and had to show us that it was an unavoidable intruder in our daily lives. It is a little like the way $e = mc^2$ suddenly moved from the status of a pure mathematical equation to the reality of an uncontrollable, murderous explosion.

"The Sandman" leaves the conflict completely unresolved; it ends in a climax that brings no relief, for Hoffmann refuses to mitigate the jarring impact of his tale. Nathanael falls in love with a wooden doll, "Olympia," manufac-

---

1. Hoffmann, "The Sandman," *Tales of Hoffmann*, 31.
2. *Critique of Judgment*, trans. J. H. Bernard, 115.

tured to act, more or less, like a human being. The trouble is, he cannot decide whether she is just a mechanism (our "physiological" view of art) or the ideal young woman, immeasurably better than any mere flesh-and-blood creature. (Is this simply Keats's choice, on the "Grecian Urn," again: art vs. life?) Clara, an actual woman, and supposedly his beloved, is associated by Nathanael with the wooden, mechanical side of Olympia, perhaps simply because Clara has the limitation of being a physical being. Once more, madness plays a role. Nathanael's attempt to destroy Clara by throwing her from a tower fails; prey to his "vile antithesis," unable to find an exit from his paradox, he circles racing around the top of the tower, screaming nonsense ("spin round, wooden doll!"), and finally throws himself over the parapet, for the only possible relief from his suffering. As though to rub in the moral, that there is no solution to Nathanael's sickness, we are shown Clara, after her lover's death, as the ultimate cliché, sitting on a bench outside a rural cottage, with two children playing at her feet. The scene gives us the full measure of what Nathanael has lost, and of what he has avoided.

The conception of the imagination as a tawdry mechanism which spins out of control and lurches into madness is pitted against the concept of the imagination as inspiration. This familiar battle in the pit of aesthetics has been close behind nonsense as a dominant scenario in this book, and it continues to call for a resolution, despite Hoffmann's clear refusal to offer one, or even to contemplate one. It may show itself to be a little more manageable, or, at least, approachable, if translated into Kantian terms.

At first glance, there would seem to be little in common between Kant's aesthetics and the scenario enacted in "The Sandman," in which the conflict between the mechanical and what I will call (for lack of a better term) the spiritual, is carried out in such a recklessly literal way. Still, there are abundant signs that Kant was not entirely immune from Nathanael's ailment. (I would not argue for a Kantian influence in "The Sandman," though, as some have done.) Circling through the vocabulary of this futile investigation, Kant too seems caught in the search for an exit. In a single paragraph, we find him struggling to clarify the relations among "delusion," "enthusiasm," "madness," "fanaticism," "monomania," and "affect," with "unbridled," "brooding passion," "irregular," "accident," "disease," and "disorderly" thrown in for good measure.[3] I believe that a better way can be found to deal with this perennial problem, but that it is located within a different area of Kant's own thinking.

---

3. Kant, *Critique of Judgment*, trans. J. H. Bernard, 116; *Kritik der Urteilskraft*, 183.

Oddly enough, Kant's apparently perverse insistence that we must all agree in our aesthetic judgments harbors a clue to a different approach. Kant's dogmatic assertion implies that the subject alone (i.e., he or we) has/have detected true imaginative art, and that all those who disagree are embracing idols, wooden puppets, inorganic, uninspired, mechanical pseudo-art. How can we justify such an unrealistic and authoritarian attitude, one that ignores quotidian experience?

My answer is that we are all just imperfect representatives of the ideal (if also, for that very reason, physically nonexistent) judge, critic, or reader in whose name we speak. When we, or Kant, demand consensus, the demand is not coming from us as individuals; it is really coming from behind us, from an ideal respondent. When we hear "Du musst dein Leben ändern," it is not even Rilke who is speaking, perhaps least of all the individual Rilke himself who is announcing that verdict, but that other, perfect judge. As individuals, we are inevitably defective: we are not pure, and therefore not free to see perfection as such. Our judgments are all clouded by our individual circumstances, the weaknesses and imperfections that we bring with us into the arena of pure judgment, where universal agreement should prevail. As Alfred de Vigny says in "La Flûte," "Des organes mauvais servent l'intelligence" ("Defective organs serve our intelligence"), or, even more to the point, Rimbaud, in "Ô saisons, ô châteaux": "Quelle âme est sans défauts?" ("What soul is without defect?").[4]

Art is not the place where we should be separated, like the wheat from the chaff, into good judges and bad judges, those who follow idols and those who are in touch with God. Art drives us together. I have said these things at the end of Chapter 6, but Kant himself had, of course, already said it for me. Art is strictly for all, never for one.[5] Art is what draws upon, strengthens, and restores the *sensus communis*. Anyone who lays claim to membership in the species of mankind "is both inclined and apt to communicate his pleasure to others and who is not contented with an object if he cannot feel satisfaction in it in common with others. Again, everyone expects and requires from everyone else this reference to universal communication [of pleasure], as it were from an original compact dictated by humanity itself."[6] A shared ground of pure judgment in beauty founds society, and from that it derives its laws.[7] (Analogues for this thought can be found in Hume, in Adam Smith, in Dr. Johnson, in Isaac D'Israeli, before Shelley.) The individual's pleasure in the aesthetic object "is inconsiderable and in itself without any marked interest,

4. Rimbaud, *Œuvres complètes,* 140, l. 2.

5. Kant, *Critique of Judgment,* trans. J. H. Bernard, 139.

6. Loc. cit.

7. Kant, *Critique of Judgment,* trans. J. H. Bernard, 140.

yet the idea of its universal communicability increases its worth in an almost infinite degree."[8] I have just heard a BBC program about the fraught history (and present, literal "worth") of the Lepinsky Stradivarius. Need one say more?

I will end this part of my chapter, on mechanistic vs. "humanistic" approaches to the arts, with an anecdote that, for me, settles the matter, if only with another question. In the 1950s, I was an assistant of I. A. Richards when he was lecturing in the Humanities 2 course at Harvard, "The Epic and the Novel." At Cambridge (UK), Richards had had the reputation of a teacher who never gave a mediocre lecture: it would have to be either dull or brilliant. This characteristic remained with Richards in America. On one occasion, in the darkened, 700-seat Norton Hall, a bat began to swing at regular intervals across the small space between the lamp on Richards's lectern and his notes, vanishing into the gloom on either side. This happened to be while Richards was talking about the "enchanters" in *Don Quixote*. Clearly, Richards was all in favor of enchantment, and relished nature's support of his predilection. Another time, Richards was talking about new developments in neuroscience, and of their possible relevance for the arts. (I can still hear him speaking, in his distinctive voice.) Despite his reputation as someone who himself applied quasi-scientific methods to criticism, he was clearly uncomfortable about the physiological approach. He expressed his doubts about "whether we ever will know" how the arts were produced by the activities of the nerves, but then, in a tone of mingled anger and indignation, his voice rising, he cried out, "or whether it would make any difference if we did know."

For me, this is the last word in the debate.

## II. NONSENSE IN RITUAL

Ritual, both tacit and overt, as both idea and practice, may constitute a fundamental part of human behavior. Still, I have no wish to appeal to the human need for ritual in its many forms, fundamental though it may be, as a final justification for nonsense. Ritual thought may be ineradicable; it may be a major motivator of our conduct; but that in itself does not give it authority over our mental processes. Still, it is an area of which nonsense is an essential feature, and, for that reason, it requires attention. Before I get back to Kant, then, let me attempt to do it at least partial justice. I will begin with the striking thesis proposed by Yuval Noah Harari in *Sapiens: A Brief History of Mankind*: the unique characteristic of our species, the ability to cooperate flexibly in large

8. Loc. cit.

numbers, is always mediated by a fiction. People can be motivated to work together on a large scale only in the name of something nonexistent—"nation," "rights," "divinity." It is the capacity to believe in the impossible that has made everything possible. One might say that the founding utterance of civilization was the pronouncement (attributed to Tertullian), surely the ultimate in nonsense: "Credo quia impossibile" ("I believe because it is impossible").

Ritual follows close behind: ritual consolidates the herd formed by nonsense. But ritual is not something to be taken lightly: it is associated with both the best and the worst in human feelings and behavior, and it seems impervious to rationalistic objections. It can overpower the hubristic claims of reason, and give us access, via the irrational, validated by the group, to experiences of immeasurable value, richness, and depth. Franz Liszt could not have been referring to the paraphrasable meaning of the text when he responded to the incomprehensible ritual, or nonsense, of a synagogue service by saying, "As the Hebrew words were pronounced, one might have said they were dark flowers separating from their stems and shedding their vibrating petals and sonorous corolla."[9] An element of unintelligibility is essential to ritual, although some have held that myth may have originated as an attempt to make sense of ritual, as itself a form of protorationalism (in the early theories of W. Robertson Smith and Sir James Frazer, among others).

In the Russian-Jewish novelist Ludmila Ulitskaya's *Medea and her Children,* a young woman, Masha, has committed suicide; the funeral service is held in a Greek that is incomprehensible to her mourners: "But all those present could clearly feel that in this bitter, inaccessible singing there was more meaning than even the wisest sage can contain within himself."[10] In such a passage, Ulitskaya makes us feel the irresistible reality of what she is describing. This is not some remote event: we know that what Ulitskaya is saying is true.

In "Rite Reasons," Dan Jones attempts to determine what it is that draws us both to initiate and to participate in ritual practices. The gist of the article is that meaningless rituals enhance our sense of group belonging: "Children copy apparently aimless sequences of actions more faithfully than sequences that move towards an obvious goal."[11] The intuition that meaningless actions must have ritual value—i.e., group bonding value—trumps any merely practical purpose. On the other hand, it is not clear why the meaningless should automatically be identified with bonding. Besides, there are other practices, such as work songs, that also promote bonding, but do not depend entirely

---

9. Ivry, "How Franz Schubert Found Himself in Shul," 12.

10. Ulitskaya, *Medea and her Children,* 306.

11. Jones, "Rite Reasons," 38.

on nonsense. I would argue, rather, that it is the sense of meaning in ritual, rather than its lack of meaning, that makes it so powerful. Language in general carries more meaning than its literal assertions convey: ritual creates a specialized version of this function. The gibberish of prayer, the magical incantation, are replete with significance. To refer to a topic considered in a previous chapter: it is not because of its sheer meaninglessness that we respond to nonsense poetry, but because we feel that it tells us something that a more rational form of language fails to convey. True, ritual language is, or has a claim to be, something more than secular poetry: but it takes the principle of the mysterious poem—say, of the most opaque "language" poem—to a higher degree. After all, we experience ritual as possessing *content*: to quote Ulitskaya again, "all those present could clearly feel that in this bitter, inaccessible singing there was *more meaning* [emphasis mine] than even the wisest sage could contain within himself."[12] In ritual, meaning overflows language, and symbols go beyond themselves.

## III. NONSENSE IN KANT

We hardly need more than religion, and that key to religion, ritual, to persuade us to take nonsense seriously. After dream, religion is perhaps our most necessary form of nonsense. Religion is a necessity of life for most people, and there are few religions that dispense with the element of miracle, an element which devotees of a different religion, or the merely secular, may experience as simply nonsense. Still, I do not mean to rest my case for nonsense on either its role in logic and scientific thought or on its dominance in the more subjective domain of religious experience. There is one more step that I wish to take in strengthening its claims to validity.

Let me get back to Kant: presumably no purveyor of nonsense, nevertheless even he, astonishingly like Blake in this respect, warns against "going mad with reason" ("mit Vernunft rasen").[13] See, also, Thomas Nash in *Lenten Stuff* on the "rawbond carcasse of reason."[14]

We are asked, not through sleight of hand, or by means of any hidden persuaders, to accept flatly improbable assertions in the text of Kant, such as several that we have seen above. To be sure, these do not represent a cavalier dismissal of facts, but a struggle to reach the meaning behind them; still, some of them are startling. One such example, already considered extensively: if a

---

12. Ulitskaya, *Medea and her Children*, 306.
13. Kant, *Critique of Judgment*, trans. J. H. Bernard, 116; *Kritik der Urteilskraft*, 183.
14. Nashe [*sic*], *Lenten Stuff*, 60.

man says that a thing is beautiful, "he does not count on the agreement of others with this judgment of satisfaction . . . but he *demands* it of them. He blames them if they judge otherwise and he denies them taste. . . . We cannot say that each man has his particular taste. . . . For this would be as much as to say that there is no taste whatever."[15] It is not the pleasure (in taste), "but the *universal validity of this pleasure,* perceived as mentally bound up with the mere judgment upon an object, which is represented *a priori* in a judgment of taste as a universal rule for the judgment and valid for everyone."[16] A "pleasure" in an individual object of art which must be "valid for everyone?"

We are being *commanded* to believe in such nonsense.

Here is another assertion, thoroughly familiar to readers of Kant, of which we are expected to make sense. We are told that the beautiful is characterized by "a purposiveness without purpose."[17] "*Beauty* is the form of the *purposiveness* of an object, so far as this is perceived in it *without any representation of a purpose.*"[18]

Is it possible to do anything without a purpose? Besides, in the absence of a purpose, how is one even to know whether one has done good or ill? Produced ugliness, or beauty? (Compare Mogens S. Kjargaard: "It is not possible to establish rules for breaches of rules.")[19] What does it mean to say that one can have purpose "without purpose"? Nothing we do is without purpose. If it were without purpose, we simply wouldn't do it: we have to *want* to do something in order to do it (unless, of course, we are being forced to do something contrary to our own purpose).

It must be, I guess, that Kant thinks, "You know what I am getting at! This is no place for niceties. If only nonsense will work to tell you what I mean, then let it be nonsense." The peremptory tone of these proclamations leaves no doubt as to their intention: "We belong together. If you don't like it, so much the worse for you." This is the same spirit in which Kant issued, with what must have been a straight face, that superbly nonsensical demand: you must not tell a lie, even to rescue somebody from murder. "Alle Menschen werden Brüder" ("All men will be brothers")—or else!

And the aesthetic imperative comprehends the ethical. It *ought* to. Peter Szendy, in *Kant chez les extraterrestres,* takes a different approach to the relation of aesthetics to social imperatives. He sees in Kant a "passage de l'esthétique au politique" ["passage from the aesthetic to the political"]

---

15. Kant, *Critique of Judgment,* trans. J. H. Bernard, 47.
16. Ibid., 131–32, emphasis in original.
17. Ibid., 62.
18. Ibid., 73.
19. Kjärgaard, *Metaphor and Parable,* 24.

(102); in fact, he speaks of aesthetic experience as being "d'emblée politique" ["immediately political"] (144).

## IV. LANGUAGE AS EXPERIENCE

Let's assume that all this is so. We do, somehow, seem to assume that Kant's magnificent nonsense makes sense. But perhaps it is not only from the content but also from the form of these implausible pronouncements that we must learn. Maybe it is, in fact, *only* in these implausible formulations that Kant could convey what he meant. Like poetry, this is a language beyond paraphrase. Scharfstein has dared to say it: there is "an intelligible outer Kant inhabited by a Kant-in-himself . . . [who] exercises the hypnotic magic of nonsensical philosophy."[20] These are not words to be parsed—this is nonsense to live by. Perhaps we expect too much of ourselves if we expect to understand language, to figure out how it works, from word to word.

It is futile to try to rephrase an idea once we have lost it. Words will not bring it back. One can't reword, because one no longer knows what one *meant*. It has to come off the boiling pot, where thoughts and words are not yet distinguished (as I may have, prematurely, suggested that they might be—see Chapter 6 Section I.C) in order to happen. At that point, thoughts and words were still too intimately wedded—only those words could carry that meaning. They were, you might say, still in love. At the source of meaning, words come of their own accord—they are not separate from meaning. The words mean what they say.

We will never know the link between words and meaning, or the source of meaning.

Kant, the great idealist, told it how it is: "Nur in der Erfahrung ist Wahrheit" ("Only in experience can truth be found").[21]

I would like to suggest that language itself, the combination of idea with word, is a special form of experience. I have hinted at this conclusion in the passage of Chapter 1 where I talked about "Jabberwocky" as being especially effective in conveying meaning because it gets around words, and goes directly to the meaning through the experience and connections of the sounds. I have also gestured towards this outcome in a previous chapter (see Chapter 6 Section I.E), where I talk about meaning as being conveyed through the aesthetic underpinning, or lining, of a sentence. By language as a special form of expe-

---

20. Scharfstein, 36.

21. Kant, *Prolegomena zu einer jeden künftigen Metaphysik,* 145, and *Prolegomena to any Future Metaphysics,* 123.

rience I certainly do not mean, in particular, that form of language which can be called active, performative, or pragmatic, such as a command. What I am considering, to simplify at the broadest level, is that, with respect to language, we exist in three ways: (1) the way which is mediated by rational expressions of a mathematical or quasi-mathematical nature, along with designations of objects or events, and the system of signs required to service that aspect of existence; (2) a second, which consists of the content of the first (one might call it "living"); and (3) a third, which I call language as experience. We usually think of the second category as our only form of experience: but language too is a form of experience, a form of experience distinct from our other, physical or emotional, experiences. It is an experience of its own kind, sui generis.[22] For that reason we can never "fathom" it, any more than we can replace a physical experience by words. In language as experience the invidious distinction between sense and nonsense begins to lose its force. I submit that Kant's deepest pronouncements appear nonsensical because they have to: they take the hypotenuse because the long way around will never get them where they are going. Sense lies outside "sense"—; it lies in language as experience.

---

In the first section of this chapter I propose a solution to the recurrent problem of art as inspiration vs. art as nonsense in terms of Kant's "sensus communis"; in the second, I suggest that language in ritual, though apparently nonsensical, is experienced as a form of extra- or, possibly, hyper-linguistic meaning; in the third, I claim that Kant sometimes makes apparently arbitrary assertions that convey his purpose more forcefully than a more reasoned form of expression would achieve; in the last, I argue not only for language in ritual, but even for language in general, as a fundamental and distinct form of experience. When language is seen in this way, "the invidious distinction between sense and nonsense begins to lose its force."

---

Some readers, however, may experience this ending as more abrupt than conclusive, and may even have lost track of the path by which it has been reached.

---

22. Hamilton, in "The Experience of Everything" (a prospectus for his lecture to the Research Group for Eighteenth-Century and Romantic Studies given at Cambridge University, January 14, 2016), following Fichte, takes a view of philosophy which is similar to my own with respect to language as such: "Every philosophical position generates an *experience* [my emphasis] of itself outside its own claims . . . there is always a 'style' in any philosophizing, and we are responsible for that as much as for the coherence of our reasoning" (18). Any attempt to take my tripartite generalization a step further would involve the concept of attentional semantics and the work of Leonard Talmy.

After having negotiated a spinney of digressions, they may even feel entitled to a new summary, though my Introduction already includes most of what I will have to say here. I concentrate now on those passages that are explicitly concerned with nonsense, avoiding the numerous tangential issues that have arisen along the way.

In my first subject area, metaphor, I point out that the margin between metaphor and nonsense has never been clearly defined, and may not even be subject to clear definition (even though the experience of metaphor itself is quite unmistakable). What is more, people with Asperger's syndrome often cannot distinguish between nonsense and metaphor: their brains deal with both in the same way, and we have no means by which to tell their brains what to do differently.

In the domain of history, in the Baroque one finds a mode of thinking in which representations systematically exceed the object represented, creating a continuous sense of discrepancy. One has to keep catching up, and reminding oneself that what one is being shown may be sheer nonsense, bombast, or inflation, with paltry reality lagging far behind. I follow the manifestations of this condition, and the efforts to deal with it, from the seventeenth century to our own.

In the chapter on poetry, as represented by Keats, I speak of the age-old controversy over contrived vs. genuine art in terms of the conflict between nonsense and inspiration. The issue in Keats is shown to have its antecedents in Kant's distinction between fanaticism (or "raving") and enthusiasm.

In the chapter on neuroscience, it is the strange behavior of language during the transition between waking and sleep that is characterized. This is one of the few situations in which one can observe what is apparently pure nonsense, though some network of associations beneath what is usually called our "stream of consciousness" may be involved.

Another of the major forms of nonsense with which I have dealt is perceptual nonsense: the powerful, involuntary, largely uncontrollable impulse to make sense out of situations that are, in themselves, objectively speaking, meaningless. (Of course, this observation raises yet again an issue that is hardly suitable material for a last-minute question, especially with Kant in the background: is there *anything* that is, in and of itself, "meaningful"?) Hamlet's shapes in clouds, and other possible shapes in nature, furnish my primary examples. Such images made by chance, or "natural" images, which are from one point of view mere nonsense, are, I try to show, basic to aesthetic experience. And, in turn, these universal, compulsory aesthetic events, dependent though they be on "nonsense," become the foundation for our ethical standards of behavior.

The last topic, language as experience, a context in which the sense/non-sense issue loses some of its urgency, is dealt with in the final pages of the text, above.

So much for the summary. It is my hope that this sketch will send the reader back to all that this outline omits.

# WORKS CITED

Abel, Lionel. *Important Nonsense*. Buffalo, NY: Prometheus, 1987.

Adamson, Robert. *Fichte*. Philadelphia: J. B. Lippincott Co.; Edinburgh: William Blackwood & Sons, 1892.

Addison, Joseph. *The Spectator: Two Volumes Complete in One*. Philadelphia: J. J. Ward, 1836.

Akhmatova, Anna. *The Complete Poems of Anna Akhmatova*. Vol. 2. Somerville, MA: Zephyr Press, 1990.

Allik, Jüri. "Do Primitive People Have Illusions?" *Dubna Psychological Journal* 3 (2013): 40–42.

Anonymous. "Observations on Mme. de Staël's Posthumous Work," *Blackwood's* 4 (September 1818): 633–47.

Aristotle. *The Politics*. Translated by T. A. Sinclair. New York: Random House, 1981.

Badgaiyan, Rajendra D. "Nonconscious Perception, Conscious Awareness and Attention." *Cognition* 21 (2012): 584–86.

———. "Nonconscious Processing and a Novel Target for Schizophrenia Research." *Open Journal of Psychiatry* 2 (2012): 335–39.

Ball, Philip. *Nature's Patterns: A Tapestry in Three Parts*. Oxford: Oxford University Press, 2011.

Baron-Cohen, Simon. *The Science of Evil*. New York: Basic Books, 2011.

Bartoli, Gabriella, Stefano Mastandrea, and Giuseppe Carrus. "The Automatic Aesthetic Evolution of Different Art and Architectural Styles." *PACA* 5, no. 2 (2011): 126–34.

Battistini, Andrea. "The Telescope in the Baroque Imagination." In *Reason and its Others: Italy, Spain, and the New World,* edited by David R. Castillo and Massimo Lollini, 3–38. Nashville, TN: Vanderbilt University Press, 2006.

Bekinschtein, Tristan A., Mathew H. Davis, Jennifer M. Rodd, and Adrian M. Owen. "Why Clowns Taste Funny: The Relationship between Humor and Semantic Ambiguity." *Journal of Neuroscience* 31, no. 26 (June 29, 2011): 9655–71.

Benjamin, Walter. *Gesammelte Schrifte*. Frankfurt am Main: Suhrkamp, 1974.

———. *Ursprung des deutschen Trauerspiels*. Frankfurt am Main: Suhrkamp, 1963.

Benzon, Bill. "Neuroaesthetics." *New Savanna* (blog). September 8, 2013. new-savanna.blogspot. in/2013/04/neuroaesthetics.html.

Bergson, Henri. *Essai sur les données immédiates de la conscience*. Geneva: Albert Skira, 1945 [1888].

Bishop, Elizabeth. *The Complete Poems*. New York: Farrar, Straus and Giroux, 1977.

Black, Max. *Models and Metaphors*. Ithaca, NY: Cornell University Press, 1962.

Blake, William. *Blake's Poetry and Designs*. Edited by Mary Lynn Johnson. New York and London: W. W. Norton, 1979.

———. *Marriage of Heaven and Hell*. 1790.

Blumenberg, Hans. *The Legitimacy of the Modern Age*. Cambridge, MA: MIT Press, 1983.

Böhme, Jakob. *Mysterium Magnum*. Stuttgart: Fr. Frommans Verlag, 1958.

Bostridge, Ian. *Schubert's Winter Journey: Anatomy of an Obsession*. New York: Alfred A. Knopf, 2015.

Bowie, Andrew. *Philosophical Variations: Music as Philosophical Language*. Malmo: NSU Press, 2010.

Brandt, Per Aage. "A Note on the Meaning of Nonsense." Personal communication, February 16, 2017.

———. *These Hands*. Austin, TX: Host Publications, 2011.

Braungart, Georg. *Leibhafter Sinn: der andere Diskurs der Moderne*. Tübingen: Max Niemeyer, 1995.

Breitenbach, Angela. *Die Analogie von Vernunft und Natur: Eine Umweltphilosophie nach Kant*. Berlin and New York: Walter de Gruyter, 2009.

Brendel, Alfred. "The Growing Charm of Dada." *New York Review of Books* 63, no. 16 (October 27, 2016): 22–25.

Brennan, Teresa. *The Transmission of Affect*. Ithaca, NY: Cornell University Press, 2004.

Breton, André. *Manifeste du surréalisme*. Paris: Pauvert, 1962.

Brown, Daniel. "Being and Naughtiness." In *Edward Lear and the Play of Poetry*, edited by James Williams and Matthew Bevis, 162–82. Oxford: Oxford University Press, 2016.

Buci-Glucksmann, Christine. *La Folie du voir : de l'esthétique baroque*. Paris: Galilée, 1986.

Caillois, Roger. *Cases d'un échiquier*. Paris: Gallimard, 1970.

———. *Méduse et cie*. Paris: Gallimard, 1960.

Caraher, Brian and Irving Massey, eds. *Literature and Contradiction*. Buffalo: State University of New York at Buffalo, 1974.

———, eds. *Literature and Iconoclasm*. Buffalo: State University of New York at Buffalo, 1976.

Carey, Benedict. "Decoding the Brain's Cacophony." *New York Times*, November 1, 2011, 1–4.

Carlyle, Thomas. "On Heroes, Hero-Worship, and the Heroic in History." In *Prose of the Victorian Period,* edited by William E. Buckler, 113–29. Boston: Houghton Mifflin, 1958.

Cascardi, Anthony J. "The Genealogy of the Sublime in the Aesthetics of the Spanish Baroque." In *Reason and its Others: Italy, Spain, and the New World,* edited by David R. Castillo and Massimo Lollini, 221–42. Nashville, TN: Vanderbilt University Press, 2006.

Centre for Research in the Arts, Social Sciences, and Humanities (CRASSH), Cambridge University. Private online message board, October 13, 2016.

Chatterjee, Anjan. "Where There Be Dragons: Finding the Edges of Neuroaesthetics." *American Society for Aesthetics* 31, no. 2 (2011): 172–94.

Chesneau, R. P. *Emblèmes sacrez sur le très-saint et très-adorable sacrement de l'eucharistie.* Paris: Florentin Lambert, 1667.

Christiansen, Irmgard. *Die Technik der allegorischen Auslegungswissenschaft bei Philon von Alexandrien.* Tübingen: J. C. B. Mohr, 1969.

Clinton, Alan. "André Breton's Skeleton Key: The Role of Automatism in Escaping the Cages of Reason." *Theory @ Buffalo* 7 (2002): 103–19.

Cohen, Leonard. *Old Ideas.* Columbia Records, 2012.

Coleridge, Samuel Taylor. *The Friend.* Bollingen Series 75. Vol. 1. Princeton, NJ: Princeton University Press, 1969.

———. *Lectures 1818—1819 on the History of Philosophy.* Bollingen Series 75. Vol. 8, no. 2. Edited by James Robert de Jager Jackson. Princeton, NJ: Princeton University Press, 2000.

———. *The Notebooks of Samuel Taylor Coleridge.* Princeton, NJ: Princeton University Press, 1957.

———. *The Selected Poetry and Prose of Coleridge.* New York: Modern Library, 1951.

Cook, Meira. *Field Marks: The Poetry of Don McKay.* Waterloo, Ontario: Wilfrid Laurier University Press, 1999.

Crawford, Donald W. "Comparative Aesthetic Judgments and Kant's Aesthetic Theory." *JAAC* 39, no. 1 (Fall 1980): 289–305.

Critchley, Macdonald. "Types of Visual Perseveration." *Brain* 74 (1951): 267–99.

Cusanus, C. *The Idiot in Four Books.* San Francisco: [California State Library], 1940.

Dalí, Salvador. *50 Secrets of Magic Craftsmanship.* Mineola, NY: Dover, 1992.

Dante. *Paradiso.*

Davidson, James. "Laugh as Long as You Can." *London Review of Books* 37, no. 14 (July 16, 2015): 33–35.

Davis, Oliver. *Jacques Rancière.* Cambridge, UK and Malden, MA: Polity Press, 2010.

Debord, Guy. *La Société du spectacle.* Paris: Buchet-Chastel, 1967.

Deleuze, Gilles. *Le Pli: Leibniz et le baroque.* Paris: Minuit, 1972.

———. *Logique du sens.* Paris: Minuit, 1969.

Dennett, Daniel. *Consciousness Explained.* Boston: Little, Brown, 1991.

Derrida, Jacques. "La mythologie blanche." *Poétique* 5 (1971): 1–52.

De Vigny, Alfred. *Œuvres complètes.* Vol. 1. Paris: Pléiade, 1948.

Dissanayake, Ellen. *Homo Aestheticus: Where Art Comes from and Why.* Seattle: University of Washington Press, 1995.

Distaso, Leonardo V. "On *Satzklang*: On the Sense and on the Nonsense." *Aisthesis* 6, no. 1 (2013): 263–73.

Dolgopolski, Sergey. *The Open Past: Subjectivity and Remembering in the Talmud.* New York: Fordham University Press, 2012.

Doy, Gen. *Picturing the Self: Changing Views of Visual Culture.* London and New York: I. B. Tauris, 2005.

Dryden, John. "Absalom and Achitophel." In *The Restoration and Eighteenth Century,* edited by Martin Price, 56–83. New York: Oxford University Press, 1973.

———. *The Works of John Dryden.* New York and Los Angeles: University of California Press; London: Cambridge University Press, 1962.

Ducasse, Isidore (the comte de Lautréamont). *Œuvres complètes.* Paris: Livre de Poche, 1963.

Dutton, Dennis. *The Art Instinct: Beauty, Pleasure, and Human Evolution.* New York, Berlin, and London: Bloomsbury, 2009.

Egginton, William. "The Baroque as a Problem of Thought." *PMLA* 124 (2009): 143–49.

Eliot, T. S. "The Love Song of J. Alfred Prufrock." In *Modern American Poetry; Modern British Poetry,* edited by Louis Untermeyer, 425–28. New York: Harcourt, Brace, 1942.

Elliott, Richard. *The Sound of Nonsense.* London: Bloomsbury Academic, 2017.

Elua, Ia, Keith Laws, and Lia Kvavilashvili. "From Mind-Pops to Hallucinations? A Study of Involuntary Semantic Memories in Schizophrenia." *Psychiatry Research* 196 (2012): 165–70.

Empson, William. *Some Versions of Pastoral.* Norfolk, CT: New Directions, 1960.

Eysenck, Hans. *Genius: The Natural History of Creativity.* Cambridge: Cambridge University Press, 1995.

Faust, Miriam and Yoed N. Kenett. "Rigidity, Chaos and Integration: Hemispheric Interaction and Individual Differences in Metaphor Comprehension." *Frontiers in Human Neuroscience* 8 (July 2014): 1–10.

Fenves, Peter. "The Scale of Enthusiasm." *HLQ* 60, nos. 1 & 2 (1998): 117–52.

Ferris, David. "Gleaning Clues on Sunny Days from the Clouds." *New York Times,* October 24, 2012, F4.

Figes, Orlando. *The Russian Revolution 1891–1924.* London: Jonathan Cape, 1996.

Findlen, Paula. "Jokes of Nature and Jokes of Knowledge: The Playfulness of Scientific Discourse in Early Modern Europe." *Renaissance Quarterly,* 43, no. 2 (1990): 292–331.

Flaubert, Gustave. "La Légende de Saint-Julien L'Hospitalier." *Œuvres de Flaubert.* Vol. 2. Paris: Pléiade, 1952, 623–48.

Forster, E. M. *Pharos and Pharillon.* London: Hogarth Press, 1967.

Forsyth, Joseph. *Remarks on Antiquities, Arts, and Letters During an Excursion in Italy in the Years 1802 and 1803.* Newark: University of Delaware; London: Associated University Presses, 2001.

Frankfurt, Henry G. *On Bullshit.* Princeton, NJ: Princeton University Press, 2005.

Gide, André. *Les Nourritures terrestres et les nouvelles nourritures.* Paris: Gallimard, [1969].

Gillain, Nathalie. "'Participer au monde par des lignes' (Henri Michaux) ou comment taire le bruit des mots : petit éloge du silence." In *Représenter à l'époque contemporaine: pratiques littéraires, artistiques et philosophiques,* edited by Isabelle Ost, Pierre Piret, and Laurent van Eynde. Bruxelles: Facultés universitaires Saint-Louis, 2010.

Gissing, George. *The Private Papers of Henry Ryecroft.* London: Phoenix House, 1953.

Glucksberg, Sam and Boaz Keysar. "How Metaphors Work." In *Metaphor and Thought,* edited by Andrew Ortony, 401–24. 2nd ed. Cambridge: Cambridge University Press, 1992.

Gold, Rinat, Miriam Faust, and Abraham Goldstein. "Semantic Integration during Metaphor Comprehension in Asperger Syndrome." *Brain & Language* 113 (2010): 124–34.

Goldman, Alvin J. *Simulating Minds: The Philosophy, Psychology, and Neuroscience of Mindreading.* New York: Oxford University Press, 2006.

Gopnik, Alison. "Cells that Read Minds?" *Slate,* April 26, 2007. www.slate.com/id/2165123.

Gray, Jeffrey. *Consciousness: Creeping up on the Hard Problem.* New York and Oxford: Oxford University Press, 2004.

Grieco, Peter J. *At the Musarium.* Buffalo, NY: Dulcet Glow Press, 2010.

———. "Portraits: for Phil." Manuscript.

Hacker, P. M. S. "Wittgenstein, Carnap and the New American Wittgensteinians." *Philosophical Quarterly* 53 (January 2003): 1–23.

Haeckel, Ernst. *Kunstformen der Natur.* Leipzig and Vienna: Verlag des bibliographischen Instituts, 1904.

Halpern, Sue. "Robots and Algorithms are Taking Over." *New York Review of Books* 62, no. 6 (April 2, 2015): 18–24.

Hamilton, Paul. "The Experience of Everything: Romantic Writing and Post-Kantian Phenomenology." Lecture, Cambridge University, January 14, 2016.

Harari, Yuval Noah. *Sapiens: A Brief History of Mankind.* New York: Vintage, 2014.

Harman, Graham. *Quentin Meillassoux: Philosophy in the Making.* Edinburgh: Edinburgh University Press, 2011.

Harris, Michael. "Let Your Mind Wander." *Discover* (June 2017): 30–35.

Hausman, Carl L. *Metaphor and Art: Interactionism and Reference in the Verbal and Nonverbal Arts.* Cambridge: Cambridge University Press, 1989.

Hawthorne, Nathaniel. *Nathaniel Hawthorne's Tales.* New York and London: W. W. Norton, 1987.

Hazlitt, William. *Collected Works.* Edited by A. R. Waller and Arnold Glover. London: J. M. Dent & co.; New York: McClure, Philips & co., 1902.

———. "Madame de Staël's Account of German Philosophy and Literature." *Morning Chronicle,* February 3, 1814, 162–66.

Heaven, Douglas. "The Obsessioneers." *New Scientist* 2971 (May 31, 2014): 38–41.

Hegel, Georg Wilhelm Friedrich. *Phenomenology of Mind.* Oxford: Oxford University Press, 1977.

Heider, Fritz and Marianne Simmel. "An Experimental Study of Apparent Behavior." *American Journal of Psychology* 57 (1944): 243–59.

Heller, Erich. *The Disinherited Mind.* Cleveland and New York: World Publishing Company, 1969.

Heller-Roazen, Daniel. *No One's Ways: An Essay on Infinite Naming.* Brooklyn: Zone Books, 2017.

Herbert, George. *The Poems of George Herbert.* London: Oxford University Press, 1964.

Hesse, Mary B. "The Explanatory Function of Metaphor." In *Logic, Methodology, and Philosophy of Science,* edited by Yehoshua Bar-Hillel, 249–59. Amsterdam: North-Holland Publishing Company, 1965.

Hilliard, Nicholas. *Unknown Man Clasping a Hand from a Cloud.* 1588. Painting. Courtesy of the Victoria and Albert Museum. www.vam.ac.uk/users/node/1961.

Hinchcliffe, Jillian and Seth Frey. "Shakespeare's Genius is Nonsense." *Nautilus* 48 (May 25, 2017).

Hobbes, Thomas. *Leviathan.* New York: E. P. Dutton; London: J. M. Dent and Sons, 1950 [1651].

Hoffmann, E. T. A. *E. T. A. Hoffmans Werke.* Vol. 2: *Nachtstücke, Klein Zaches genannt Zinnoben; Die Serapionsbrüder.* Frankfurt am Main: Insel, 1967.

———. *The Tales of Hoffmann.* New York: Frederick Ungar, 1963.

Hogan, Patrick Colm. *Beauty and Sublimity: A Cognitive Aesthetics of Literature and the Arts.* Cambridge: Cambridge University Press, 2016.

Hogarth, William. *Credulity, Superstition, and Fanaticism.* 1762. Etching.

Holstein, Baroness de Staël. *Germany.* Vol. 3. London: John Murray, 1814.

Homer. *The Complete Works of Homer.* New York: Modern Library, 1950.

———. *The Odyssey.* Translated by Robert Fagles. New York: Penguin, 1997.

Hopkins, Gerard Manley. *Gerard Manley Hopkins.* Oxford and New York: Oxford University Press, 1992.

———. *Gerard Manley Hopkins: The Major Works.* Oxford: Oxford University Press, 2009.

———. *Journals and Papers of Gerard Manley Hopkins.* New York: Oxford University Press, 1959.

Hugh of St. Victor. *Œuvres complètes du pseudo-Denys l'Aréopagite.* Paris: Aubier, 1943.

Hume, David. *A Treatise of Human Nature.* Edited by L. A. Selby-Bigge. Oxford: Clarendon Press, 1973.

Husserl, Edmund. *Ideas: General Introduction to Pure Phenomenology.* New York and London: Collier, 1967.

Issa, Naom P. and Ari Rosenberg. "Peripheral Mechanisms That Underlie Sensory Illusions." In *A Field Guide to a New Meta-Field: Bridging the Humanities-Neurosciences Divide,* edited by Barbara Maria Stafford, 108–22. Chicago: University of Chicago Press, 2011.

Ivry, Benjamin. "How Franz Schubert Found Himself in Shul." *The Forward,* January 30, 2015, 11–12.

Jackson, John Hughlings. *Selected Writings.* Vol. 2. New York: Basic Books, 1958 [1874].

Jacobson, Roni. "Your Pun-Divided Attention." *Scientific American* 315, no. 6 (December 2016): 17.

James, Henry. *The Art of the Novel: Critical Prefaces.* London and New York: Charles Scribner's Sons, 1937.

James, William. *Principles of Psychology.* New York: Henry Holt, 1902.

Janson, Horst W. "The 'Image Made by Chance' in Renaissance Thought." In *De Artibus Opuscula XL: Essays in Honor of Erwin Panofsky,* edited by Millard Meiss, 254–66. New York: New York University Press, 1961.

Jay, Martin. "Scopic Regimes of Modernity." In *Vision and Visuality,* edited by Hal Foster, 19. Seattle: Bay Press, 1988.

Jones, Christopher P., ed. *Philostratus: The Life of Apollonius of Tyana.* Vol. 2. Cambridge, MA: Harvard University Press, 2005.

Jones, Dan. "Rite Reasons: Why Your Brain Loves Pointless Rituals." *New Scientist* 3004 (January 17, 2015): 36–39.

Kahneman, Daniel. *Thinking, Fast and Slow.* New York: Farrar, Straus and Giroux, 2011.

Kandel, Erich. *The Age of Insight*. New York: Random House, 2012.

Kant, Immanuel. *Critique of Judgment*. Translated by Werner Pluhar. Indianapolis, IN: Hackett, 1987.

———. *Critique of Judgment*. Translated by J. H. Bernard. New York: Hafner, 1972.

———. *Gesammelte Schriften*. Berlin: Akademie der Wissenschaften Berlin, 1900.

———. *Kants Werke: Akademie-Textausgabe*. Vol. 5, *Kritik der praktischen Vernunft, Kritik der Urteilskraft*. Berlin: Walter de Gruyter, 1968.

———. *Kritik der Urteilskraft*. Stuttgart: Reclam, 1971.

———. *Prolegomena to any Future Metaphysics*. New York: Macmillan; London: Collier Macmillan, 1950.

———. *Prolegomena zu einer jeden künftigen Metaphysik*. Hamburg: Felix Meiner, 1957.

Kazemzadeh, Max. "Apophenoetics: Virtual Pattern Recognition, the Origins of Creativity and Augmenting the Evolution of Self." *Technoetic Arts* 10, no. 1 (2012): 115–23.

Keats, John. *Selected Poems and Letters*. Edited by Douglas Bush. Boston: Houghton Mifflin, 1959.

Keegan, Paul. "Housman Country: Into the Heart of England." *London Review of Books* 38, no. 22 (November 17, 2016): 27–30.

Kemp, Martin. *Structural Intuitions: Seeing Shapes in Art and Science*. Charlottesville: University of Virginia Press, 2016.

Kemp, Martin and Margaret Walker, eds. *Leonardo on Painting*. New Haven, CT: Yale University Press, 2001.

Kheirbek, Mazen A. and René Hen. "Add Neurons Subtract Anxiety." *Scientific American* 311 (July 2014): 62–67.

Kidd, Stephen E. *Nonsense and Meaning in Ancient Greek Comedy*. Cambridge: Cambridge University Press, 2014.

Kiš, Danilo. *Hourglass*. New York: Farrar, Straus and Giroux, 1990.

Kittay, Eva Feder. *Metaphor: Its Cognitive Force and Linguistic Structure*. Oxford: Clarendon Press, 1987.

———. "Metaphor." *Encyclopedia of Philosophy: Supplement*. New York: Macmillan Reference USA, 1996.

Kjärgaard, Mogens Stiller. *Metaphor and Parable: A Systematic Analysis of the Special Structure and Cognitive Function of the Synoptic Similes and Parables Qua Metaphors*. Leiden: E. J. Brill, 1986.

Kleist, Heinrich von. *Kleists Aufsatz über das Marionettentheater: Studien und Interpretationen*. Berlin: Schmidt, 1967.

———. *The Selected Prose of Heinrich von Kleist*. Translated by Peter Wortsman. New York: Archipelago Books, 2009.

Knausgaard, Karl Ove. *My Struggle: Book Three: Boyhood*. Brooklyn: Archipelago, 2014.

Kovalevskaya, Sofya. *A Russian Childhood*. New York: Springer-Verlag, 1978.

Kotkin, Stephen. "If Stalin had died . . ." *New York Review of Books* 61, no. 17 (November 6, 2014): 34–35.

LaCoss, Don. "Our Lady of Darkness: Decadent Arts and the Magnetic Sleep of Magdeleine G." In *Neurology and Literature, 1860–1920,* edited by Anne Stiles, 52–73. New York: Palgrave/ Macmillan, Houndmills, 2007.

Lakatos, Imre. *The Methodology of Scientific Research Programmes: Philosophical Papers Volume I.* Cambridge: Cambridge University Press, 1980.

Lakoff, George. "The Contemporary Theory of Metaphor." In *Metaphor and Thought,* edited by Andrew Ortony, 1. 2nd ed. Cambridge: Cambridge University Press, 1992.

Lakoff, George and Rafael Nuñez. *Where Mathematics Comes From: How the Embodied Mind Brings Mathematics into Being.* New York: Basic Books, 2000.

Lange, Donald. "A New Coleridge-Mills Letter: Were There Two Meetings between Keats and Coleridge?" *Modern Language Review* 72, no. 4 (October 1977): 769–72.

Lau, Beth. *Keats's Reading of the Romantic Poets.* Ann Arbor: University of Michigan Press, 1991.

Lear, Edward. *The Complete Nonsense of Edward Lear.* New York: Dover, 1951.

Lecercle, Jean-Jacques. *Philosophy of Nonsense: The Intuitions of Victorian Nonsense Poetry.* London and New York: Routledge, 1994.

Lefebve, Jean. *L'image fascinante et le surréel.* Paris: Plon, 1965.

Leibniz, Gottfried Wilhelm. *Nouveaux essais sur l'entendement humain.* Vol. 4. Paris: Flammarion, 1921.

———. *Œuvres philosophiques.* Vol. 1. Paris: Félix Alcan, 1900.

Léon, Xavier. *La Philosophie de Fichte.* Paris: Alcan, 1902.

Leopardi, Giacomo. *Canti.* Milan: Rizzoli, 1953.

Lewis, C. Day. *The Poetic Image.* London: Johnathan Cape, 1964.

Lewis, Rhodri. "Shakespeare's Clouds and the Image Made by Chance." *Essays in Criticism* 62 (2012): 1–24.

Libet, Benjamin. *Mind Time: The Temporal Factor in Consciousness.* Cambridge, MA: Harvard University Press, 2004.

Lipps, Theodor. "Aesthetische Faktoren der Raumanschauung." In *Beiträge zur Psychologie und Physiologie der Sinnesorgane: Hermann von Helmholtz als Festgruss zu seinem siebzigsten Geburtstag,* edited by T. W. Engelmann, E. Javal, A. Koenig, J. von Kries, T. Lipps, L. Matthiessen, W. Preyer, and W. Uhthoff, 217–307. Hamburg: Leopold Voss, 1891.

———. "Das Wissen von fremden Ichen." *Psychologische Untersuchungen* 1 (1907): 694–722.

Livingstone, Margaret. *Vision and Art: The Biology of Seeing.* New York: Harry N. Abrams, 2002.

Llewellyn, Sue. "Such Stuff as Dreams Are Made on? Elaborative Encoding, the Ancient Art of Memory and the Hippocampus." *Behavioral and Brain Sciences* 36, no. 6 (December 2013): 589–607.

Llinas, Rodolfo and Denis Paré. "Of Dreaming and Wakefulness." *Neuroscience* 44, no. 3 (1991): 521–35.

Lyotard, Jean-François. *Discours, figure.* Paris: Klincksieck, 1971.

Mallgrave, Harry Francis and Eleftherios Ikonomou. *Empathy, Form, and Space: Problems in German Aesthetics 1873–1893.* Santa Monica, CA: Getty Center for the History of Art and the Humanities, 1994.

Mantegna, Andrea. *St. Sebastian* of Vienna. Erich Lessing Culture and Fine Arts Archive.

Marion, Jean-Luc. *Negative Certainties*. Translated by Stephen E. Lewis. Chicago: University of Chicago Press, 2015.

Mars-Jones, Adam. "Sight, Sound and Sex." *London Review of Books* 38, no. 6 (March 17, 2016): 43–45.

Marvell, Andrew. *The Norton Anthology of English Literature*. 3rd ed. New York: W. W. Norton, 1974.

Massey, Irving J. *Find You the Virtue: Ethics, Image, and Desire in Literature*. Fairfax, VA: George Mason University Press, 1987.

———. "Freud before Freud: K. A. Scherner (1825–1889)." *Centennial Review* 34, no. 4 (1990): 567–76.

———. *The Neural Imagination: Aesthetic and Neuroscientific Approaches to the Arts*. Austin: University of Texas Press, 2009.

———. *Philo-Semitism in Nineteenth-Century German Literature*. Tübingen: Max Niemeyer, 2000.

———. "A Rationality Larger than the Material Universe." *Criticism* 59, no. 2 (Spring 2008): 339–43.

———. "Shelley's 'Music, When Soft Voices Die': Text and Meaning." *Journal of English and Germanic Philology* 59 (1960): 430–38.

———. "Two Types of Visual Metaphor." *Criticism* 19, no. 4 (1977): 285–95.

———. *The Uncreating Word*. Bloomington: University of Indiana Press, 1970.

Mavromatis, Andreas. *Hypnagogia: The Unique State of Consciousness between Wakefulness and Sleep*. London: Thyrsos Press, 2010.

McMahon, Jennifer. "The Perceptual Constraints on Pictorial Realism." *Contemporary Aesthetics* 4 (January 18, 2006).

McManus, I. C. and Ben Wu. "'The Square is . . . Bulky, Heavy, Contented, Plain, Good-Natured, Stupid . . . ': A Cross-Cultural Study of the Aesthetics and Meaning of Rectangles." *PACA* 7, no. 2 (May 2013): 130–39.

Meillassoux, Quentin. *After Finitude: An Essay on the Necessity of Contingency*. London: Continuum, 2008.

Meisel, Martin. *Chaos Imagined: Literature, Art, Science*. New York: Columbia University Press, 2015.

Melikian, Souren. "Exhibition: New York: From Figural to Abstract: Julio Gonzalez." *New York Times,* June 1, 2002.

Merker, Björn. "Consciousness without a Cerebral Cortex. A Challenge for Neuroscience and Medicine." *Behavioral and Brain Sciences* 30, no. 1 (February 2007): 63–81.

Merleau-Ponty, Maurice. *Phénoménologie de la perception*. Paris: Gallimard, 1945.

———. *Phenomenology of Perception*. London: Routledge and Kegan Paul, 1962.

Michael, Charles R. "Retinal Processing of Visual Images." *Scientific American* 220 (May 1969): 104–17.

Mihov, Konstantin M., Markus Denzler, and Jens Förster. "Hemispheric Specialization and Creative Thinking: A Meta-Analytic Review of Lateralization of Creativity." *Brain and Cognition* 72 (2010): 442–48.

Miller, Hillis. *The Linguistic Moment*. Princeton, NJ: Princeton University Press, 1985.

Montero, Barbara. "Proprioception as an Aesthetic Sense." *Journal of Aesthetics and Art Criticism* 64, no. 2 (Spring 2006): 231–42.

Moody, Raymond. *Donner du sense au non-sens.* Quebec: Guy Tredaniel, 2016.

Moran, Richard. "Kant, Proust, and the Appeal of Beauty." *Critical Inquiry* 38, no. 2 (Winter 2012): 298–329.

Muecke, Stephen. "What if Objects Were Beautiful Without a Human Standing By to Judge Them to Be So?" *Aesthetics after Finitude* (blog), October 18, 2013. aestheticsafterfinitude.blogspot.com.

Nabokov, Vladimir. *Speak, Memory.* New York: G. P. Putnam, 1951.

Nashe [*sic*], Thomas. *Lenten Stuff.* Menston, Yorkshire: Scolar Press, 1971.

Netzley, Ryan. "Sameness and the Poetics of Nonrelation: Andrew Marvell's 'The Garden.'" *PMLA* 132, no. 2 (May 2017): 580–95.

Newman, John Henry. *An Essay in Aid of a Grammar of Assent.* Notre Dame, IN: University of Notre Dame Press, 1979.

Nielsen, Tore A. "Describing and Modeling Hypnagogic Imagery Using a Systematic Self-Observation Procedure." *Dreaming* 5 (1995): 75–94.

Nietzsche, Friedrich. *Nietzsches Werke: Klassiker-Ausgabe.* Leipzig: Alfred Kröner, [1919–1921].

Nikolaus von Kues [Cusanus]. *Philosophisch-Theologische Schriften.* Vol. 3. Wien: Verlag Herder, 1964–1967.

Nooteboom, Cees. *Rituals.* San Diego, CA and New York: Harvest, 1984.

Noreika, Valdas, Andrés Canales-Johnson, Justin Koh, Mae Taylor, Irving Massey, and Tristan A. Bekinschtein. "Intrusions of a Drowsy Mind: Neural Markers of Phenomenological Unpredictability." *Frontiers in Psychology* 6 (March 12, 2015). https://doi.org/10.3389/fpsyg.2015.00202.

Oates, Whitney J. and Eugene O'Neill Jr., eds. *The Complete Greek Drama.* New York: Random House, 1938.

Orr, H. Allen. "The Biology of Being Good to Others." *New York Review of Books* 62, no. 5 (March 19, 2015): 27–29.

Orwell, George. *How to Shoot an Elephant.* London: Harcourt, Brace & World, 1950.

Osgood, Charles G., ed. *Boccaccio on Poetry.* Indianapolis, IN and New York: Bobbs-Merrill, 1956.

Ovid. *Metamorphoses.*

Peirce, Charles Sanders. *The Philosophy of Peirce.* London: Routledge and Kegan Paul, 1956.

Penfield, Wilder and Theodore Rasmussen. *The Cerebral Cortex of Man: A Clinical Study of Localization of Function.* New York: Macmillan, 1950.

Phillips, Catherine, ed. *Gerard Manley Hopkins.* Oxford and New York: Oxford University Press, 1992.

Phillips, Flip, J. Farley Norman, and Amanda M. Beers. "Fechner's Aesthetics Revisited." *Seeing and Perceiving* 23, no. 3 (2010): 263–71.

Philo of Alexandria. *Philo.* Translated by F. H. Colson and G. H. Whitaker. London: William Heinemann; New York: G. P. Putnam's Sons, 1929–1962.

Pitcher, George. "Wittgenstein, Nonsense, and Lewis Carroll." *Massachusetts Review* 6, no. 3 (Spring 1965): 591–611.

Plato. *The Dialogues of Plato.* New York: Random House, 1937.

Platonov, Andrey. *Soul.* London: Harvill Press, 2003.

Poe, Edgar Allan. "Marginalia." In *Introduction to Poe: A Thematic Reader,* edited by Eric W. Carlson, 535–37. Atlanta, GA: Scott, Foresman and Co., 1967.

Pope, Alexander. *Selected Poetry and Prose.* Toronto: Rinehart, 1959.

Porter, James I. *The Origins of Aesthetic Thought in Ancient Greece: Matter, Sensation, and Experience.* Cambridge: Cambridge University Press, 2010.

Potter, Michael and Tom Ricketts, eds. *The Cambridge Companion to Frege.* Cambridge: Cambridge University Press, 2010.

Powell, Corey S. "Weirdlands of Mars." *Discover* 35, no. 5 (June 2014): 58 and 60.

Price, Uvedale. *On the Picturesque.* Otley: Woodstock Books, 2000.

Pym, Barbara. *Quartet in Autumn.* London: Pan Books, 2004.

Rabin, Roni Caryn. "A Few Strokes of the Past in an Artist Who Lost Her Memory." *New York Times,* September 19, 2011, 4.

Ramachandran, V. S. and William Hirstein. "The Science of Art: A Neurological Theory of Aesthetic Experience." *Journal of Consciousness Studies* 6, nos. 6–7 (1999): 15–51.

Rancière, Jacques. *The Flesh of Words: The Politics of Writing.* Stanford, CA: Stanford University Press, 2004.

Reid, Lynette. "Wittgenstein's Ladder; the *Tractatus* and Nonsense." *Philosophical Investigations* 21, no. 2 (April 1998): 97–151.

Richards, I. A. *Philosophy of Rhetoric.* New York and Oxford: Oxford University Press, 1936.

———. *Practical Criticism: A Study in Literary Judgment.* London: Kegan Paul Trench Trubner, 1930.

Ricoeur, Paul. *La Métaphore vive.* Paris: Éditions du Seuil, 1975.

———. *The Rule of Metaphor: Multi-Disciplinary Studies in the Creation of Meaning in Language.* London: Routledge and Kegan Paul, 1978 [1975].

Rilke, Rainer Maria. *The Selected Poetry of Rainer Maria Rilke.* Edited by Stephen Mitchell. New York: Random House, 1982.

———. *Translations from the Poetry of Rainer Maria Rilke.* Translated by M. D. Herter Norton. New York: W. W. Norton, 1938.

Rimbaud, Arthur. *Œuvres complètes.* Paris: Pléiade, 1963.

Robbe-Grillet, Alain. *Pour un nouveau roman.* Paris: Minuit, 1963.

Robson, David. "Memory—The Ultimate Guide." *New Scientist* 216, no. 2885 (October 6, 2012): 32–33.

Rothenberg, David. *Survival of the Beautiful: Art, Science, and Evolution.* London: Bloomsbury Press, 2011.

Sacks, Oliver. *Musicophilia: Tales of Music and the Brain.* New York: Alfred A. Knopf, 2007.

Saxe, Rebecca. "Against Simulation." *Trends in Cognitive Science* 9, no. 4 (2005): 174–79.

Schacter, Daniel L. et al. "Remembering the Past to Imagine the Future." *Nature Reviews Neuroscience* 8 (September 2007): 657–61.

Scharfstein, Ben-Ami. *The Nonsense of Kant and Lewis Carroll.* Chicago: University of Chicago Press, 2014.

Scheibmayr, Werner. *Niklas Luhmanns Systemtheorie und Charles Peirces Zeichensystem.* Tübingen: Niemeyer, 2004.

Schiller, Johann Christoph Friedrich von. "On Simple and Sentimental Poetry." *Aesthetical Essays of Friedrich Schiller*, 1902.

Schlegel, Friedrich. *Schriften zur Literatur*. München: Deutscher Taschenbuch Verlag, 1972.

Scott, Heidi C. M. *Chaos and Cosmos: Literary Roots of Modern Ecology in the British Nineteenth Century*. University Park: Pennsylvania State University Press, 2014.

Seneca, L. Annaeus. *Treatises*. New York: American Book Co., 1877.

Shakespeare, William. *Antony and Cleopatra*. Edited by John Wilders. London: Routledge, 1995.

———. *Hamlet*. Edited by Ann Thompson and Neil Taylor. London: Routledge, 2006.

———. *King Lear*. Edited by Kenneth Muir. Cambridge, MA: Harvard University Press, 1959.

———. *Love Poems and Sonnets of William Shakespeare*. New York: Doubleday, 1991.

———. *The Tempest*. New York: Simon and Schuster, 2004.

Shelley, Percy Bysshe. *Selected Poetry*. Boston and New York: Houghton Mifflin Company, 1968.

Shermer, Michael. *The Believing Brain: From Ghosts and Gods to Politics and Conspiracies*. New York: St. Martin's Griffin, 2011.

Shetty, Priya. "Mirror Neurons Not All They Are Cracked up to Be." *New Scientist* 202, no. 2710 (May 27, 2009): 9.

Sieburth, Richard. "The Poetics of Futurity." *TLS* 5703 (July 20, 2012): 13–15.

Simpson, David. "A Positive Future." *London Review of Books* 31, no. 6 (March 26, 2009): 14–17.

Skov, Martin and Oshin Vartanian, eds. *Neuroaesthetics*. Amityville, NY: Baywood Publishing Co., 2009.

Sloan, Kim. *Alexander and John Robert Cozens: The Poetry of Landscape*. New Haven, CT: Yale University Press, 1986.

Smart, Christopher. *Abimelech, an Oratorio. The Poetical Works of Christopher Smart, II: Religious Poetry 1763–1771*. Edited by Marcus Walsh and Karina Williamson. Oxford: Clarendon, 1983.

Smith, Daniel B. *Muses, Madness, and Prophets; Hearing Voices and the Borders of Sanity*. New York: Penguin, 2008.

Sokal, Alan. "Transgressing the Boundaries: towards a Transformative Hermeneutics of Quantum Gravity." *Social Text* 46/47 (Spring–Summer 1996): 217–52.

Solmsen, Friedrich. "Nature as Craftsman in Greek Thought." *Journal of the History of Ideas* 24, no. 4 (1963): 473–96.

Sovran, Tomar. *Relational Semantics and the Anatomy of Abstraction*. New York: Routledge, 2014.

Spalding, J. M. K. and O. L. Zangwill. "Disturbance of Number-Form." *Journal of Neurology, Neurosurgery, and Psychiatry* 13 (1950): 24–29.

Sparshott, F. E. "'As,' or The Limits of Metaphor." *New Literary History* 6 (Autumn 1974): 74–94.

Stebbing, Peter. "A Universal Grammar for Visual Composition?" *Leonardo* 37 (2004): 63–70.

Stenstrom, Philippe, Kieran Fox, Elizaveta Solomonova, and Tore Nielsen. "Mentation During Sleep Onset Theta Bursts in a Trained Participant: A Role for NREM Stage 1 Sleep in Memory Processing?" *International Journal of Dream Research* 5, no. 1 (2012): 37–46.

Stevenson, Robert Louis. *An Inland Voyage, Travels with a Donkey, The Silverado Squatters*. London: J. M. Dent, 1988.

Stewart, Lauren, Vincent Walsh, Uta Frith, and John Rothwell. "Transcranial Magnetic Stimulation Produces Speech Arrest but not Song Arrest." In *The Biological Foundations of Music,* edited by Robert J. Zatorre and Isabelle Peretz, 433–35. New York: New York Academy of Sciences, 2001.

Strand, Mark. *Darker: Poems.* New York: Atheneum, 1970.

Sutherland, Robert D. *Language and Lewis Carroll.* The Hague and Paris: Mouton, 1970.

Szendy, Peter. *Kant chez les extraterrestres: philosofictions cosmopolitiques.* Paris: Minuit, 2011.

Tallis, Raymond. *Aping Mankind: Neuromania, Darwinitis and the Misrepresentation of Humanity.* Durham: Acumen, 2011.

———. *Logos: The Mystery of How We Make Sense in the World.* New York: Columbia University Press, 2018.

Tennyson, Alfred (Lord). *Selections from Tennyson.* New York: F. S. Crofts, 1940.

Thoreau, Henry David. *A Week on the Concord and Merrimack Rivers, Walden; or Life in the Woods, The Main Woods, Cape Cod.* New York: The Library of America, 1985.

Tretjakova, Jelena. "An Insight into Contemporary Theory of Metaphor." *The 53rd International Scientific Conference Proceedings,* April 2011. dukonference.lv/files/proceedings_of_conf/53konf/valodnieciba_literaturzinatne/Tretjakova.pdf.

Turner, Jane, ed. *Dictionary of Art.* London and New York: Macmillan Publishers Limited and Grove's Dictionaries Inc., 1996.

Turner, Mark and Gilles Fauconnier. "Conceptual Integration and Formal Expression." *Metaphor and Symbolic Activity* 10, no. 3 (1995): 183–204.

Ulitskaya, Ludmila. *Medea and her Children.* New York: Schocken, 2004.

Valéry, Paul. *Monsieur Teste.* Paris: Gallimard, 1946.

van Gogh, Vincent. *Painted with Words: The Letters to Émile Bernard.* New York: Rizzoli, 2007.

Verlaine, Paul. *Œuvres poétiques complètes.* Paris: Robert Laffont, 1992.

———. *One Hundred and One Poems by Paul Verlaine: A Bilingual Edition.* Translated by Norman R. Shapiro. Chicago: University of Chicago Press, 2010.

Vico, Giambattista. *The New Science.* New York: Anchor, 1961.

Volkelt, Johannes. *Die Traum-Phantasie.* Stuttgart: Meyer & Zeller, 1875.

Vrahimis, Andreas. "Nonsense and Absurdity: Carnap's Use of Husserl's Theory of Meaning." *Review of Contemporary Philosophy* 10 (2011): 133–40.

Vygotsky, L. S. *Thought and Language.* Cambridge, MA: MIT Press, 1962.

Watkin, William. *The Literary Agamben: Adventures in Logopoiesis.* London and New York: Continuum, 2010.

Whitfield, T. W. Allan and Lucila R. de Destefani. "Mundane Aesthetics." *Psychology of Aesthetics, Creativity, and the Arts* 5, no. 3 (2011): 291–99.

Whorf, Benjamin Lee. *Language, Thought and Reality: Selected Writings of Benjamin Lee Whorf.* Boston: MIT Press, 1956.

Wickert, Max. "Ave atque Vale." *Earth's Daughters* 59/60 (2002): 42.

Wilde, Oscar. "From 'The Critic as Artist.'" In *Victorian Poetry and Poetics,* edited by Walter E. Houghton and G. Robert Stange, 754–60. Boston: Houghton Mifflin, 1959.

Williams, James and Matthew Bevis, eds. *Edward Lear and the Play of Poetry.* Oxford: Oxford University Press, 2016.

Windt, Jennifer M. and Valdas Noreika. "How to Integrate Dreaming into a General Theory of Consciousness—A Critical Review of Existing Positions and Suggestions for Future Research." *Consciousness and Cognition* 20 (2011): 1091–107.

Winter, Alison. *Mesmerized: Powers of Mind in Victorian Britain.* Chicago: University of Chicago Press, 1998.

Witmore, Michael. *Culture of Accidents: Unexpected Knowledge in Early Modern England.* Stanford, CA: Stanford University Press, 2001.

Wittgenstein, Ludwig. *Tractatus Logico-Philosophicus.* Abingdon and New York: Routledge, 2014.

Wordsworth, William. *Selected Poems and Prefaces.* Edited by Jack Stillinger. Boston: Houghton Mifflin, 1965.

Zaidel, Dahlia W. *Neuropsychology of Art: Neurological, Cognitive, and Evolutionary Perspectives.* New York: Psychology Press, 2005.

Zeki, Semir. *Inner Vision: An Exploration of Art and the Brain.* New York: Oxford University Press, 1999.

Zeman, Adam. *A Portrait of the Brain.* New Haven, CT: Yale University Press, 2008.

Zhadova, Larissa A. *Malevich: Suprematism and Revolution in Russian Art 1910–1930.* London: Thames and Hudson, 1982.

# INDEX

Abel, Lionel, 22, 26n13, 45n50

Abrams, M. H. (Meyer Howard), 19, 48

Achilles, 23, 27, 34, 42, 45

Adamson, Robert, 11n15

Addison, Joseph, 90, 90n3

Aeolian harp, 29

aesthetics, 6, 9, 14, 28, 45, 47, 49, 60, 62–68, 63n17, 71n47, 76, 80, 85n50, 92–93, 112, 122, 124–26, 129n47, 131–35, 138–48, 150–51, 154–56, 160–61, 163; and automaticity, 118, 118n14, 124–25, 128, 132, 143, 148; democratization of, 129, 132; disagreement in, 133, 151; empirical, 145–46; of form(s), 60, 63, 84; Kantian, 6, 132, 134; neuroaesthetics, 89–90, 92, 94–95, 142, 146n105; and meaning, 56, 131, 134; and patterns, 115, 118–20, 127–28; as a physiological response, 63, 116, 143–46, 155; and psychology, 60, 62, 65, 112; and structure, 30, 65

Akhmatova, Anna, 86, 86n54, 88

aleatory techniques in art, 29

*Alice in Wonderland* (Carroll), 66

allegory and allegoresis, 29–31, 37, 39, 105, 154

Allik, Jüri, 48n72

*The American* (James), 84, 110, 112, 127

amusias, 61

Anabaptism, 75

Anthony, Earl of Shaftesbury. *See* Shaftesbury

aphasia, 61, 113; fluent (Wernicke's), 113

architecture, 60, 63–64, 67, 118, 133, 137

Aristotle, 78, 105, 118, 118n13

Arnheim, Rudolph, 68

Art Nouveau, 66

Artaud, Antonin, 108

Asperger's syndrome, 13, 44, 73, 163

atmosphere and atmospherics, 66, 107, 111

attention, 2, 28, 44n47, 50–51, 61, 67, 84, 113, 115, 117–18, 118n11, 141–42, 162n22

automaticity, 64–65, 107, 114, 118–20, 121n25, 124–25, 128–29, 132, 140, 143–44, 147–48, 154

Avio, Sara, 102

*Bacchae* (Euripides), 75

Bach, Johann Sebastian, 58, 91

Badgaiyan, Rajendra D., 113n65

Ball, Philip, 8

Baron-Cohen, Simon, 119

179

## COGNITIVE APPROACHES TO CULTURE

Frederick Luis Aldama, Patrick Colm Hogan, Lalita Pandit Hogan, and
Sue J. Kim, Series Editors

This series takes up cutting edge research in a broad range of cognitive sciences inso-
far as this research bears on and illuminates cultural phenomena such as literature,
film, drama, music, dance, visual art, digital media, and comics, among others. For
the purpose of the series, "cognitive science" is construed broadly to encompass work
derived from cognitive and social psychology, neuroscience, cognitive and generative
linguistics, affective science, and related areas in anthropology, philosophy, computer
science, and elsewhere. Though open to all forms of cognitive analysis, the series is
particularly interested in works that explore the social and political consequences of
cognitive cultural study.

*Necessary Nonsense: Aesthetics, History, Neurology, Psychology*
    IRVING MASSEY

*Shaming into Brown: Somatic Transactions of Race in Latina/o Literature*
    STEPHANIE FETTA

*Resilient Memories: Amerindian Cognitive Schemas in Latin American Art*
    ARIJ OUWENEEL

*Permissible Narratives: The Promise of Latino/a Literature*
    CHRISTOPHER GONZÁLEZ

*Literatures of Liberation: Non-European Universalisms and Democratic Progress*
    MUKTI LAKHI MANGHARAM

*Affective Ecologies: Empathy, Emotion, and Environmental Narrative*
    ALEXA WEIK VON MOSSNER

*A Passion for Specificity: Confronting Inner Experience in Literature and Science*
    MARCO CARACCIOLO AND RUSSELL T. HURLBURT